Informatik-Fachberichte 289

Herausgeber: W. Brauer
im Auftrag der Gesellschaft für Informatik (GI)

Norbert Fuhr (Hrsg.)

Information Retrieval

GI/GMD-Workshop
Darmstadt, 23./24. Juni 1991

Proceedings

Springer Fachmedien Wiesbaden GmbH

Herausgeber

Norbert Fuhr
Universität Dortmund, Fachbereich Informatik
Postfach 500 500, W-4600 Dortmund 50

CR Subject Classification (1991): H.3, H.5.1-2, J.1-4

ISBN 978-3-540-54618-4   ISBN 978-3-642-76981-8
DOI 10.1007/978-3-642-76981-8

Satz: Reproduktionsfertige Vorlage vom Autor

33/3140-543210 – Gedruckt auf säurefreiem Papier

Vorwort

Am 23. und 24. Juni 1991 fand in Darmstadt die erste deutschsprachige Informatik-Tagung auf dem Gebiet des Information Retrieval (IR) statt. Hier trafen sich mehr als 100 IR-Forscher und -Praktiker, um über Entwicklungsstand und Perspektiven in diesem Gebiet zu diskutieren. In den letzten Jahren haben neue technische Entwicklungen, insbesondere im Bereich der Speicherung großer Datenmengen, zu einer weiten Verbreitung von IR-Systemen geführt. Leider basieren aber fast alle derzeit auf dem Markt angebotenen Systeme noch auf der gleichen Konzeption, die bereits den Anfang der 70er Jahre (auf Großrechnern) verfügbaren Systemen zugrundelag. Fortschritte sind allenfalls im Bereich der Benutzerschnittstellen auszumachen, die aber die grundlegenden Schwächen der Systeme nur unzureichend kompensieren können. Unberücksichtigt bleiben dagegen wesentliche Ergebnisse der IR-Forschung, die z.B. belegen, daß durch Rankingmethoden in Kombination mit robusten linguistischen Erschließungsverfahren nicht nur die Retrievalqualität deutlich verbessert werden kann, sondern durch den Verzicht auf Boolesche Anfragesprachen auch die Bedienung des Systems wesentlich erleichtert wird. Mit der Veranstaltung dieses Workshops (als geplanter Auftakt einer in regelmäßigen Abständen stattfindenden Tagungsreihe) sollen Forschungsergebnisse aus dem Bereich des IR einem breiteren Kreis von Wissenschaftlern und Praktikern zugänglich gemacht werden.

Die in diesem Band versammelten Beiträge (13 angenommene von 21 eingereichten) geben einen guten Überblick über die derzeitigen IR-Forschungsaktivitäten im deutschsprachigen Raum. Die ersten sieben Aufsätze sind dabei dem Bereich des „klassischen" IR zuzurechnen, also dem Textretrieval und der Textindexierung. H.P. Frei, S. Meienberg und P. Schäuble stellen in ihrem Beitrag „The Perils of Interpreting Recall and Precision Values" eine Evaluierungsstudie vor, bei der sie ein neues Qualitätsmaß mit der bislang üblichen Bewertung mittels Precision und Recall vergleichen. Die beschriebenen Experimente zeigen, daß das von ihnen entwickelte Maß insbesondere im Hinblick auf die statistischen Eigenschaften der seitherigen Bewertungsmethode eindeutig vorzuziehen ist. Die Arbeit „Evaluating Weighted Search Terms as Boolean Queries" von H.P. Frei und S. Meienberg beschreibt effiziente Algorithmen zur Implementierung von Rankingverfahren im Zugangssystem zu einem Booleschen IR-System. Die erzielten Ergebnisse lassen sich allerdings auch in dem Sinne interpretieren, daß nur durch die (längst überfällige) Implementierung von Rankingverfahren innerhalb des eigentlichen IR-Systems akzeptable Antwortzeiten erreichbar sind. Die beiden folgenden Beiträge beschäftigen sich mit Problemen der automatischen Indexierung auf der Grundlage des Darmstädter Indexierungsansatzes. Für das hierbei benötigte Indexierungswörterbuch, das automatisch aus einer großen Menge von vorliegenden intellektuell indexierten Dokumenten erstellt werden kann, stellt K. Tzeras ein Verfahren zur Aufwandsabschätzung vor. Über die endgültige Zuteilung bzw. Nicht-Zuteilung von Deskriptoren bei der automatischen Indexierung entscheidet eine sogenannte Indexierungsfunktion; U. Pfeifer beschreibt hierzu neue Ansätze, die eine verbesserte Indexierungsqualität liefern. Aus dem an der TU Berlin laufenden Projekt ATLAS („Archiv für Technik-, Lebenswelt- und Alltagssprache") heraus sind die nächsten zwei Beiträge entstanden: J. Willenborg beschreibt einen objektorientierten Ansatz zur Erstellung und Pflege von Thesauri, und in „ATLAS/ti - ein Interpretations-Unterstützungs-System" von T. Muhr wird ein neuartiges System vorgestellt, mit dem die in den Geisteswissenschaften übliche Arbeit mit Texten unterstützt werden soll. Der abschließende Beitrag aus dem Bereich des Textretrieval „Elektronische Ablage und Archivierung auf der Basis eines Database Management Information Retrieval Systems" von H. Amstutz und B. Holländer-Thönssen beschreibt die Anforderungen an IR-Systeme aus Anwendersicht, wobei deutlich wird, daß hier eine Reihe zusätzlicher, entscheidender Anforderungen an solche Systeme gestellt wird, während die in der Forschung überwiegend diskutierten Problemkreise von untergeordneter Bedeutung sind.

Die folgenden drei Beiträge stammen aus dem Gebiet des Faktenretrieval. K. Englmeier präsentiert ein wissensbasiertes Zugangssystem zu öffentlich angebotenen statistischen Datenbanken.

W. Augsburger, H.K. Rieder und J. Schwab haben ein System für die innerbetriebliche Anwendung konzipiert, das sowohl die Verdichtung der in großem Umfang anfallenden betriebswirtschaftlichen Daten erlaubt, als auch deren laufende Überwachung. In „Forensisches Informationssystem Handschriften — Ein Beispiel für ein klassifizierendes Rechercheverfahren" stellt M. Münzenberger eine interessante neue Anwendung von IR-Verfahren vor.

Die letzten drei Beiträge beschäftigen sich mit der Verknüpfung von Hypertext- und IR-Ansätzen. J. Herrmann und P. Meiser beschreiben ein System zur Unterstützung der Recherche in Volltextdatenbanken, in dem der zugrundeliegende Thesaurus mit Hilfe eines Hypertext-Systems besser zugänglich gemacht wird. D. Merkl, A Min Tjoa und S. Vieweg setzen ein Hypertextsystem ein, um bei der Suche in juristischen Volltexten die Verweise zwischen verschiedenen Dokumenten dem Benutzer zu präsentieren. J. Herczeg, H. Hohl und M. Ressel zeigen am Beispiel eines Reiseinformationssystems, wie die Informationsuche durch das Angebot verschiedener Anfragemöglichkeiten verbessert werden kann.

Abschließend möchte ich allen herzlich danken, die durch ihre Mitarbeit zum Gelingen dieser Tagung beigetragen haben:

- den Autoren der angenommenen und abgelehnten Beiträge für ihre Mühe und Arbeit sowie für die Disziplin bei der Erstellung der druckfertigen Manuskripte,
- der Gesellschaft für Mathematik und Datenverarbeitung (GMD) und der Gesellschaft für Informatik (GI) für ihre Bereitschaft, diese Tagung zu tragen,
- den Mitgliedern des Programmkomitees für ihre wertvolle Unterstützung, und
- dem Herausgeber der Reihe „Informatik-Fachberichte", Herrn Prof. W. Brauer für die schnelle Zusage zur Publikation des Tagungsbandes in dieser Reihe.

Besonderer Dank gilt Herrn Dr. D. Böcker für die Organisation der Tagung sowie Frau U. Kischel und Frau U. Sotnik für ihre tatkräftige Unterstützung bei dieser Aufgabe. Ebenso möchte ich meinem Mitarbeiter, Herrn U. Pfeifer, für seine vielfältige Hilfe herzlich danken.

Dortmund, im Juli 1991   Norbert Fuhr

Inhaltsverzeichnis

The Perils of Interpreting Recall and Precision Values

H.P. Frei, S. Meienberg, P. Schäuble

Swiss Federal Institute of Technology (ETH) Zurich
Department of Computer Science
8092 Zurich, Switzerland

1. Introduction

"The measurement of performance is necessary to evaluate Information Retrieval systems" [Los 91] seems to be a generally accepted opinion in the Information Retrieval (IR) community. An important factor of whether a user is able to benefit from using an IR system is the *effectiveness* of the retrieval method implemented in the system.

A widely applied effectiveness measure consists of computing recall and precision values [Sal 83, pp. 164]. This traditional effectiveness measure is appropriate in connection with static document collections, a sufficient number of queries, and complete relevance assessments. Often, recall and precision values are used when retrieval methods are evaluated with respect to standard test collections such as the CACM test collection or the CISI test collection [Fox 83]. These test collections are static and they contain an almost sufficient large number of queries.

The traditional recall and precision measure is inappropriate when retrieval algorithms that retrieve information from Wide Area Networks (WANs) are evaluated [Fre 89]. As pointed out in [Fre 91], there are several reasons that recall and precision values are inappropriate to evaluate such retrieval methods. The principle reason, however, is that information available in WANs is dynamic and its size is orders of magnitude greater than the size of the usual test collections.

To overcome these problems with the traditional recall and precision measure, a new effectiveness measure has been developed. This measure, which we call *the usefulness measure,* is described in [Fre 91]. In this paper, experiments are described where retrieval methods are compared by both the traditional recall and precision measure and the new usefulness measure. The results show the perils of interpreting recall and precision values. In particular, we present the evaluation of two retrieval methods where recall and precision imply completely wrong conclusions whereas the usefulness measure points in the correct direction.

2. Recall and Precision

In this section, we briefly review the recall and precision measure. In particular, we show how a recall-precision graph is computed given a retrieval method and a test collection, i.e. a set of documents, a set of queries, and relevance assessments belonging to these documents and queries.

A retrieval method is represented by a retrieval function RSV that assigns every query q and every document d a so-called Retrieval Status Value RSV(q,d). The real valued RSV(q,d) constitutes an estimation of the retrieval system on how relevant document d is with respect to the query q.

For every query q, the retrieval function induces an equivalence relation $\equiv_q$ in the following way.

$$d \equiv_q d' \quad \text{iff} \quad RSV(q,d) = RSV(q,d')$$

Furthermore, the complete ordering of the real numbers induces a complete ordering on the set of equivalence classes induced by $\equiv_q$. This ordering is denoted by $\geq_q$.

$$[d] \geq_q [d'] \quad \text{iff} \quad RSV(q,d) \geq RSV(q,d')$$

It should be noted that the definition of the relation $\geq_q$ is independent of the documents d and d' representing the equivalence classes [d] and [d']. We will write $[d] >_q [d']$ if $[d] \geq_q [d']$ and $[d] \neq [d']$. Because D is assumed to be a finite set there is a finite chain

$$[d_1] >_q [d_2] >_q \ldots >_q [d_k]$$

which contains each equivalence class induced by $\equiv_q$. This chain is called the *ranked list* induced by the retrieval function RSV for the query q.

The *effectiveness* of a retrieval system expresses how well the produced output, i.e. ranked list, satisfies the information need. It is assumed that the user inspects the first i classes $[d_1], \ldots, [d_i]$ of the ranked list. The value i depends on the user. A recall-oriented user inspects more classes than a precision-oriented user. In an optimal case, the items of every class are equally relevant and, for each $i \in \{1, \ldots, k\}$, every item of the first i classes meets the user's need better than any item of the remaining k-i classes.

The recall-precision graph is determined by means of a *test collection*. A test collection consists of a set of items D, a set of queries Q, and relevance assessments. The relevance assessments divide, for each query q, the item collection D into a set of relevant items D_q^{rel} and a set of non-relevant items D_q^{non}. In order to avoid useless relevance assessments, we assume subsequently that both D_q^{rel} and D_q^{non} are non-empty. The recall-precision graph is obtained in the following way [Sal 83, p. 164]. First of all, for every query q, the ranked list

$$[d_1] >_q \ldots >_q [d_k]$$

is determined. Secondly, k pairs consisting of a recall and a precision value are computed. A pair (ρ_i, π_i) expresses the degree of satisfaction of the user's need of information by the response $[d_1] \cup \ldots \cup [d_i]$. The response does not usually contain every relevant item. This is measured by the recall ρ_i which is the portion of relevant items that are contained in the response. On the other hand, the response usually contains non-relevant items. This is measured by the precision π_i which is the portion of the response which contains relevant items.

$$\rho_i := \frac{|D_q^{rel} \cap D_i|}{|D_q^{rel}|}$$

$$\pi_i := \frac{|D_q^{rel} \cap D_i|}{|D_i|}$$

where the response is denoted by D_i and consists of the first i classes the user inspects:

$$D_i := [d_1] \cup ... \cup [d_i].$$

When computing ρ_i and π_i, division by zero will not occur because we assumed D_q^{rel} to be non-empty and D_i is non-empty by definition.

In the next step, for every query q, a function Π_q is defined that assigns each recall value $\rho \in]0,1]$ to the corresponding precision value in the following way.

$$\Pi_q(\rho) := \max\{\pi_i \mid \rho_i \geq \rho\}$$

The objective of this rounding up is to replace a sawtooth curve by a monotonically decreasing curve where each recall value corresponds to a unique precision value [Sal 83, p. 167]. In the last step, the average function is obtained from

$$\Pi(\rho) := \frac{1}{|Q|} \sum_{q \in Q} \Pi_q(\rho).$$

When drawing $\Pi(\rho)$ for $0<\rho\leq1$, a recall-precision graph is obtained as shown in Figures 1a and 2a. A major advantage of recall-precision graphs is that they can easily be interpreted. How well such interpretations reflect reality will be discussed in Section 5. In the next section, a recently developed effectiveness measure, called the usefulness measure, is presented; it will be compared with the traditional recall and precision measure.

3. The Usefulness Measure

In this section, we briefly review the usefulness measure which has been introduced in [Fre 91]. It is a relative measure which compares a retrieval method A and a retrieval method B with respect to their retrieval effectiveness. The retrieval method A is given by the retrieval function RSV_A which determines for every query q and for every document d the Retrieval Status Value $RSV_A(q,d)$. Likewise, the retrieval method B is given by the retrieval function RSV_B. The usefulness measure is based on a probability space where the experimental setting consists of a retrieval system and a community of users who need information. The retrieval system provides access to a dynamic collection of documents. Furthermore, the information need of the users is also assumed to be dynamic. Without loss of generality, we assume that, at every moment, the retrieval system is used by one and only one user. We call her or him the current user. Given such an experimental setting, the value

$$P(D,p,q,r)$$

denotes the probability that (1) D is equal to the current document collection of the system, (2) p is the current user, (3) q is the query by which p expresses her or his current need of information, and (4) the current user is willing to specify relevance assessments for at most 2r documents.

Given a document collection D, a query q, and a threshold r, the answer set $R_A(D,q,r)$ of the algorithm A is defined as follows: If the document collection D contains more than r documents, the answer set $R_A(D,q,r)$ consists of the r documents with the highest RSV_A value.

The answer set $R_B(D,q,r)$ is defined analogously and it also contributes at most r documents. Since we are comparing the two algorithms A and B, the set of documents the system actually delivers to the user is the union of the answer sets of A and B:

$$R(D,q,r) := R_A(D,q,r) \cup R_B(D,q,r).$$

This set of documents, $R(D,q,r)$, contains at most 2r documents. If $r \leq |D|$ the answer set $R(D,q,r)$ contains at least r documents and if $r \geq |D|$ the answer set $R(D,q,r)$ is equal to D.

In the process of determining the effectiveness, a decision has to be made on how relevant the retrieved items are to the user. In contrast to classical relevance assessments, where the entire document collection is divided into sets of relevant and non-relevant documents, we propose that the current user specifies only relative relevance assessments and only for the documents contained in the answer set. Such relative relevance assessments are represented by *preference relations* $<_p$ where p denotes the current user. The preference $d <_p d'$ signifies that the user p judges d to be less useful than d'. When determining the usefulness, at different moments, the current user is asked to specify preferences for the documents contained in the answer set. More precisely, the current user p whose information need is represented by q specifies preferences between the items contained in the answer set $R(D,q,r)$. This set of preferences is equal to

$$\pi_p \cap R^2(D,q,r)$$

where

$$\pi_p \quad := \{(d,d') \mid d <_p d'\},$$
$$R^2(D,q,r) \quad := R(D,q,r) \times R(D,q,r).$$

The pairs of π_p represent the preferences of the user p. The pairs of $\pi_p \cap R^2(D,q,r)$ represent the known preferences explicitly specified by the user p. In addition to π_p, we specify π_A and π_B determined by the RSV values of the retrieval algorithms A and B respectively:

$$\pi_A \quad := \{(d,d') \mid RSV_A(q,d) < RSV_A(q,d')\}$$
$$\pi_B \quad := \{(d,d') \mid RSV_B(q,d) < RSV_B(q,d')\}$$

Furthermore, we introduce two random variables $X(D,p,q,r)$ and $Y(D,p,q,r)$. The former denotes the portion of preferences satisfied by A minus the portion of inverse preferences satisfied by A, i.e. preferences $d <_p d'$ for which $RSV_A(q,d) > RSV_A(q,d')$. The latter denotes the portion of preferences satisfied by B minus the portion of inverse preferences satisfied by B. These random variables are closely related to the R_{norm} measure suggested by Peter Bollmann [Fuh 87].

$$X(D,p,q,r): = \frac{|R^2(D,q,r) \cap \pi_p \cap \pi_A| - |R^2(D,q,r) \cap \pi_p^{-1} \cap \pi_A|}{|R^2(D,q,r) \cap \pi_p|}$$

$$Y(D,p,q,r): = \frac{|R^2(D,q,r) \cap \pi_p \cap \pi_B| - |R^2(D,q,r) \cap \pi_p^{-1} \cap \pi_B|}{|R^2(D,q,r) \cap \pi_p|}$$

In contrast to the random variables $X(D,p,q,r)$ and $Y(D,p,q,r)$, the actual values obtained from an experiment are denoted by $x(D,p,q,r)$ and $y(D,p,q,r)$ respectively. The value $u_{A,B}$ determining the usefulness of B relative to A is obtained with k experiments. Every experiment corresponds to an event (D_i,p_i,q_i,r_i) where $0 \leq i < k$. Informally, the value $u_{A,B}$ indicates how often, on the average, the values $x(D_i,p_i,q_i,r_i)$ are smaller than the values $y(D_i,p_i,q_i,r_i)$. In what follows we abbreviate these values by x_i and y_i respectively.

Given k samples of events (D_i, p_i, q_i, r_i), the values x_i and y_i are calculated according to the formulas given above. The sum of the positive ranks, w_+ is computed as follows.

1. Calculate the differences $y_i - x_i$ and discard the differences that are equal to zero. They do not contribute to the comparison of A and B.

2. Rank the absolute values $|y_i - x_i|$ of the differences $y_i - x_i$ in increasing order. If there are ties ($|y_i - x_i| = |y_j - x_j|$), each $|y_i - x_i|$ is assigned the average value of the ranks for which it is tied.

3. Restore the signs of the $|y_i - x_i|$ to the ranks, obtaining signed ranks.

4. Calculate w_+, the sum of those ranks that have positive signs.

If method B is consistently better than method A, many differences with positive signs obtain high ranks. This ranking means that w_+ is high if B is consistently better than A. However, a high value w_+ does not indicate whether B is only slightly better than A, or B is much better than A.

The usefulness $u_{A,B}$ is defined to be the normalized deviation of w_+ from μ, the expectation of W_+ that is obtained when X_i and Y_i have the same distribution. The value k is reduced to the number of valid experiments (i.e. without experiments yielding zero differences, $y_i - x_i = 0$) which will be called k_0.

$$u_{A,B} = \frac{w_+ - \mu}{\mu}$$

where

$$\mu = \frac{k_0(k_0 + 1)}{4}$$

The value $u_{A,B}$ indicates how often, on the average, the values y_i are greater than the values x_i. In order to obtain an indication of how much the y_i's are greater than the x_i's, we define an *adjusted usefulness* which also includes the zero differences.

$$u_{A,B}^* = u_{A,B} \frac{1}{k} \; \left| \sum_{i=0}^{k-1} (y_i - x_i) \right|$$

The adjusted usefulness $u_{A,B}^*$ is small if $u_{A,B}$ is small. In this case, there are few queries for which B is more effective than A. On the other hand, if $u_{A,B}$ is close to 1, we can distinguish two cases. First, if $u_{A,B}^*$ is also close to 1 then there are many queries for which B is considerably more effective than A. Second, if $u_{A,B}^*$ is small then there are many queries for which B is only slightly more effective than A.

If A is more effective than B the expectation of $U_{A,B}$ is negative. Remember that a negative value $u_{A,B}$ indicates that A is more effective than B. Because of purely chance fluctuations, a positive value $u_{A,B}$ can be obtained even though A is more effective than B. Let $u_{A,B}$ be a positive value obtained by k experiments which indicates that B performs better than A. Then, a small probability

$$P_k(U_{A,B} \geq u_{A,B})$$

means that it is unlikely that $u_{A,B}$ indicates an improvement by B, although B is less effective than A. In [Wae 69, p. 267] the value $P_k(U_{A,B} \geq u_{A,B})$ is called an *error probability*, i.e. the probability of *rejecting* the hypothesis that A is more effective than B even though the hypothesis is true. Rejecting the hypothesis means that B is regarded as being more effective than A. If $k \geq 20$, the error probability is obtained by the following formula, where Φ denotes the cumulative distribution function of the normal distribution:

$$P_k(U_{A,B} \geq u_{A,B}) \approx 1 - \Phi(\frac{w_+ - \mu}{\sigma})$$

where

$$\mu = \frac{k_0(k_0 + 1)}{4}$$

$$\sigma^2 = \frac{k_0(k_0 + 1)(2k_0 + 1)}{24}$$

The new measure concentrates on the *usefulness* of the information items for the user to whom they are delivered. In addition, *relative* judgements are used rather than the more rigid absolute (relevant - non-relevant) classification. In other words: the judge may indicate a rank order of the information items delivered. This ranking constitutes a significant advantage, as a human examiner makes *relative* judgements easily and consistently by comparing two or several items. This observation has been confirmed by various authors.

Another advantage of the proposed method is that it is possible to determine how stable a usefulness value is for a given environment. This calculation is accomplished with a statistical test which has been shown to be both applicable and useful in such experiments. An error probability determines the reliability of the usefulness value.

4. Unweighted vs. Weighted Terms

In this section, we focus on a comparison where a retrieval method B is clearly more effective than another retrieval method A. We show that both the traditional recall and precision measure and the new usefulness measure reveal that method B performs better than method A. The retrieval methods A and B are described below.

A) Every document is assumed to consist of several fields (title, author, abstract, descriptors, etc.). The indexing procedure of the retrieval method A processes the title, author, and abstract fields to extract tokens that are not in van Rijsbergen's stop list [Rij 78, p. 18]. The queries are processed analogously. An *unweighted* term is assigned to the document or the query if a corresponding token has been extracted (binary indexing). The retrieval status value (RSV) of a document with respect to a query is the number of terms that are assigned to both the document and the query (coordination level matching).

B) The indexing procedure of the retrieval method B processes the descriptor fields in addition to the title, author, and abstract fields to extract tokens that are not in the stop list. The tokens are reduced by means of Porter's word reduction algorithm [Por 80] and the frequencies of the reduced words are determined. Every document representation and every query representation consists of a set of *weighted* terms where the weight is obtained by multiplying the term frequency by the inverse document frequency. The RSV of a document with respect to a query is the cosine of the document representation and the query representation.

A test collection of abstracts from CACM [Fox 83] is used to compare the retrieval methods A and B described above. Out of the 64 queries belonging to the test collection we used those 52 queries which yield at least one relevant document. The recall vs. precision graph (Figure 1a) as well as the usefulness measure (Figure 1b) show that the retrieval method B is clearly better than A, which was to be expected.

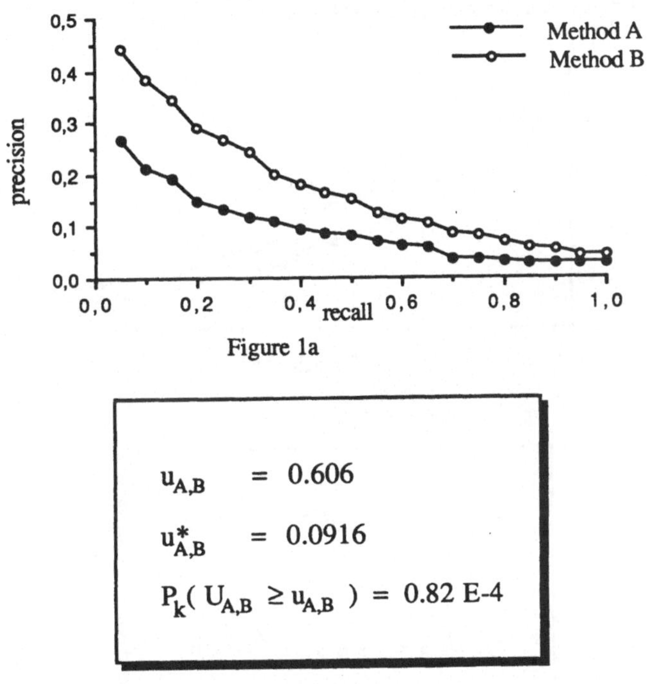

Figure 1a

$$u_{A,B} \quad = \quad 0.606$$

$$u^{*}_{A,B} \quad = \quad 0.0916$$

$$P_k(\ U_{A,B} \geq u_{A,B}\ ) = 0.82\ E\text{-}4$$

Figure 1b

5. Words vs. Reduced Words as Indexing Terms

In this section, we analyze a particular comparison of two retrieval methods where the recall and precision measure and the usefulness measure disagree as to which method is more effective. A close inspection reveals that the usefulness measure seems to reflect reality better than the recall and precision values.

We specially selected a subset of 24 queries[1] of the CACM test collection to compare the effectiveness of the following two retrieval methods:

A') The retrieval method A' is identical to the retrieval method B of the previous experiment except that the words are not reduced.

B') The retrieval method B' includes word reduction and is therefore identical to the retrieval method B of the previous experiment.

The recall vs. precision graph (Figure 2a) shows a higher effectiveness for method B' compared to method A'; on the other hand, the usefulness measure indicates that A' and B' perform equally well (Figure 2b). More precisely, B' seems to be slightly better than A' but the error probability is so high (40%) that neither of the two algorithms qualifies for higher effectiveness. Hence, the recall and precision measure and the usefulness measure disagree as to which method performs better.

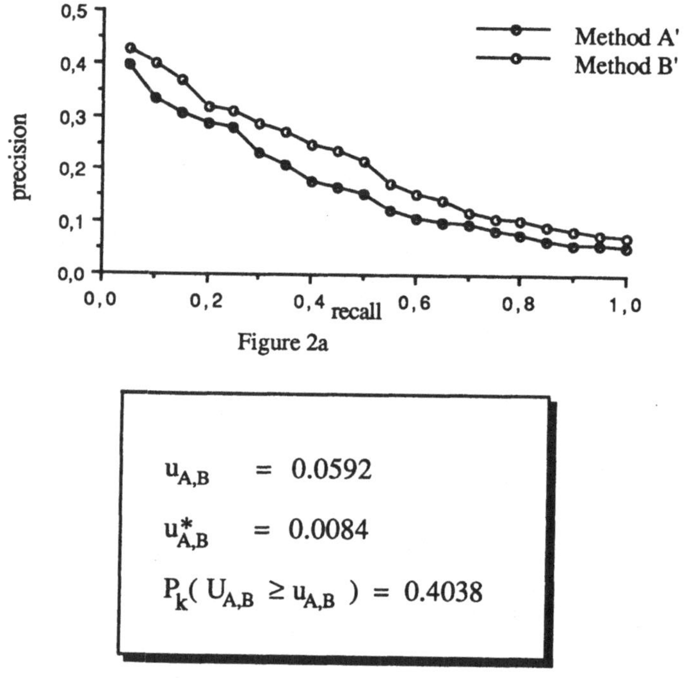

Figure 2a

$$u_{A,B} = 0.0592$$

$$u^{*}_{A,B} = 0.0084$$

$$P_k(\,U_{A,B} \geq u_{A,B}\,) = 0.4038$$

Figure 2b

As a consequence of these results we analysed the recall vs. precision graphs of every query carefully. It was found that the averaged recall vs. precision graph (Figure 2a) shows that B' performs better than A' because of *outliers*. As shown in Section 2, the recall vs. precision graph represents arithmetic means of several precision values. Arithmetic means are known to be very sensitive to outliers. Such outliers raised

---

[1] The subset includes the following queries: 1, 3, 4, 5, 7, 12, 13, 14, 19, 20, 23, 26, 29, 31, 33, 36, 38, 40, 43, 49, 57, 60, 61, 64.

the recall vs. precision curve of B' above the curve of A' even though both methods perform similarly. This is confirmed by alternative recall vs. precision graphs where the *median* of precision values is taken instead of the arithmetic mean. Figure 3 shows such an alternative recall vs. precision graph of the retrieval methods A and B described in Section 4. It expresses the same result as the standard recall vs. precision graph (Figure 1a) and as the usefulness measure (Figure 1b). However, the alternative recall vs. precision graph (Figure 4) is inconsistent with the standard recall vs. precision graph (Figure 2a), but it is consistent with the usefulness measure (Figure 2b). Thus, the usefulness measure seems to represent the real retrieval effectiveness better than the standard recall vs. precision graph.

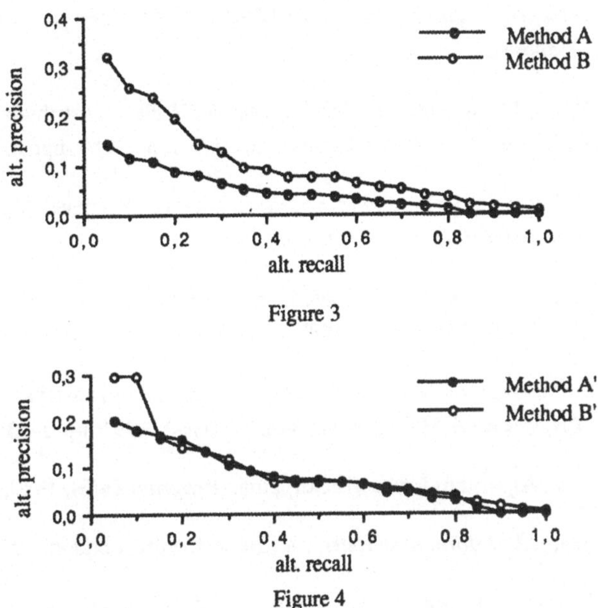

Figure 3

Figure 4

6. Conclusions

When interpreting recall and precision values, one encounters the following four different types of perils. At first glance, recall and precision values seem to represent the absolute effectiveness of a retrieval method; however, it is well known that these values strongly depend on the test collection as shown in [Sch 89, p. 8]. Hence, recall and precision values of a retrieval method should only be interpreted *relative* to the recall and precision values of another method that have been determined by the *same* test collection. The second type of peril is related to the number of queries which is used to determine the recall and precision values. In contrast to the usefulness measure (Section 3), the recall and precision measure does not indicate when *too few queries* are used. The third type of peril is due to the *rounding up* of the precision values (see [Sal 83, pp. 164] or [Sch 89, pp. 6] for details). The recall and precision graphs partially hide a bad effectiveness when the precision values of the medium recall range are below the precision values of the high recall range. Finally, there is a type of peril due to *outliers* as shown in Section 5. With regard to the perils mentioned above, we strongly feel that the usefulness measure is a much better indication of effectiveness than the traditional recall and precision measure. Only in cases when complete relevance assessments are available, modified recall and precision graphs (as presented in section 5) may be helpful in addition to the usefulness measure. In these cases the median of the precision values should be used rather than their average.

References

[Fox 83] Fox, E.A.: *Characterization of Two New Experimental Collections in Computer and Information Science Containing Textual and Bibliographic Concepts.* Report 83-561, Dept. of CS, Cornell University, 1983.

[Fre 89] Frei, H.P., Wyle, M.: Retrieving Highly Dynamic, Widely Distributed Information. *Proc. 12th Int. SIGIR Conf. ACM Press,* Cambridge, MA, June 1989, pp. 108-115.

[Fre 91] Frei, H.P., Schäuble, P.: Determining the Effectiveness of Retrieval Algorithms. *Information Processing & Management,* Vol. 27, No. 2, 1991.

[Fuh 87] Fuhr, N., Müller, P.: Probabilistic Search Term Weighting - Some Negative Results. *Proc. 10th Int. SIGIR Conf.,* ACM Press, 1987, pp. 13-18.

[Los 91] Losee, R.M.: An Analytic Measure Predicting Information Retrieval System Performance. *Information Processing & Management,* Vol. 27, No. 1, 1991, pp. 1-13.

[Por 80] Porter, M.F.: An Algorithm for Suffix Stripping. *Program* 14(3), 1980, pp. 130-137.

[Rij 78] van Rijsbergen, C.J.: *Information Retrieval.* Butterworths, London, 1978.

[Sal 83] Salton, G., McGill, M.J.: *Introduction to Modern Information Retrieval.* McGraw-Hill, New York, 1983.

[Sch 89] Schäuble, P.: *Information Retrieval Based on Information Structures.* Informatik-Diss. ETH, No. 15, vdf Verlag, Zürich, 1989.

[Wae 69] Van der Waerden, B.L.: *Mathematical Statistics.* Springer-Verlag, Berlin 1969.

Evaluating Weighted Search Terms as Boolean Queries

H.P. Frei, S. Meienberg

Swiss Federal Institute of Technology (ETH) Zurich
Department of Computer Science
8092 Zurich, Switzerland

A method for automatically generating Boolean queries from weighted search terms is described. The method is intended to exploit traditional Boolean Information Retrieval Systems in a more user-friendly way. In addition, the method partitions the answer set delivered by the Boolean system into sorted subsets of information items. This, in turn, allows control of the size of an answer set by simply adjusting retrieval status value thresholds. The principal advantage of the method we present is that its computational complexity is low in comparison to many other known methods. It is shown that efficiency can be improved significantly by a query reduction method. In addition, we introduce a more sophisticated method which further enhances retrieval effectiveness through the use of maximum term frequencies.

1. Introduction

Most of the commercially available Information Retrieval (IR) Systems rely on the ability to search for character strings in large texts as well as on a Boolean retrieval logic. The reason for the existence of these methods is not their user friendliness, but the fact that both of these techniques are relatively easy to implement. In addition, the documents of most of the existing large document collections are indexed by a relatively small number of index terms. For these reasons, to obtain information on a critical subject using a Boolean IR system requires the formulation of an elaborate Boolean expression. This is a complicated matter and requires a great deal of experience by the searcher. Even search specialists are often overwhelmed by the complexity of the queries they have to formulate [Coo 88].

Since in a Boolean expression search terms are either present or absent, it is not possible to express that a particular search term be more desirable than another. The most significant deficiency of Boolean IR systems is the fact that they merely partition the document collection into two sets, the retrieved items and those not retrieved. The items within these two sets are not ranked. In other words, if a query is formulated in a way that is too general, the answer set tends to be a very large collection of unranked documents. It is difficult for the user to assess such a reply and to extract the information that she or he was originally looking for.

The motivation for this work was to exploit better the large amount of information stored in the Boolean IR systems of today. We chose to approach this goal in two ways:
- First of all, the user friendliness is improved by allowing the user to express her or his information need with a number of weighted search terms.
- Secondly, the quality of the query result is enhanced by ranking the documents in the answer set.

The methods we present here take a search request consisting of a number of weighted search terms and translate it automatically into a Boolean query which is then submitted to a conventional Boolean IR system. The answer set is partitioned into subsets of decreasing relevance taking into account the weights indicated by the user. This allows the user both to inspect the documents in a ranked order and to define threshold values in order to limit the size of the answer set.

Ranking algorithms are a natural part of the retrieval method in many non-Boolean IR systems, viz. in the case of vector space models or fuzzy IR [Pan 86]. The retrieval functions then used, deliver a number of subsets; each subset is composed of information items with identical Retrieval Status Values (RSV). Though ideally such a subset would consists of *only one element*, in real life environments this is hardly ever the case.

[Nor 81] compared hundreds of different ranking functions in Boolean environments, he also disclosed that most of them operate on excessively indexed document collections. Unfortunately, such collections are used seldom, except of course, in experimental IR environments. In this paper we restrict ourselves to those document collections which form the basis of most Boolean IR systems: documents indexed by descriptors in a purely binary sense (presence or absence of a descriptor). Some of the attempts for ranking the results of such systems are:
- Boolean queries with *soft Boolean operators* [Pai 84]. Search terms are connected by only one, but generally applicable operator which—in the two extreme cases—can take on the function of Boolean AND and Boolean OR.
- Boolean queries with *extended Boolean operators* [Sal 83]. Search terms are connected by a general operator which may function in the framework of the Boolean and the vector space model.
- Boolean queries with *weighted search terms* [Rad 82]. The search terms are weighted but are connected by the classical Boolean operators. However, there are some problems with the operator NOT.
- Non-Boolean queries consisting of *weighted search terms* [Fre 83]. The query is specified as a virtual document by a set of weighted search terms; the Boolean operator NOT becomes obsolete with the introduction of negative weights.

In what follows, we concentrate on weighted search terms and transform these terms into common Boolean queries which can then be processed by a classical commercial Boolean IR system.

2. Weighted Terms as Queries

We assume that there is a set T of n terms t_i and a collection D of documents d which are indexed by a set of $t_i \in T$. A query is expressed by a vector $q = (q_0, q_1, ..., q_{n-1})$ with the q_i's implying the importance of every search term t_i to the user; these weights q_i are numbers in the interval [0,1].

Given are
- a collection D of documents d indexed by $(t_0, t_1, ..., t_{n-1})$,
- a document is represented by a vector $d = (d_0, d_1, ..., d_{n-1})$,
- a user query $q = (q_0, q_1, ..., q_{n-1})$,
- a retrieval function RSV which returns a real valued retrieval status value RSV(q,d) for every query - document pair,
- a number of desired documents $N \leq |D|$.

The retrieval function RSV we are using is the conventional scalar vector product:

$$RSV(q,d) = \sum_{i=0}^{n-1} q_i \cdot d_i$$

However, all the d_i's in a Boolean system are either 1 (descriptor present) or 0 (descriptor absent). For our purposes we are assigning weights to these otherwise strictly Boolean descriptors. These weights are computed by exclusively making use of the information contained in the document collection similar to the suggestions in [Sal 88b]:
- number of documents in the collection $|D|$;
- document frequency of a term $df(t)$;
- term frequency $tf(t,d)$ of term t in document d.

This results in the following descriptor weighting function:

$$d_i = idf(t_i) \cdot \frac{tf(t_i,d)}{1+tf(t_i,d)}$$

where $idf(t) = 1 - \frac{df(t)}{|D|}$ signifies the inverse document frequency and $\frac{tf(t_i,d)}{1+tf(t_i,d)}$ the normalized term frequency. Our definition of inverse document frequency and normalized term frequency has the property that the values are numbers in the intervall [0,1].

This seems to be a particularly appropriate approach as this RSV emphasizes terms with high user weights, takes into account how evenly a descriptor is distributed in the document collection, and favors descriptors which occur many times in an individual document. Furthermore the RSV values are numbers in the intervall [0,n]. In addition, Boolean IR systems usually provide the document frequency and the number of documents in the collection; the term frequency could also be provided by the system.

When τ signifies an RSV threshold and A the answer set delivered by the retrieval function at least the following conditions should hold:
a.) $RSV(q,d) < \tau \Rightarrow d \notin A$
b.) $|A| \geq N$
c.) $|A|$ as small as possible

Condition a.) means that for a given query q, a document d with an RSV smaller than τ cannot be an element of A. However, it is possible that a document d can produce an RSV greater than or equal to τ and still not be an element of the answer set A. The conditions b.) and c.) are necessary because there may exist documents d and d' with $RSV(q,d) = RSV(q,d')$ and $d \neq d'$. In other words, changing the threshold value τ slightly, may already affect several documents.

Given a user query q consisting of a number of weighted terms $(q_0, q_1, ..., q_{n-1})$ our task is to find a Boolean query Q which expresses the request q of the user, as well as a threshold value τ which ensures that the user gets at most the desired number of documents N. This Q will—as stated at the outset—then be executed by a traditional Boolean IR system.

3. Boolean Queries in Disjunctive Normal Form

When evaluating Boolean queries, we use the fact that each Boolean expression can be written in a *disjunctive normal form* consisting of a disjunction of so-called *elementary logical conjuncts* (ELC). Thus, a Boolean query containing m different search terms can be expressed as a disjunction of such ELCs which themselves have the property of containing the m search terms of the original Boolean query exactly once:

$$\bigwedge_{j=0}^{m-1} (\mu_j \, t_{i_j}) \text{ , where } \mu_j \text{ stands for either the negation or the identity of term } t_{i_j}$$

First, we concentrate on how such an ELC is evaluated. Given is a query expressed by a *single* ELC, which we call elc, consisting of m search terms and a collection consisting of binary indexed documents. If elc is evaluated by a classical Boolean retrieval function, the answer set is defined as

$$\alpha(elc) = \{d \in D \mid \forall \, j = 0..m-1:$$
$$((tf(t_{i_j}, d) > 0) \wedge \mu_j \text{ is the identity}) \vee$$
$$((tf(t_{i_j}, d) = 0) \wedge \mu_j \text{ is the negation})\}$$

Hence, every document d of the answer set $\alpha(elc)$ has the following properties:
- $tf(t_{i_j},d) = 0$ for all those t_{i_j} which are negated in elc,
- $tf(t_{i_j},d) > 0$ for all those t_{i_j} which are not negated in elc.

Since Boolean queries do not usually consist of a single ELC, we have to evaluate a disjunction of ELCs. The interesting fact is, that the answer set of such a query is the *union of all disjunctive answer sets* produced by the individual ELCs [Jam 79].

As already mentioned, our goal is to *simulate* the retrieval function RSV defined in section 2 with a *strictly Boolean* function. Inspecting $\alpha(elc)$ and using the above properties we can define a minimum RSV value minv for every ELC elc, such that $\forall \, d \in \alpha(elc)$:

$$RSV(q,d) \geq minv(elc)$$

where
$$minv(elc) = \frac{1}{2} \cdot \sum_{j=0}^{m-1} q_{i_j} \cdot idf(t_{i_j}) \cdot \delta_j$$
$$\delta_j = 1, \text{ if } \mu_j \text{ is the identity}$$
$$0 \text{ otherwise}$$

The factor $\frac{1}{2}$ is a consequence of our definition of the normalized term frequency.

In order to evaluate our user query consisting of weighted terms, we are looking for a first approximation to a possible answer set. An obvious and easy way to determine such an approximation is by considering the *disjunction of all search terms* t_i having a weight q_i greater than zero. Writing this Boolean expression in disjunctive normal form, its evaluation will produce an answer set partitioned into disjunct subsets. Each of these subsets is the result of the evaluation of an individual ELC. The subsets are then sorted according to their descending minv so as to pre-rank (partially) the documents of the answer set.

It is to be noted that this pre-ranking is not identical to the ranking imposed by our RSV function as term frequencies are neglected. As a result, it is possible for documents belonging to the answer set of an ELC with a low minv to have a higher RSV than other documents belonging to the answer set of an ELC with a higher minv.

4. Forward- and Backward-Strategy

We distinguish two different strategies both of which convert a weighted query q into a Boolean query Q. The *Forward-Strategy* starts out with an empty answer set A and broadens this set by continuously decreasing the RSV threshold value τ. The *Backward-Strategy* starts out with the answer set A consisting of the documents obtained by the above-mentioned disjunction of all the search terms. It then reduces the answer set A by continuously increasing the RSV threshold value τ.

The first step of the *Forward-Strategy* is to establish the first approximation of the answer set A as described in section 3 (disjunct subsets sorted according to descending minv). Starting from an empty answer set A, the disjunctive result sets of the sorted ELCs are added to A until the number of documents in A is greater than or equal to the number of desired documents N, or until all the ELCs are processed. If ELC^m signifies the set of all the different ELCs generated by m different search terms then the algorithm is as follows:

```
A := {};
(* a ∧ c *)
while (N > |A|) and (ELCᵐ ≠ {}) do
        find elc ∈ ELCᵐ such that minv(elc) = max{minv(elc') | elc' ∈ ELCᵐ};
        ELCᵐ := ELCᵐ - {elc};
        A := A ∪ α(elc);
od;
(* a ∧ b∧ c *)
sort A by RSV
(* the assertions a, b, and c correspond to the conditions formulated in section 2 *)
```

Forward-Strategy using Minimum-Values

The final step in this algorithm is the sorting of A according to decreasing RSV values. This step may be computationally demanding. As term frequencies are usually not explicitly available in commercial IR systems, the individual documents of the answer set may have to be scanned to determine these frequencies.

In order to improve system performance the term weighting function could also be reduced to the inverse document frequency—which may result in a loss of retrieval effectiveness [Sal 88b]. Furthermore, there will be no need for an additional sorting of the documents because the minimum values of the ELCs will be identical to the RSV of the documents in their result sets.

The complexity of this Forward-Strategy depends on the number of ELCs to be evaluated. Given m search terms, there are 2^m-1 different ELCs. It has been pointed out in [Bov 84] that the retrieval expense on the host side can be significantly reduced by evaluating search statements in a more systematic way. The idea is to build up complex Boolean queries step by step rather than evaluating a complex statement in one go. A search tree is then generated representing various possible combinations of the search terms present or absent.

As mentioned above, the *Backward-Strategy* starts out with the answer set A resulting from the disjunction of all the search terms occurring in the weighted query. This set can be decomposed into the disjunctive subsets determined by the ELCs. Subsequently, the set A is reduced successively by the subset with the smallest minv until the desired number of documents N is reached.

$$A := \{d \in D \mid \exists j; 0 \le j \le m\text{-}1: tf(t_{ij}, d) > 0\};$$

find elc $\in$ ELC^m such that minv(elc) = min$\{$minv(elc') $\mid$ elc' $\in$ ELC$^m\}$;
(* a $\wedge$ b *)
while N $\le$ |A| - | α(elc)| **do**
    ELC^m := ELC^m - {elc};
    A := A - α(elc);
    find elc $\in$ ELC^m such that minv(elc) = min$\{$minv(elc') $\mid$ elc' $\in$ ELC$^m\}$;
od;
(* a $\wedge$ b$\wedge$ c *)
sort A by RSV
(* the assertions a, b, and c correspond to the conditions formulated in section 2 *)

Backward-Strategy using Minimum-Values

The Backward-Strategy as well as the Forward-Strategy delivers as it's answer set a number of unranked documents. A sorting of all the documents of A is therefore necessary. Nevertheless, the Backward-Strategy can be more efficient than the Forward-Strategy when the number of desired documents N is high compared to the number of documents assigned to the initial answer set A.

5. Query Reduction and the Use of Maximum Values

Instead of sending each single ELC to the host, the ELC result set sizes can be estimated [Sal 88a]. This makes it possible to build up a set of ELCs applying Forward- or Backward-Strategy, where the sum of the estimated result set sizes of these ELCs is close to the number of desired documents N.

The resulting query which is a disjunction of all the ELCs in this set, can now be reduced—thus avoiding superfluous query evaluations. Primarily, the query is reduced by eliminating all the negated terms in the remaining conjuncts which converts the set of ELCs into a set of positive logical conjuncts (PLC) as stated in Lemma 2.

Positive logical conjuncts (PLC) do not contain negated search terms and are defined in the following way:

$$\bigwedge_{j=0}^{k-1} t_{ij}$$

Every ELC can be converted into its corresponding PLC by simply omitting the negated search terms. Similar to the ELCs there exists a minv for all the PLCs:

$$minv(plc) = \frac{1}{2} \cdot \sum_{j=0}^{k-1} q_{ij} \cdot idf(t_{ij})$$

Lemma 1:

If there is a PLC plc which is part of another PLC plc', then the following holds:

a.) $\alpha(plc') \subseteq \alpha(plc)$

b.) $minv(plc') > minv(plc)$

Condition a.) implies that the answer set of plc' has to be a subset of the answer set of plc, because plc is a part of plc' and, therefore, defines a less restrictive query.

Condition b.) is trivial and follows from the definition of the minimum value minv. **q.e.d.**

Lemma 2:

Let ELC' be a subset of the set ELC^m (of all the different ELCs generated by m search terms), so that those $elc \in ELC^m$ with the r lowest minv values are *not* contained in ELC'. ELC' can then be reduced to PLC' by eliminating all negated search terms from all $elc \in ELC'$. The answer set of the disjunction of all $plc \in$ PLC' and the answer set of the disjunction of all $elc \in ELC'$ can be shown to be identical, as follows:

1.)   Base case:

    Let ELC' be ELC^m and PLC' be PLC^m (the set of all the different PLCs generated by subsets of m search terms), then the result set of the disjunction of all $plc \in$ PLC' and of all $elc \in ELC'$ are identical.

2.)   Induction step:

    When successively removing the ELC elc' with the lowest minv from the above ELC' and the corresponding PLC plc' from PLC', the following conditions hold:

    a.)   All documents containing all the nonnegated terms of elc' and not containing any negated terms of elc' are removed from the result set of the disjunction of all $elc \in$ ELC'.

    b.)   Every plc" that is a subquery of plc' has a smaller minv than plc' and is already removed from PLC'. As stated in Lemma 1, the result set of plc' is a subset of the result set of plc".

    c.)   Every plc" which contains plc' as a subquery has a higher minv than plc' and is still present in PLC'. As stated in Lemma 1, the result set of plc" is a subset of the result set of plc'.

    d.)   From conditions b.) and c.) follows that all documents containing all the nonnegated terms of elc' and not containing any negated terms of elc' are removed from the result set of the disjunction of all $plc \in$ PLC' and thus both above mentioned result sets are identical. **q.e.d.**

The query is further reduced by omitting all conjuncts which are redundant according to Lemma 1. This reduced, more compact query which is the disjunction of all the remaining PLCs can now be evaluated by the IR system using a search tree.

Example:

Given are a set $T = \{t_0, t_1, t_2, t_3, t_4, t_5, t_6, t_7, t_8, t_9\}$ of index terms and a weighted query q:

$$q = (0.0,\ 0.0,\ 0.8,\ 0.0,\ 0.0,\ 0.9,\ 0.0,\ 0.1,\ 0.0,\ 0.2)$$

The first step is the translation of the weighted query q into disjunctive normal form. Therefore we generate the ELCs and sort them by their minv.

no.	ELC	minv	corresponding PLC
elc_0	$t_2 \wedge t_5 \wedge t_7 \wedge t_9$	1.0	$t_2 \wedge t_5 \wedge t_7 \wedge t_9$
elc_2	$t_2 \wedge t_5 \wedge \neg t_7 \wedge t_9$	0.95	$t_2 \wedge t_5 \wedge t_9$
elc_1	$t_2 \wedge t_5 \wedge t_7 \wedge \neg t_9$	0.9	$t_2 \wedge t_5 \wedge t_7$
elc_3	$t_2 \wedge t_5 \wedge \neg t_7 \wedge \neg t_9$	0.85	$t_2 \wedge t_5$
elc_8	$\neg t_2 \wedge t_5 \wedge t_7 \wedge t_9$	0.6	$t_5 \wedge t_7 \wedge t_9$
elc_4	$t_2 \wedge \neg t_5 \wedge t_7 \wedge t_9$	0.55	$t_2 \wedge t_7 \wedge t_9$
elc_{10}	$\neg t_2 \wedge t_5 \wedge \neg t_7 \wedge t_9$	0.55	$t_5 \wedge t_9$
elc_6	$t_2 \wedge \neg t_5 \wedge \neg t_7 \wedge t_9$	0.5	$t_2 \wedge t_9$
elc_9	$\neg t_2 \wedge t_5 \wedge t_7 \wedge \neg t_9$	0.5	$t_5 \wedge t_7$
elc_5	$t_2 \wedge \neg t_5 \wedge t_7 \wedge \neg t_9$	0.45	$t_2 \wedge t_7$
elc_{11}	$\neg t_2 \wedge t_5 \wedge \neg t_7 \wedge \neg t_9$	0.45	t_5
elc_7	$t_2 \wedge \neg t_5 \wedge \neg t_7 \wedge \neg t_9$	0.4	t_2
elc_{12}	$\neg t_2 \wedge \neg t_5 \wedge t_7 \wedge t_9$	0.15	$t_7 \wedge t_9$
elc_{14}	$\neg t_2 \wedge \neg t_5 \wedge \neg t_7 \wedge t_9$	0.1	t_9
elc_{13}	$\neg t_2 \wedge \neg t_5 \wedge t_7 \wedge \neg t_9$	0.05	t_7

The next step is the "Forward-Strategy" query reduction: This produces sets of ELCs which can be reduced to a more compact query according to Lemma 1 and 2.

set of ELCs	reduced query
$\{elc_0\}$	$t_2 \wedge t_5 \wedge t_7 \wedge t_9$
$\{elc_0, elc_2\}$	$t_2 \wedge t_5 \wedge t_9$
$\{elc_0, elc_2, elc_1\}$	$(t_2 \wedge t_5 \wedge t_9) \vee (t_2 \wedge t_5 \wedge t_7)$
$\{elc_0, elc_2, elc_1, elc_3\}$	$t_2 \wedge t_5$
$\{elc_0, elc_2, elc_1, elc_3, elc_8\}$	$(t_2 \wedge t_5) \vee (t_5 \wedge t_7 \wedge t_9)$
$\{elc_0, elc_2, elc_1, elc_3, elc_8, elc_4\}$	$(t_2 \wedge t_5) \vee (t_5 \wedge t_7 \wedge t_9) \vee (t_2 \wedge t_7 \wedge t_9)$
$\{elc_0, elc_2, elc_1, elc_3, elc_8, elc_4, elc_{10}\}$	$(t_2 \wedge t_5) \vee (t_5 \wedge t_9) \vee (t_2 \wedge t_7 \wedge t_9)$
$\{elc_0, elc_2, elc_1, elc_3, elc_8, elc_4, elc_{10}, elc_6\}$	$(t_2 \wedge t_5) \vee (t_5 \wedge t_9) \vee (t_2 \wedge t_9)$
$\{elc_0, elc_2, elc_1, elc_3, elc_8, elc_4, elc_{10}, elc_6, elc_9\}$	$(t_2 \wedge t_5) \vee (t_5 \wedge t_9) \vee (t_2 \wedge t_9) \vee (t_5 \wedge t_7)$
$\{elc_0, elc_2, elc_1, elc_3, elc_8, elc_4, elc_{10}, elc_6, elc_9, elc_5\}$	$(t_2 \wedge t_5) \vee (t_5 \wedge t_9) \vee (t_2 \wedge t_9) \vee (t_5 \wedge t_7)$ $\vee (t_2 \wedge t_7)$
$\{elc_0, elc_2, elc_1, elc_3, elc_8, elc_4, elc_{10}, elc_6, elc_9, elc_5, elc_{11}\}$	$t_5 \vee (t_2 \wedge t_9) \vee (t_2 \wedge t_7)$
$\{elc_0, elc_2, elc_1, elc_3, elc_8, elc_4, elc_{10}, elc_6, elc_9, elc_5, elc_{11}, elc_7\}$	$t_5 \vee t_2$
$\{elc_0, elc_2, elc_1, elc_3, elc_8, elc_4, elc_{10}, elc_6, elc_9, elc_5, elc_{11}, elc_7, elc_{12}\}$	$t_5 \vee t_2 \vee (t_7 \wedge t_9)$
$\{elc_0, elc_2, elc_1, elc_3, elc_8, elc_4, elc_{10}, elc_6, elc_9, elc_5, elc_{11}, elc_7, elc_{12}, elc_{14}\}$	$t_2 \vee t_5 \vee t_9$
$\{elc_0, elc_2, elc_1, elc_3, elc_8, elc_4, elc_{10}, elc_6, elc_9, elc_5, elc_{11}, elc_7, elc_{12}, elc_{14}, elc_{13}\}$	$t_2 \vee t_5 \vee t_7 \vee t_9$

The main problem of both methods following the Forward- and Backward-Strategy using minimum values is the fact that the property

a'.) $RSV(q,d) \geq \tau \Rightarrow d \in A$

does not hold, i.e. it is possible that a document d can produce an RSV greater than or equal to τ and still not be an element of the answer set A (cf. section 2).

In order to eliminate this problem, we first have to envisage the RSV function defined in section 2. As we have defined a minimum value minv for every ELC, we can also define a maximum RSV value *maxv* in a similar way. Proposing that we know the maximum term frequency *maxtf* of each search term in the query (which is admittedly rather difficult to obtain from commercially available IR systems) we can evaluate the maximum RSV for each ELC, such that $\forall d \in \alpha(elc)$:

$$RSV(q,d) \leq maxv(elc)$$

where
$$maxv(elc) = \sum_{j=0}^{m-1} q_{ij} \cdot idf(t_{ij}) \cdot \frac{maxtf(t_j)}{1+maxtf(t_j)} \cdot \delta_j$$

$$\delta_j = 1, \text{ if } \mu_j \text{ is the identity}$$
$$0 \text{ otherwise}$$

Knowing the maximum RSV of each ELC, we now can work out a strategy which takes into account property a'.) in addition to the properties a.) to c.) of section 2.

Firstly, all the ELCs are evaluated and then sorted according to their descending maximum RSV values maxv. As in the Forward-Strategy using minimum values we start with an empty answer set A and add the disjunctive result sets of the ELCs to A. Each time an ELC is processed, the maximum value of the next ELC becomes the threshold value τ.

All documents with an RSV greater than τ belong definitively to the result set A as no document in any of the following ELCs can have an RSV greater than τ. Therefore, the algorithm stops as soon as the number of documents in the result set A with an RSV greater than τ is greater than or equal to the number of desired documents N. To satisfy condition a.) of section 2, all documents with an RSV smaller than τ must be removed from the answer set A.

Applying the proposed method, it is necessary to evaluate at least the RSV of each document in the answer set A. This can be rather complex if term frequencies are not provided by the system. Nevertheless, this method can be effective because both properties a.) *and* a'.) of sections 2 and 5 hold. On the other hand, the method requires at least *maximum* term frequencies to be available from the host system.

6. Experiments

The Forward-Strategy we introduced in this paper has been applied to the commercial IR system "Data-Star" of Radio Suisse using the INSPEC database. Firstly, we evaluated each ELC as a self-contained query until the desired number of documents N were retrieved. In a second experiment we combined the Forward-Strategy with the query reduction method described in section 5. Finally we used a search tree [Bov 84] to evaluate the Boolean statements in a more systematic manner.

Each of the above techniques was applied to queries with eight and ten weighted search terms. The number of desired documents N was set to 100. As an informal indicator of efficiency we measured the number of basic Boolean operations (AND, OR, NOT) and the number of queries transferred to the Data-Star host.

Weighted query containing eight search terms:

Forward-Strategy		query reduction
	1344 operations 200 queries	199 operations 76 queries
search tree	107 operations 115 queries	90 operations 61 queries

Weighted query containing ten search terms:

Forward-Strategy		query reduction
	8253 operations 927 queries	432 operations 169 queries
search tree	191 operations 201 queries	110- operations 86 queries

The results show clearly that a high number of operations and queries are necessary when the pure Forward-Strategy without further aid is applied. This would result in a great deal of computation and long response times making this method feasible only for a small number of search terms (at most about four terms). Our experiments demonstrate that the efficiency is significantly enhanced by applying the query reduction method and/or using a search tree.

When comparing the query reduction method with the application of a search tree, the following points should be borne in mind:
The Forward-Strategy combined with the query reduction method generates about twice as many operations as the Forward-Strategy using a search tree. On the other hand, it generates a smaller number of queries. However, it is to be noted that not all the operations of the query reduction method are actually performed, because the IR host automatically stops further execution of a Boolean statement as soon as an intermediate result set is empty. Furthermore, the query reduction method has no need for the NOT-operator which is computationally more demanding than the operators OR and AND [Sal 89].

Unfortunately, the use of search trees requires the storage of a relatively large number of intermediate result sets on the host. However, this space requirement can be significantly reduced by first applying the reduction process to the query.

7. Conclusions

Many attempts have been made and sophisticated methods proposed to improve the retrieval effectiveness of commercial reference, fact, and text data bases. However, most of these methods are computationally expensive or difficult to apply in existing real life environments.

The paramount advantage of the proposed method using minimum RSV values is its simplicity which makes it easily applicable to any commercial IR system relying on Boolean retrieval logic. Another advantage is that user needs may be expressed by weighted search terms. Finally, the query results consist of partially sorted, size-restricted lists of documents, enhancing significantly the user friendliness of traditional IR systems.

Furthermore, a more sophisticated method increasing retrieval effectiveness by the use of maximum term frequencies has been introduced. This method is more complex and requires additional information to be provided by the host system.

Finally, it has to be stated that—despite all the efforts proposed in this paper—weighted retrieval can be much more efficient when implemented on the host side. All the information for generating a ranked result list is then directly available and there is no need for expensive and time-consuming transmission of this data to the front-end for processing. Unfortunately none of the commercially available large IR systems which rely on Boolean retrieval logic, have implemented such a mechanism on their host as yet.

References

[Bov 84]   Bovey, J.D., Robertson, S.E.: An algorithm for weighted searching on a Boolean system. *Information Technology: Research and Development 3(1)*, 1984, pp. 84-87.

[Coo 88]   Cooper, W.S.: Getting beyond Boole. Information Technology: *Information Processing & Management 24 (3)*, 1988, pp. 243-248.

[Fre 83]   Frei, H.P., Jauslin, J.-F.: Graphical Presentation of Information and Services: A User-Oriented Interface. *Information Technology: Research and Development 2 (1)*, Jan. 1983, pp. 23-42.

[Jam 79]   Jamieson, S.H.: The economic implementation of experimental retrieval techniques on a very large scale using an intelligent terminal. *Proc. 2nd Int. Conf. on Inf. Storage and Retr.*, Dallas, 1979, pp. 45-51.

[Nor 81]   Noreault, T., McGill, M., Koll, M.B.: A Performance Evaluation of Similarity Measures, Document Term Weighting Schemes and Representations in a Boolean Environment. In: Oddy, R.N. et al. *Information Retrieval Research*, Butterworths, London, 1981.

[Pai 84]   Paice, C.D.: Soft evaluation of Boolean search queries in information retrieval systems. *Information Technology: Research and Development 3 (1)*, Jan. 1984.

[Pan 86]   Panyr, J.: Die Theorie der Fuzzy-Mengen und Information-Retrieval Systeme. *Nachr. f. Dokum. 37 (3)*, 1986.

[Rad 82] Radecki, T.: Reducing the Perils of Merging Boolean and Weighted Retrieval. *Journal of Documentation 38 (3)*, 1982, pp. 207-211.

[Sal 83] Salton, G., Fox, E.: Extended Boolean Information Retrieval. *Communication of the ACM 26 (11)*, 1983, pp. 1022-1036.

[Sal 88a] Salton, G.: A Simple Blueprint for Automatic Boolean Query Processing. *Information Processing & Management 24 (3)*, 1988, pp. 269-280.

[Sal 88b] Salton, G., Buckley, C.: Term-Weighting Approaches in Automatic Text Retrieval. *Information Processing & Management 24 (5)*, 1988, pp. 513-523.

[Sal 89] Salton, G.: Automatic Text Processing: The Transformation, Analysis, and Retrieval of Information by Computer. *Addison-Wesley Publishing Company,* 1989.

Zur Aufwandsabschätzung bei der Entwicklung eines Indexierungswörterbuches

Kostas Tzeras
Technische Hochschule Darmstadt, Fachbereich Informatik
Fachgebiet Datenverwaltungssysteme II
Alexanderstr. 6, W–6100 Darmstadt,
Germany

Zusammenfassung

Für die automatische Indexierung mit einem vorgegebenen Deskriptorensystem wird ein Wörterbuch benötigt, das möglichst viele Fachausdrücke des Anwendungsgebietes durch Relationen mit Deskriptoren verbindet. Werden die in einem solchen Indexierungswörterbuch erfaßten Relationen aus der Verarbeitung von Texten gewonnen, so ergibt sich eine Beziehung zwischen der Anzahl der Texte und der Größe und Leistungsfähigkeit des Wörterbuches. Die Beschreibung derartiger Beziehungen ist besonders vor Beginn der Entwicklung eines automatischen Indexierungssystems von großem Interesse. H. Hüther hat sich in mehreren Arbeiten mit diesem Problem beschäftigt und verschiedene Schätzverfahren theoretisch hergeleitet. Für eines der von ihm vorgeschlagenen Schätzverfahren zur Abschätzung der Größe eines Indexierungswörterbuches in Abhängigkeit von der Anzahl der zugrundeliegenden Texte werden im vorliegenden Beitrag die Leistungsfähigkeit und die Anwendbarkeit untersucht.

1 Einleitung

Bei Systemen zur wissensbasierten Verarbeitung von Texten in natürlicher Sprache werden in der Regel umfangreiche Wörterbücher benötigt. Das in einem Wörterbuch erfaßte Wissen bildet die Grundlage für die automatische Verarbeitung der komplexen natürlichen Sprache.

Da globale Wörterbücher, die für viele Anwendungsmöglichkeiten in vielen Fachgebieten einsatzfähig wären, praktisch nicht erstellbar sind, hängt das in einer solchen Wissensbasis abgelegte Wissen stark von der jeweiligen Aufgabenstellung ab.

Hat man sich für bestimmte Wissensarten und -repräsentationen im Rahmen einer Entwicklung entschieden, so stellt sich die Frage der Gewinnung von Wörterbuchdaten. Hierfür bieten sich zwei, gegenseitig oft ergänzende Vorgehensweisen an: der Einsatz von Experten aus dem Anwendungsgebiet bzw. die Anwendung automatisch-heuristischer Verfahren zur Extraktion des Wissens aus einer Menge von Texten. In beiden Fällen ist vor Beginn der obengenannten Phase einer Entwicklung die Frage der Abhängigkeit zwischen Systemqualität und Aufwand für den Aufbau des Wörterbuches von besonderem Interesse.

Die Beantwortung dieser zunächst sehr allgemein gestellten Frage setzt eine Konkretisierung der Begriffe Aufwand und Qualität voraus, die nur innerhalb einer gegebenen Aufgabenstellung vorgenommen werden kann. Darüberhinaus werden Verfahren zur Aufwandsabschätzung benötigt, da das sukzessive Aufbauen und Testen verschiedener Wörterbuchvarianten aus wirtschaftlichen und praktischen Gründen oft nicht durchführbar ist.

Der vorliegende Beitrag beschäftigt sich in erster Linie mit der Problematik der Aufwandsabschätzung bei der Entwicklung einer speziellen Art von Wörterbüchern, die für die automatische Indexierung mit einem vorgegebenen Deskriptorensystem erforderlich sind. Diese Wörterbücher werden aus der Verarbeitung einer Menge von Texten automatisch gewonnen, so daß sich eine Beziehung zwischen der Anzahl der Texte und der Größe und Leistungsfähigkeit des Wörterbuches ergibt. Die Realisierung einer möglichst zuverlässigen Aufwandsabschätzung wird dabei als ein erster Schritt auf dem Weg zur Untersuchung der Zusammenhänge zwischen Aufwand und Qualität im Kontext der automatischen Indexierung angesehen.

Zur Aufwandsabschätzung bei der Entwicklung eines Indexierungswörterbuches wurden von Hüther [Hüther 89] verschiedene Schätzverfahren hergeleitet. Für eines der von ihm vorgeschlagenen Verfahren sollen in dem vorliegenden Beitrag die Leistungsfähigkeit und die Anwendbarkeit untersucht werden.

Zunächst werden in Abschnitt 2 die Repräsentation, Gewinnung und Rolle des Wörterbuchwissens innerhalb des im Fachgebiet Datenverwaltungssysteme II der Technischen Hochschule Darmstadt entwickelten automatischen Indexierungssystems AIR/PHYS erläutert. Der Indexierungsansatz wird dabei nur soweit beschrieben, wie es für den Zweck dieses Beitrags notwendig ist. Bei Interesse an dem gesamten Indexierungsansatz wird hier auf [Lustig 86] und [Fuhr et al. 91] verwiesen.

Abschnitt 3 enthält eine Beschreibung des Schätzverfahrens, während die experimentellen Ergebnisse zur Beurteilung der Leistungsfähigkeit des Schätzverfahrens in Abschnitt 4 vorgestellt werden. Dabei werden die Daten aus der Produktion des Wörterbuches PHYS/PILOT herangezogen, das als Bestandteil des automatischen Indexierungssystems AIR/PHYS aus 392 000 Referatetexten entwickelt wurde. In Abschnitt 5 werden Strategien der Stichprobenerhebung für die Berechnung möglichst zuverlässiger Schätzwerte diskutiert, deren Eignung durch weitere Experimente belegt wird. Abschließend werden die Möglichkeiten der Anwendung des Schätzverfahrens für die Untersuchung der Zusammenhänge zwischen Aufwand zum Aufbau des Indexierungswörterbuches und Qualität der damit erzielten Indexierungsergebnisse skizziert.

2 Wörterbücher für die automatische Indexierung

Bei der betrachteten Konzeption wird die Aufgabenstellung, Texte automatisch zu indexieren, als die maschinelle Zuteilung von Schlagwörtern aus einem vorgegebenen Vokabular (Deskriptoren) an Referatetexte (Abstracts), die in englischer Sprache vorliegen, aufgefaßt. Die Bedingung, daß die zur Indexierung zugelassenen Deskriptoren vorgegeben sind, bedeutet, daß die Indexierung nicht „am Text kleben" darf. Ein automatisches Indexierungssystem muß daher die wichtigsten Stellen eines Textes herausfinden und durch Deskriptoren darstellen. Hierfür wird ein Wörterbuch benötigt, dessen Relationen jeweils einen Fachausdruck des Anwendungsgebietes mit einem Deskriptor verbinden. Prozedural gesehen, läßt sich die automatische Indexierung auf die Teilaufgabe zurückführen, automatisch zu entscheiden, ob ein Deskriptor s aus der Menge der zugelassenen Deskriptoren bezüglich eines zu indexierenden Referatetextes d relevant ist (Indexierungsentscheidung).

Zunächst werden ausgehend vom maschinenlesbaren Referatetext bestimmte Texteigenschaften aufgrund vorgegebener Kriterien identifiziert. Als Texteigenschaft soll hier das Vorkommen eines Terms (bedeutungtragendes Wort bzw. Mehrwortgruppe, chemische Formel, fachspezifische Abkürzung, usw.) betrachtet werden, das durch die Sicherheit der Identifikation[1] und die Signifikanz in bezug auf das Referat[2] attribuiert wird.

Die aus sämtlichen Texteigenschaften und globalen Angaben über das Referat[3] bestehende Repräsen-

---

[1] Wort wird in Grundform/Stammform identifiziert, Mehrwortgruppe besteht aus 3 Komponenten, wobei zwischen diesen zwei Wörter stehen, die nicht zur Mehrwortgruppe gehören, usw.

[2] Vorkommensort (z.B. Titel/Abstract), Vorkommenshäufigkeit im Text, usw.

[3] Art des Referates, Länge des Referates, Anzahl identifizierter Terms, usw.

tation des zu indexierenden Textes bildet die Voraussetzung für den Einsatz des im Indexierungswörterbuch erfaßten Wissens.

Das Indexierungswörterbuch verbindet möglichst viele Terms durch Relationen mit Deskriptoren und ermöglicht die Erstellung von Hinweisen von Terms des Textes auf eine Menge von Deskriptoren. Das in einem Indexierungswörterbuch erfaßte Wissen wird durch Term-Deskriptor-Paare repräsentiert, welche aufgrund semantischer oder statistischer Kriterien gebildet werden.

Term-Deskriptor-Paare, die aufgrund semantischer Kriterien wie Synonymie, Ober-, Unterbegriff, verwandter Begriff u.ä. gebildet werden, können aus bestehenden Nachschlagewerken[4] direkt übernommen werden. Term-Deskriptor-Paare, die aufgrund statistischer Kriterien gebildet werden, müssen durch eine aufwendige Auswertung von Referatetexten und intellektueller Indexierung einer Dokumentmenge gewonnen werden. Letztere Paare bilden die für die automatische Indexierung sehr wichtige Relation Z.

Die statistische Relation Z zwischen einem Term t und einem Deskriptor s beruht auf dem Assoziationsfaktor z. Bei Vorliegen einer sehr großen intellektuell indexierten Dokumentmenge wird z (im folgenden z-Wert genannt) wie folgt berechnet:

$$z(t, s, U) = \frac{h(t, s, U)}{f(t, U)}.$$

Dabei bezeichnet

U	eine Menge von Formen des Vorkommens,
$f(t, U)$	die Anzahl der Dokumente, in denen der Term t in eine zu U gehörenden Form des Vorkommens auftritt (Termhäufigkeit), und
$h(t, s, U)$	die Anzahl derjenigen unter diesen Dokumenten, denen der Deskriptor s intellektuell zugeteilt wurde (Paarhäufigkeit).

Der z-Wert approximiert die Wahrscheinlichkeit, daß beim zugrundeliegenden Indexierungsvokabular ein Indexierungsfachmann den Deskriptor s einem Dokument zuteilen würde, falls der Term t in eine zu U gehörenden Form des Vorkommens im Referat des Dokuments[5] identifiziert wird.

Ist eine formal verifizierbare Definition der erlaubten Formen des Vorkommens gegeben, so kann die Eigenschaft „ein Term t kommt in einem Dokument vor" algorithmisch identifiziert und die Relation Z aus einer Menge intellektuell indexierter Dokumente automatisch gewonnen werden. Im folgenden wird das Argument U nicht weiter in den Bezeichnungen mitgeführt, da sich die Betrachtungen auf eine feste Menge U beziehen[6].

Aus praktischen und statistischen Gründen werden nur solche z-Werte in das Indexierungswörterbuch übernommen, die mit geeigneten Konstanten c_1 und c_2 die Bedingungen $z(t, s) \geq c_1$ und $h(t, s) \geq c_2$ erfüllen.

Die Approximation der oben beschriebenen Wahrscheinlichkeit durch den z-Wert wirft eine Reihe von Problemen auf, die im Rahmen des vorliegenden Beitrags nicht ausführlicher behandelt werden können. Es sei hier aber auf das wesentliche Problem der niedrigen statistischen Sicherheit des z-Wertes für kleine Häufigkeiten $h(t, s)$ und $f(t)$ hingewiesen[7]. Weiterhin muß sich die Festlegung der Menge U von Formen des Vorkommens, der Schwellenwerte c_1 und c_2, wie auch der verwendeten Dokumentmenge von Überlegungen hinsichtlich der statistischen Sicherheit der zu gewinnenden Relationen leiten lassen (vgl. auch [Fuhr et al. 86]).

---

[4] Thesauri, Sachregister usw.

[5] einschl. Titel.

[6] Für den Aufbau des Wörterbuches PHYS/PILOT wurde z.B. bei Einzelwörtern Übereinstimmung in der Grundform, bei Mehrwortgruppen Grundformübereinstimmung und maximal sechs andere Wörter zwischen den Komponenten der Mehrwortgruppe zugelassen.

[7] Über grundsätzliche Probleme bei probabilistischen Modellen vgl. auch [Fuhr & Hüther 89].

Das Indexierungssystem findet in einem Text einen Hinweis $t \rightarrow s$ von einem Term t auf einen Deskriptor s genau dann, wenn es den Term t als in dem Text vorkommend erkennt und eine Relation zwischen t und s im Wörterbuch feststellt. Ein Hinweis wird durch verschiedene Eigenschaften beschrieben, wie z.B. die Form des Vorkommens des Terms t, Angaben über die Relation zwischen t und s und weitere Informationen über s und t.

Nach Erstellung der Hinweise von Terms des Textes auf eine Menge von Deskriptoren werden die Relevanzbeschreibungen gebildet. Die Relevanzbeschreibung $x(s,d)$ eines Deskriptors s bezüglich eines Dokuments d enthält alle Hinweise von Terms des Textes auf den Deskriptor s, und auch Eigenschaften, die nicht einem einzelnen Hinweis zuzuordnen sind[8].

Die Relevanzbeschreibung $x(s,d)$ kann als die Zusammenfassung der Texteigenschaften betrachtet werden, die vom System zur Entscheidung über die Zuteilung bzw. Nicht-Zuteilung des Deskriptors s herangezogen werden können.

Die für die Entscheidung erforderliche Bewertung der Relevanzbeschreibung erfolgt durch eine Indexierungsfunktion $a(x)$. Die Indexierungsfunktion ordnet jeder Relevanzbeschreibung x ein Indexierungsgewicht $g = a(x)$ zu, das die Wahrscheinlichkeit approximiert, daß ein Indexierungsfachmann den Deskriptor s dem Text d zuteilen würde, falls die Relevanzbeschreibung $x(s,d) = x$ vorliegt. Die von der Indexierungsfunktion gelieferten Gewichte können durch die Einführung eines Schwellenwertes g_0 auf die Gewichte 0 (Nicht-Zuteilung) bzw. 1 (Zuteilung) abgebildet werden, so daß sich eine ungewichtete Indexierung ergibt.

Für die Entwicklung von Indexierungsfunktionen wird eine Stichprobe von intellektuell indexierten Dokumenten verwendet, auf der ein probabilistischer Klassifikationsalgorithmus angewendet wird. Verschiedene Algorithmen für die Klassifikation von Objekten auf der Basis von Stichproben korrekter Entscheidungen wurden in der Literatur vorgeschlagen. In Zusammenhang mit der automatischen Indexierung wurden verschiedene Ansätze experimentell untersucht und evaluiert (vgl. [Beinke-Geiser et al. 86], [Knorz 83], [Pfeifer 90], [Faißt 90]).

Die bisher beschriebene Konzeption verdeutlicht die zentrale Rolle des Wörterbuches innerhalb des automatischen Indexierungssystems. Das in einem Wörterbuch erfaßte Wissen bestimmt weitgehend die Entscheidungsbasis für die Indexierungsfunktion und dementsprechend auch die Qualität des Indexierungssystems. Das Indexierungswörterbuch muß bezüglich der darin erfaßten Terms so vollständig wie möglich sein, denn Textwörter, über die es keine Angaben enthält, bleiben bei der automatischen Indexierung unberücksichtigt. Weiterhin müssen die unsicheren Angaben, die durch die Verwendung statistisch-heuristischer Verfahren in das Wörterbuch gelangen, mit einer akzeptablen Quote an Folgefehlern weiterverarbeitet werden können.

Die in diesem Abschnitt vorgestellte Relation Z macht sowohl in quantitativer als auch in qualitativer Hinsicht den wichtigsten Bestandteil[9] eines Indexierungswörterbuches aus, und trägt somit entscheidend zur Qualität der Indexierungsergebnisse bei. Die Gewinnung der Relation Z bestimmt weitgehend den Aufwand für die Entwicklung eines Indexierungswörterbuches.

3 Ein Schätzverfahren für den Umfang der Relation Z

In [Hüther 89] werden verschiedene Möglichkeiten zur Schätzung des Umfangs der Relation Z vorgeschlagen, über deren Leistungsfähigkeit jedoch keine Aussagen gemacht werden.

Eine Möglichkeit, die Anzahl der verschiedenen Term-Deskriptor-Paare der Relation Z in Abhängigkeit von der Anzahl der zugrundeliegenden Dokumente abzuschätzen, besteht darin, aufgrund einer kleinen Stichprobe von Dokumenten eine Teilmenge der Relation Z zu bilden, um dann mittels einer Hochrechnung einen Erwartungswert für den Umfang der gesamten Relation Z zu erhalten.

---

[8] z.B. Länge des Referatetextes von d, Anzahl der Hinweise von Terms des Textes auf den Deskriptor s, usw.

[9] Für das aus 392 000 Referatetexten entwickelte Wörterbuch PHYS/PILOT wurden z.B. aus insgesammt 878 674 Term-Deskriptor-Paaren, 805 853 aufgrund der Relation Z gebildet.

Das Schätzverfahren basiert auf sogenannten Paartoken, wobei mit Paartoken das „Vorkommen" eines Term-Deskriptor-Paares in einem Dokument in dem Sinne gemeint ist, daß der Term im Referatetext vorkommt und der Deskriptor dem Dokument intellektuell zugeteilt ist.

Im folgenden wird mit (t, s) ein Term-Deskriptor-Paar bezeichnet, wobei t den Term und s den Deskriptor repräsentiert. Für ein Dokument wird die Bezeichnung d verwendet. Die Anzahl der zur Entwicklung des Wörterbuches zur Verfügung stehenden Dokumente (Korpus) wird mit n bezeichnet, während die Anzahl der Dokumente einer Stichprobe aus dem Korpus mit n_s bezeichnet wird. Weiterhin wird das Vorkommen eines Paares (t, s) in einem Dokument d, also das Paartoken (t, s), mit $((t, s), d)$ bezeichnet.

$D(n)$ bezeichnet die Menge der Dokumente des Korpus[10], $D(n_s)$ die Menge der Dokumente der Stichprobe, wobei $D(n_s)$ eine Teilmenge von $D(n)$ ist. Für einen Term t, der in mindestens einem Dokument des Korpus $D(n)$ vorkommt, bezeichnet $D(t, n)$ die Menge der Dokumente von $D(n)$, in denen t vorkommt. Analog bezeichnet $D(s, n)$ die Menge der Dokumente von $D(n)$, denen der Deskriptor s zugeteilt wurde, und $D(t, s, n)$ die Menge der Dokumente von $D(n)$, in denen t vorkommt und denen s zugeteilt wurde.

Es ergeben sich somit folgende Definitionen:

$$
\begin{aligned}
D(n) &= \{d \,|\, d \in \text{Korpus}\} \\
D(n_s) &= \{d \,|\, d \in \text{Stichprobe}\} \\
D(t, n) &= \{d \,|\, d \in D(n), t \text{ kommt in } d \text{ vor }\} \\
D(s, n) &= \{d \,|\, d \in D(n), s \text{ wurde } d \text{ zugeteilt }\} \\
D(t, s, n) &= D(t, n) \cap D(s, n)
\end{aligned}
$$

Weiterhin wird mit $Z(n)$ die Menge der Term-Deskriptor-Paare, aus denen die über $D(n)$ gewonnene Relation Z besteht, bezeichnet:

$$
Z(n) = \{(t, s) \,|\, z(t, s) \geq c_1, h(t, s) \geq c_2\}.
$$

Mit $Z(h, f, n)$ wird die Teilmenge von $Z(n)$ bezeichnet, deren Paare (t, s) eine Paarhäufigkeit $h(t, s)$ von h und eine Termhäufigkeit $f(t)$ von f haben:

$$
Z(h, f, n) = \{(t, s) \in Z(n) \,|\, h(t, s) = h, f(t) = f\}.
$$

Aus der Menge $Z(h, f, n)$ und der Stichprobe $D(n_s)$ wird die Menge der Paartoken

$$
(Z(h, f, n), D(n_s)) = \{((t, s), d) \,|\, (t, s) \in Z(h, f, n), d \in D(t, s, n) \cap D(n_s)\}
$$

gebildet. Diese Menge besteht aus denjenigen Paartoken der Stichprobe, deren Paare (t, s) einen bestimmten z-Wert (bzw. Paarhäufigkeit h und Termhäufigkeit f) bezüglich des gesamten Korpus bilden. Man beachte, daß die Menge $(Z(h, f, n), D(n_s))$ nicht aus Paaren, sondern aus Paartoken besteht. So kommt beispielsweise ein Paar (t, s), das eine Paarhäufigkeit von h und eine Termhäufigkeit von f bildet und in den 17 Dokumenten $d_1, d_2, \ldots, d_{17}$ der Stichprobe vorkommt, 17 Mal in $(Z(h, f, n), D(n_s))$ vor. Es bildet dann die Elemente $((t, s), d_1), ((t, s), d_2), \ldots, ((t, s), d_{17})$.

Als Erwartungswert $E(|(Z(h, f, n), D(n_s))|)$ für die Anzahl der Paartoken einer zufällig gewählten Stichprobe $D(n_s)$ erhält man:

$$
E(|(Z(h, f, n), D(n_s))|) = |(Z(h, f, n), D(n))| \cdot \frac{n_s}{n}. \tag{1}
$$

---

[10] Dabei wird angenommen, daß $D(n)$ repräsentativ für das jeweilige Fachgebiet ist.

Für ein Paar $(t,s) \in Z(h,f,n)$ gilt $|D(t,s,n)| = h$ und damit für die Anzahl der Paare mit einer bestimmten Paarhäufigkeit h und Termhäufigkeit f

$$|Z(h,f,n)| = \frac{|(Z(h,f,n),D(n))|}{h}. \tag{2}$$

Aus (1) und (2) ergibt sich

$$E(|(Z(h,f,n),D(n_s))|) = |Z(h,f,n)| \cdot h \cdot \frac{n_s}{n} \tag{3}$$

und weiter folgender Schätzwert für $|Z(h,f,n)|$:

$$E^*(|Z(h,f,n)|) = |(Z(h,f,n),D(n_s))| \cdot \frac{n}{h \cdot n_s}. \tag{4}$$

(4) ermöglicht Schätzungen für die Anzahl der z-Werte mit einer bestimmten Paarhäufigkeit h und Termhäufigkeit f bezüglich des gesamten Korpus. Durch Summation über alle möglichen Werte von h und f, wobei nur solche h- und f-Werte betrachtet werden, die mit geeigneten Konstanten c_1 und c_2 die Bedingungen $h \geq c_2$ und $\frac{h}{f} \geq c_1$ erfüllen, erhält man einen Schätzwert für den Umfang der Relation Z:

$$E^*(|Z(n)|) = \frac{n}{n_s} \sum_{h \geq c_2} \frac{1}{h} \sum_{h \leq f \leq \frac{h}{c_1}} |(Z(h,f,n),D(n_s))|. \tag{5}$$

Die Ermittlung der Anzahlen $|(Z(h,f,n),D(n_s))|$ erfordert die Berechnung der z-Werte bezüglich des gesamten Korpus, allerdings nur für die in den Dokumenten der Stichprobe vorkommenden Paare. Man muß für jedes in einem Dokument $d \in D(n_s)$ vorkommende Paar (t,s) feststellen, zu welcher Menge $(Z(h,f,n),D(n_s))$ das Tripel $((t,s),d)$ gehört. Der Schätzwert ergibt sich dann aus der Hochrechnung der Anzahl der Elemente dieser Mengen mittels der Gleichung (5).
Ebenso wie aus $D(n_s)$ Schätzungen für $Z(n)$ möglich sind, können aus der Dokumentmenge $D(n_s) \cap D(n')$ Schätzungen für $Z(n')$ mit $n' \leq n$ vorgenommen werden. Dabei ist $D(n')$ eine Teilmenge von $D(n)$, die Stichprobe $D(n_s)$ braucht jedoch nicht unbedingt eine Teilmenge von $D(n')$ zu sein. Ist $|(D(n_s) \cap D(n'))|$ ausreichend groß, so ergibt sich der Schätzwert für $|Z(n')|$ aus:

$$E^*(|Z(n')|) = \frac{n'}{n_s} \sum_{h \geq c_2} \frac{1}{h} \sum_{h \leq f \leq \frac{h}{c_1}} |(Z(h,f,n'),D(n_s) \cap D(n'))|. \tag{6}$$

(6) ist für $n' = n$ äquivalent zu (5), da für $n' = n$, $D(n_s) \cap D(n') = D(n_s)$ gilt.
Summiert man in (6) nur über bestimmte h- und f-Werte, so erhält man weitere Schätzfunktionen. Ein Schätzwert für die Anzahl der Term-Deskriptor-Paare mit einer bestimmten Paarhäufigkeit ergibt sich aus (7); ein weiterer Schätzwert für die Anzahl der Paare mit einer bestimmten Paar- und Termhäufigkeit aus (8):

$$E^*(|Z(h,n')|) = \frac{n'}{n_s} \frac{1}{h} \sum_{(h \leq f \leq \frac{h}{c_1})} |(Z(h,f,n'),D(n_s) \cap D(n'))|, \tag{7}$$

$$E^*(|Z(h,f,n')|) = \frac{n'}{n_s} \frac{1}{h} |(Z(h,f,n'),D(n_s) \cap D(n'))|. \tag{8}$$

4 Beurteilung der Leistungsfähigkeit des Schätzverfahrens

4.1 Zielsetzung und Aufbau der Experimente

Für die Beurteilung der Leistungsfähigkeit des in Abschnitt 3 vorgestellten Schätzverfahrens wurden die Daten aus der Produktion des Wörterbuches PHYS/PILOT herangezogen. Die Relation Z dieses Wörterbuches wurde aufgrund von 392 000 Dokumenten berechnet und enthält u.a. 159 930 verschiedene Term-Deskriptor-Paare mit einem Wort als Term. Jedes dieser Paare bildet einen z-Wert von mindestens 0,3 (Konstante c_1) und eine Paarhäufigkeit von mindestens 3 (Konstante c_2). Diese Schwellenwerte wurden heuristisch festgelegt, wobei pragmatische Aspekte und Erfahrungswerte aus früheren Arbeiten berücksichtigt wurden. Weitere Informationen über die Relation Z des Wörterbuches PHYS/PILOT sind der Tabelle 1 zu entnehmen.

Anzahl Dokumente	392 000
Art der Dokumente	Referatetexte einschl. Titel
Quelle der Dok.	PHYSICS/BRIEFS
Zeitraum	Januar 80 bis Februar 85
mittlere Anzahl bedeutungstragender Wörter pro Dokument	60
mittlere Anzahl manuell zugeteilter Deskriptoren pro Dokument	8.8
Anzahl Einzelwort-Deskriptor-Paare	159 930
Anzahl Mehrwortgruppen-Deskriptor-Paare	620 617
Anzahl Formelbezeichner-Deskriptor-Paare	25 306

Tabelle 1: Angaben über die Relation Z des Wörterbuches PHYS/PILOT

Ziel der durchgeführten Experimente war in erster Linie die Überprüfung der Genauigkeit und der Streuung der Schätzwerte bei unterschiedlich großen Stichproben. Weiterhin sollte die Analyse der experimentellen Ergebnisse die Kriterien für eine erfolgreiche Anwendung des Schätzverfahrens aufzeigen, bzw. auf Schwächen des Schätzverfahrens im Hinblick auf die praktische Anwendung hinweisen.

Es wurden insgesamt 18 Schätzungen für die Größe der Relation Z mit einem Wort als Term durchgeführt. Auf Schätzungen mit Mehrwortgruppen als Terms wurde verzichtet, da frühere Experimente auf einen ähnlichen Verlauf der Schätzungen schließen lassen [Tzeras 88]. Um zu überprüfen, inwieweit sich die Schätzwerte mit einer Verdopplung des Stichprobenumfangs verbessern, wurden Schätzungen mit geschachtelten Stichproben im Umfang von 100, 200 und 400 Dokumenten durchgeführt. Die Stichproben wurden aus den 392 000 Dokumenten des für die Produktion des PHYS/PILOT Wörterbuches verwendeten Korpus durch die Kombination eines geschichteten und eines systematischen Auswahlverfahrens gezogen.

4.2 Ergebnisse der Schätzungen für den Umfang der Relation Z

In Tabelle 2 werden die Ergebnisse der durchgeführten Schätzungen dargestellt. Die Schätzungen sind nach der Größe der jeweils verwendeten Stichprobe unterteilt. Für jede Schätzung wird in Spalte 2 die kleinste Dokumentnummer (Anfangswert), die Schrittweite und die Anzahl der gezogenen Dokumente der Stichprobe angegeben[11]. Die mit $|D(n_s)|$ gekennzeichnete Spalte enthält die Anzahl

---

[11] Um eine Stichprobe von n Elementen zu ziehen, wurde eine Zahl a zwischen 1 und 1000 zufällig bestimmt und danach die Dokumente mit den Nummern $a + 1003 * i$ (wobei $0 \leq i \leq n - 1$) herausgegriffen.

Test Nr.	Auswahlverfahren für $D(n_s)$			$|D(n_s)|$	$E^*(|Z(n')|)$	%DIFF
	Anfangswert	Schrittweite	Anzahl			
1	3	1003	100	92	152 660	−4.54
2	56	1003	100	94	219 189	+37.05
3	265	1003	100	93	156 031	−2.43
4	312	1003	100	93	196 310	+22.74
5	586	1003	100	92	167 508	+4.73
6	788	1003	100	93	107 915	−32.52
7	3	1003	200	186	162 039	+1.31
8	56	1003	200	188	170 668	+6.71
9	265	1003	200	187	143 037	−10.56
10	312	1003	200	187	159 008	−0.57
11	586	1003	200	186	155 392	−2.83
12	788	1003	200	187	122 871	−23.17
13	3	1003	400	372	146 166	−8.60
14	56	1003	400	374	158 592	−0.83
15	265	1003	400	373	164 838	+3.06
16	312	1003	400	373	156 570	−2.10
17	586	1003	400	372	151 948	−4.99
18	788	1003	400	373	152 995	−4.33

Exakter Wert $|Z(n')| = 159\,930$

Tabelle 2: Ergebnisse der Schätzungen für den Umfang der Relation Z

der Dokumente der jeweiligen Stichprobe. Da die Numerierung der Dokumente nicht fortlaufend ist, ist die Anzahl der Dokumente unter $|D(n_s)|$ nicht gleich der Anzahl der gezogenen Dokumente aus Spalte 2. Aus dem gleichen Grund enthalten einige Stichproben 1 bis 2 Dokumente weniger als andere Stichproben der gleichen Größenordnung.

In der mit $E^*(|Z(n')|)$ gekennzeichneten Spalte ist der jeweils berechnete Schätzwert, in der mit %DIFF gekennzeichneten Spalte die prozentuale Abweichung von dem exakten Wert $|Z(n')|$ angegeben.

Wie aus den Ergebnissen der Tabelle 2 hervorgeht, liegen die prozentualen Abweichungen der einzelnen Schätzwerte weitgehend unter der 5%-Grenze (Tests Nr 1, 3, 5, 7, 10, 11, 14, 15, 16, 17, 18). Es sind jedoch auch Abweichungen bis +37,05% (Test Nr. 2) bzw. −32,52% (Test Nr. 6) zu beobachten. Bei Verdopplung der Größe einer Stichprobe, wobei alle Dokumente der anfänglichen Stichprobe in der größeren enthalten sind, ergibt sich nicht immer ein besserer Schätzwert. Die Schätzwerte der Tests Nr. 1, 4 und 5 haben sich zwar nach der ersten Verdopplung (Tests Nr. 7, 10, 11) verbessert, jedoch nach der zweiten Verdopplung (Tests Nr. 13, 16, 17) verschlechtert. Test Nr. 3 hat bei der ersten Verdopplung (Test Nr. 9) einen schlechteren, bei der zweiten Verdopplung (Test Nr. 15) einen besseren Schätzwert geliefert.

Aus dieser ersten Analyse der experimentellen Ergebnisse läßt sich schließen, daß die Berechnung ziemlich genauer Schätzwerte bereits mit Stichproben von 100 aus 392 000 Dokumenten möglich ist. Die Ergebnisse deuten jedoch darauf hin, daß die Streuung der Schätzwerte bei Stichproben der betrachteten Größenordnung erheblichen Schwankungen unterworfen ist. Für eine nähere Untersuchung der Zusammenhänge zwischen Streuung der Schätzwerte und Stichprobengröße wurden verschiedene Streuungsmaßzahlen herangezogen. Tabelle 3 enthält die Abwei-

Tests Nr.	Abweichung des Mittelwertes	Mittlere Abweichung	Standard-abweichung	Viertel-wertabstand	Variations-breite
1–6	6 672.17	27 734.66	35 744.87	43 650	111 274
7–12	−7 760.83	12 043.16	17 320.21	19 002	47 797
13–18	−4 745.17	6 381.16	7 510.24	6 644	18 672
1–6	4.17%	17.34%	22.35%	27.29%	69.57%
7–12	−4.85%	7.53%	10.82%	11.88%	29.88%
13–18	−2.96%	3.98%	4.69%	4.15%	11.67%

Tabelle 3: Absolute und relative Streuungsmaßzahlen

chung des Mittelwertes, die mittlere Abweichung und die Standardabweichung der Schätzwerte aus den Tests Nr. 1 bis 6, 7 bis 12 und 13 bis 18 in bezug auf den exakten Wert $|Z(n')|$. Weiterhin enthält Tabelle 3 den Viertelwertabstand und die Variationsbreite der nach Stichprobengröße gruppierten Schätzwerte. Diese Zahlen werden sowohl absolut als auch als Prozentsatz des exakten Wertes angegeben.

Im Vergleich zu den einzelnen Tests ist zunächst eine deutliche Abnahme der Streuung bei Vergrößerung der Stichprobengröße zu beobachten. Der Verlauf der mittleren Abweichung und der Standardabweichung deutet auf eine durchschnittliche Halbierung der Streuung bei einer Verdopplung der Stichprobe hin. Dies wird auch durch den Verlauf des Viertelwertabstands und der Variationsbreite belegt.

Aufgrund der vorliegenden Analyse der experimentellen Ergebnisse läßt sich die Leistungsfähigkeit des Schätzverfahrens folgendermaßen beurteilen:

- Die Schätzwerte bei Stichproben der betrachteten Größenordnung sind ziemlich unstabil und können sehr stark vom exakten Wert abweichen.

- Größere Stichproben liefern im Schnitt genauere und stabilere Schätzwerte.

Die große Streuung der Schätzwerte ist vermutlich auf den kleinen Umfang der bisher verwendeten Stichproben zurückzuführen. Wie in Abschnitt 5.2 nachgewiesen wird, lässt sich die Streuung durch den Übergang zu größeren Stichproben erheblich verringern.

5 Strategien der Stichprobenerhebung für die Berechnung zuverlässiger Schätzwerte

5.1 Auswahl „guter" Stichproben

Eine Möglichkeit für die Berechnung möglichst zuverlässiger Schätzwerte besteht darin, Kriterien für die Güte einer Stichprobe aufzustellen, um dann im Rahmen einer Vorauswahl repräsentative Stichproben herauszufiltern. Ausgehend von dieser Überlegung wurde daher untersucht, welche Eigenschaften einer Stichprobe mit der Genauigkeit des daraus berechneten Schätzwertes in einem systematischen Zusammenhang stehen.

Als mögliche Eigenschaft wurde zunächst die Verteilung der Textlängen und der Indexierungstiefen der Dokumente aus der Stichprobe untersucht. Ein χ^2-Anpassungstest wurde für die Überprüfung der Hypothese, daß die Textlängen im Korpus und in einer gegebenen Stichprobe die gleiche Verteilung haben, durchgeführt. Gleichzeitig wurden für eine gegebene Stichprobe die Indexierungstiefen untersucht.

Test Nr.	%DIFF	r	$Q(n_1,\ldots,n_r;\\ p_1^0,\ldots,p_r^0)$	Wert der χ^2-Verteilung mit r Freiheitsgraden am Punkt $Q(\vec{n};\vec{p^0})$	$Q(\vec{n};\vec{p^0})\\ < \chi^2_{r,0.95}$
1	−4.54	15	13.69	0.45	ja
2	+37.05	15	22.35	0.90	ja
3	−2.43	15	9.56	0.15	ja
4	+22.74	15	11.85	0.31	ja
5	+4.73	15	28.70	0.98	nein
6	−32.52	15	11.22	0.26	ja
7	+1.31	26	23.48	0.39	ja
8	+6.71	26	25.89	0.53	ja
9	−10.56	26	23.50	0.40	ja
10	−0.57	26	24.58	0.46	ja
11	−2.83	26	26.77	0.58	ja
12	−23.17	26	24.84	0.47	ja
13	−8.60	50	49.70	0.51	ja
14	−0.83	50	51.73	0.58	ja
15	+3.06	50	52.06	0.61	ja
16	−2.10	50	47.21	0.41	ja
17	−4.99	50	62.41	0.89	ja
18	−4.33	50	46.36	0.38	ja

Tabelle 4: χ^2-Anpassungstests bzgl. der Textlängen

Bezeichnet man mit

N : die Anzahl der Dokumente des Korpus,

n : die Anzahl der Dokumente einer Stichprobe,

N_i : die Häufigkeit der Dokumente im Korpus mit einer Textlänge von i und

n_i: die Häufigkeit der Dokumente in der Stichprobe mit der Textlänge i,

so beträgt die Wahrscheinlichkeit p_i (bzw. p_i^0), daß ein zufällig ausgewähltes Dokument aus der Stichprobe (bzw. dem Korpus) die Länge i hat, $\frac{n_i}{n}$ (bzw. $\frac{N_i}{N}$).
Stellt man nun als Nullhypothese

$$H_0 : (p_1,\ldots,p_r) = (p_1^0,\ldots,p_r^0)$$

bei der Gegenhypothese

$$H_1 : (p_1,\ldots,p_r) \neq (p_1^0,\ldots,p_r^0)$$

auf, so kann man mit Hilfe der χ^2–Abstandsfunktion

$$Q(n_1,\ldots,n_r;p_1^0,\ldots,p_r^0) = \sum_{i=1}^{r} \frac{(n_i - np_i^0)^2}{np_i^0}$$

testen, ob die Textlänge im Korpus und in einer gegebenen Stichprobe die gleiche Verteilung haben.

Test Nr.	%DIFF	r	$Q(n_1,\ldots,n_r;\ p_1^0,\ldots,p_r^0)$	Wert der χ^2-Verteilung mit r Freiheitsgraden am Punkt $Q(\vec{n};\vec{p^0})$	$Q(\vec{n};\vec{p^0}) < \chi^2_{r,0.95}$
1	−4.54	9	2.68	0.02	ja
2	+37.05	9	10.02	0.65	ja
3	−2.43	9	5.98	0.26	ja
4	+22.74	9	13.19	0.85	ja
5	+4.73	9	9.59	0.62	ja
6	−32.52	9	12.48	0.81	ja
7	+1.31	18	18.74	0.59	ja
8	+6.71	18	14.48	0.30	ja
9	−10.56	18	15.74	0.39	ja
10	−0.57	18	21.50	0.75	ja
11	−2.83	18	21.43	0.74	ja
12	−23.17	18	17.51	0.51	ja
13	−8.60	34	48.91	0.95	ja
14	−0.83	35	29.75	0.28	ja
15	+3.06	35	26.22	0.14	ja
16	−2.10	35	37.59	0.65	ja
17	−4.99	34	29.00	0.29	ja
18	−4.33	34	53.62	0.98	nein

Tabelle 5: χ^2-Anpassungstests bzgl. der Paartoken

Um die Näherung der Testgröße bei zutreffender Nullhypothese H_0 durch χ^2_{r-1} statistisch abzusichern, wurden die Häufigkeiten n_i bzw. $n \cdot p_i^0$ auf geeignete Intervalle so abgebildet, daß $n \cdot p_i^0 \geq 10$ für $i = 1,\ldots,r$ gilt.

Tabelle 4 zeigt, daß die Nullhypothese H_0 auf dem Signifikanzniveau $\alpha = 0.05$ für fast alle Stichproben nicht verworfen wird. Weiterhin erkennt man keinerlei Korrelation zwischen den Abweichungen der einzelnen Schätzwerte und den Werten der χ^2-Verteilung an den Punkten $Q(\vec{n},\vec{p^0})$.

Ähnliche Ergebnisse wurden auch bzgl. der Indexierungstiefen festgestellt, so daß die betrachteten Eigenschaften sich als ungeeignet für die Auswahl „guter" Stichproben erwiesen haben.

Ein besseres Kriterium für die Güte einer Stichprobe ist die Anzahl der gebildeten Paartoken pro Dokument. Diese Anzahl kann durch das Produkt aus Textlänge und Indexierungstiefe für jedes Dokument aus der Stichprobe bzw. des Korpus angenähert werden. Analog zu den bisher betrachteten Fällen läßt sich dann überprüfen, ob die Paartoken im Korpus und in einer gegebenen Stichprobe die gleiche Verteilung haben. Tabelle 5 zeigt, daß diese Nullhypothese auf dem Signifikanzniveau $\alpha = 0.05$ für fast alle Stichproben nicht verworfen wird. Weiterhin erkennt man eine gewisse Korrelation zwischen den Abweichungen der einzelnen Schätzwerte und der Werte der χ^2-Verteilung an den Punkten $Q(\vec{n},\vec{p^0})$ in dem Sinne, daß für kleine Werte der χ^2-Verteilung (d.h. kleiner als 0,3) die Abweichungen die 5%-Grenze nicht übersteigen.

Man kann daher mit Hilfe der Entscheidungsregel „Werte der χ^2-Verteilung am Punkt der berechneten Testgröße kleiner als 0,1" die „guten" von den „schlechten" Stichproben relativ sicher trennen. Es hat sich jedoch im Rahmen weiterer Experimente herausgestellt, daß Stichproben, die obengenannte Bedingung erfüllen, schwer zu finden sind. In einer Reihe von 30 gezogenen Stichproben der Größe 100 hat keine das obengenannte Kriterium erfüllt.

Die bisher betrachteten Eigenschaften können also aufgrund dieser Ergebnisse nicht für die Beurteilung der Güte einer Stichprobe verwendet werden. Sie deuten vielmehr darauf hin, daß Stichproben von bis zu 400 Dokumenten nicht nur bezüglich der berechneten Schätzwerte, sondern auch bezüglich plausibler Eigenschaften, erhebliche Unregelmäßigkeiten aufweisen. Die beobachtete Schwierigkeit der Auswahl repräsentativer Stichproben kleinen Umfangs kann auf systematische Abhängigkeiten innerhalb der einzelnen Dokumente zurückgeführt werden. Die Auswirkungen dieser Abhängigkeiten lassen sich durch den Übergang zu größeren Dokumentstichproben bzw. durch die Verwendung von sogenannten Paartoken-Stichproben beseitigen.

5.2 Übergang zu größeren Stichproben

Die in Abschnitt 4.2. festgestellten Schwankungen der Schätzwerte bei Stichproben von bis zu 400 Dokumenten können durch den Übergang zu wesentlich größeren Stichproben vermieden werden. Eine günstige Eigenschaft des Schätzverfahrens kann für die kontrollierte Berechnung von Schätzwerten mit Stichproben dieser Größenordnung ausgenutzt werden. Der Mittelwert mehrerer Schätzwerte, die mit n disjunkten Stichproben der gleichen Größenordnung berechnet werden, ist nämlich äquivalent zum Schätzwert, der vom Schätzverfahren geliefert wird, wenn als Stichprobe die Vereinigung dieser n Stichproben verwendet wird ([Tzeras 88]). So kann z.B. der Mittelwert der Schätzungen Nr. 13 bis 18 aus Tabelle 2 als eine Schätzung auf der Basis einer – aus der Vereinigung der 6 Stichproben bestehenden – etwa 2400-elementigen Stichprobe angesehen werden.
Es bietet sich daher die Vorgehensweise an, anstatt einer einzigen Schätzung mehrere durchzuführen, und als Schätzwert den Mittelwert der einzelnen Schätzwerte zu nehmen. Betrachtet man die Ergebnisse aus Tabelle 3, erscheint es bereits für einen aus 6 Schätzungen mit 400-elementigen Dokumentstichproben berechneten Schätzwert unwahrscheinlich, daß er über 5% vom exakten Wert abweichen wird.

5.3 Übergang zu Paartoken-Stichproben

Die Schwierigkeit der Auswahl repräsentativer Dokumentstichproben kleinen Umfangs kann durch den Übergang zu sogenannten Paartoken-Stichproben überwunden werden. Die grundlegende Idee besteht darin, anstelle aller Paartoken, die aufgrund einer kleinen Dokumentstichprobe gebildet werden, nur einen kleinen Anteil der Paartoken, die aufgrund einer wesentlich größeren Dokumentstichprobe gebildet werden, für die Schätzung zu verwenden. Bezeichnet man mit n_s die Anzahl der Elemente einer Stichprobe der bisherigen Größenordnung (mit 100 bis 400 Dokumenten) und mit n_s' die Anzahl der Elemente einer Dokumentstichprobe mit $n_s' \gg n_s$, so ist die Menge der aufgrund von $D(n_s')$ gebildeten Paartoken durch

$$(Z(h,f,n), D(n_s')) = \{((t,s),d) | (t,s) \in Z(h,f,n), d \in D(t,s,n) \cap D(n_s'))\}$$

definiert. Mit $(Z(h,f,n), D(n_s'))'$ wird eine zufällig gewählte Stichprobe aus $(Z(h,f,n), D(n_s'))$ mit

$$|(Z(h,f,n), D(n_s'))'| \approx \frac{p}{100} \cdot |(Z(h,f,n), D(n_s'))|$$

bezeichnet, wobei $(Z(h,f,n), D(n_s'))' \subset (Z(h,f,n), D(n_s'))$ und $0 \leq p \leq 100$ gilt.
Die in Abschnitt 3 hergeleitete Gleichung (6) lässt sich dementsprechend für eine Dokumentstichprobe vom Umfang n_s', bei der nur ein bestimmter Prozentsatz $p\%$ der Paartoken für die Schätzung verwendet wird, folgendermaßen umformen:

$$E^*(|Z(n')|) = \frac{100 \cdot n'}{n_s' \cdot p} \sum_{h \geq c_2} \frac{1}{h} \sum_{h \leq f \leq \frac{h}{c_1}} |(Z(h,f,n'), D(n_s') \cap D(n'))'|. \tag{9}$$

Test Nr.	Auswahlverfahren für $D(n'_s)$			$|D(n'_s)|$	$E^*(|Z(n')|)$	$\%DIFF$
	Anfangswert	Schrittweite	Anzahl			
1	1	11	10000	9333	170 963	+6.90
2	3	11	10000	9334	167 038	+4.44
3	5	11	10000	9333	142 307	−11.02
4	7	11	10000	9333	157 956	−1.23
5	9	11	10000	9334	179 504	+12.24
6	11	11	10000	9334	163 758	+2.39
7	1	11	20000	18666	155 021	+3.07
8	3	11	20000	18667	161 882	+1.22
9	5	11	20000	18667	139 711	−12.64
10	7	11	20000	18666	156 124	−2.38
11	9	11	20000	18667	177 649	+11.08
12	11	11	20000	18667	174 631	+9.19
13	1	11	40000	35466	159 090	+0.53
14	3	11	40000	35467	167 179	+4.53
15	5	11	40000	35467	149 832	−6.31
16	7	11	40000	35466	168 784	+5.54
17	9	11	40000	35467	163 740	+2.38
18	11	11	40000	35467	171 218	+7.06

Exakter Wert $|Z(n')| = 159\,930$

Tabelle 6: Ergebnisse der Schätzungen für den Umfang der Relation Z auf der Basis von Paartoken-Stichproben

Das auf diese Weise modifizierte Schätzverfahren wurde im Rahmen von 18 weiteren Schätzungen mit dem ursprünglichen Schätzverfahren verglichen. Die Schätzungen beziehen sich hier ebenfalls auf die Relation Z mit einem Wort als Term und basieren auf 100 Mal größere Dokumentstichproben, wobei jedoch nur 1% der jeweils gebildeten Paartoken verwendet wird[12]. Um zu überprüfen inwieweit sich die Schätzwerte mit einer Verdopplung des Stichprobenumfangs verbessern, wurden hier ebenfalls Schätzungen mit geschachtelten Stichproben durchgeführt. Gleichzeitig wurde wie bei den Schätzungen aus Abschnitt 4.2 ein z-Wert von mindestens 0,3 und eine Paarhäufigkeit von mindestens 3 gefordert.
Die in den Tabellen 6 und 7 vorgestellten Ergebnisse sind im Vergleich zu den Ergebnissen aus Tabellen 2 und 3 deutlich besser. Auch die Streuungsmaßzahlen aus Tabelle 7 deuten auf eine deutliche Abnahme der Schwankungen der Schätzwerte um den exakten Wert. Verwendet man daher Stichproben von über 40 000 Dokumenten, so dürften sich zuverlässige Schätzwerte (mit Abweichungen im 5%-Bereich) berechnen lassen.

6 Mögliche Anwendungen des Schätzverfahrens

Das vorgestellte Schätzverfahren für den Umfang der Relation Z kann aufgrund der Ergebnisse aus den Abschnitten 4 und 5 als ziemlich zuverlässig beurteilt werden. Seine Anwendung kann zu einem frühen Zeitpunkt einer Systementwicklung nützliche Informationen über die Größe des Inde-

---

[12] Durch diese Wahl von n'_s und p wurde eine Vergleichbarkeit mit den in Abschnitt 4.2 vorgestellten Ergebnissen angestrebt.

Tests Nr.	Abweichung der Mittelwerte	Mittlere Abweichung	Standard- abweichung	Viertel- wertabstand	Variations- breite
1–6	3 657.67	10 190.00	12 141.61	13 007	37 197
7–12	906.33	10 551.00	12 788.56	19 610	37 938
13–18	3 377.17	7 023.17	7 911.51	9 694	21 386
1–6	2.28%	6.37%	7.59%	8.13%	23.26%
7–12	0.57%	6.59%	8.00%	12.26%	23.72%
13–18	2.1%1	4.39%	4.95%	6.06%	13.37%

Tabelle 7: Absolute und relative Streuungsmaßzahlen der Schätzwerte

xierungswörterbuches in Abhängigkeit von den zur Entwicklung des Wörterbuches zur Verfügung stehenden Dokumenten liefern. So können z.B. wichtige Entscheidungen bezüglich der Gewinnung von Wörterbuchdaten bei der Einführung der automatischen Indexierung in einem neuen Fachgebiet unterstützt werden.

Weiterhin kann das Schätzverfahren für die Untersuchung der Beziehung zwischen Umfang und Leistungsfähigkeit eines Indexierungswörterbuches verwendet werden. In [Hüther 90] werden dazu weitere Schätzverfahren vorgeschlagen, die unter Benutzung von Häufigkeitsverteilungen der Relation Z Erwartungswerte für die Vollständigkeit des Wörterbuches liefern. Eine mögliche Anwendung des hier behandelten Schätzverfahrens besteht darin, die benötigten Häufigkeitsverteilungen mit Hilfe der Gleichungen (7) bzw. (8) abzuschätzen, um dann die Beziehung zwischen Umfang und Vollständigkeit für verschiedene Wörterbuchvarianten mit Hilfe der obengenannten Erwartungswerte zu untersuchen. Erwartungswerte für weitere wichtige Qualitätsmaße eines Wörterbuches sind auch denkbar und werden zur Zeit im Fachgebiet Datenverwaltungssysteme II untersucht.

Prinzipiell ist eine Anwendung des Schätzverfahrens auch außerhalb der automatischen Indexierung denkbar und zwar im Rahmen von Entwicklungen, bei denen statistische Verfahren der Wissensakquisition aus Texten eingesetzt werden. Dies müsste jedoch innerhalb einer gegebenen Aufgabenstellung diskutiert werden.

Literatur

Beinke-Geiser, U.; Lustig, G.; Putze-Meier, G. (1986). Indexieren mit dem System DAISY. In: Lustig, G. (ed.): *Automatische Indexierung zwischen Forschung und Anwendung*, pages 73–97. Olms, Hildesheim.

Faißt, S. (1990). *Entwicklung von Indexierungsfunktionen auf der Basis probabilistischer Entscheidungsbäume.* Diplomarbeit, TH Darmstadt, FB Informatik, Datenverwaltungssysteme II.

Fuhr, N.; Hüther, H. (1989). Optimum Probability Estimation from Empirical Distributions. *Information Processing and Management 25(5)*, pages 493–507.

Fuhr, N.; Jäger-Beck, R.; Schwantner, M. (1986). Die Gewinnung von statistischen Relationen zwischen Terms und Deskriptoren. In: Lustig, G. (ed.): *Automatische Indexierung zwischen Forschung und Anwendung*, pages 43–51. Olms, Hildesheim.

Fuhr, N.; Hartmann, S.; Knorz, G.; Lustig, G.; Schwantner, M.; Tzeras, K. (1991). AIR/X - a Rule-Based Multistage Indexing System for Large Subject Fields. In: *Proceedings of the RIAO'91, Barcelona, Spain, April 2-5, 1991.*

Hüther, H. (1989). *Wachstumsfunktionen in der automatischen Indexierung.* Dissertation, TH Darmstadt, FB Informatik, Datenverwaltungssysteme II.

Hüther, H. (1990). On the Interrelationship of Dictionary Size and Completeness. In: Vidick, J.-L. (ed.): *Proceedings of the 13th International Conference on Research and Development in Information Retrieval,* pages 313–326. ACM, New York.

Knorz, G. (1983). *Automatisches Indexieren als Erkennen abstrakter Objekte.* Niemeyer, Tübingen.

Lustig, G. (ed.) (1986). *Automatische Indexierung zwischen Forschung und Anwendung.* Olms, Hildesheim.

Pfeifer, U. (1990). *Entwicklung log-linearer und linear-iterativer Indexierungsfunktionen .* Diplomarbeit, TH Darmstadt, FB Informatik, Datenverwaltungssysteme II.

Tzeras, K. (1988). *Schätzfunktionen für die Relation Z.* Diplomarbeit, TH Darmstadt, FB Informatik, Datenverwaltungssysteme II.

Entwicklung linear-iterativer und logistischer Indexierungsfunktionen

Ulrich Pfeifer*
Technische Hochschule Darmstadt

1 Einführung

Im Fachgebiet Datenverwaltungssysteme II des Fachbereichs Informatik an der Technischen Hochschule Darmstadt wird seit 1977 an dem Problem der automatischen Indexierung gearbeitet (siehe [Lustig 86]). Das hierbei entwickelte Indexierungssystem AIR/PHYS wird seit 1985 im Fachinformationszentrum Karlsruhe bei der Inputproduktion für die Physikdatenbank PHYS eingesetzt (siehe [Biebricher et al. 88]).

Unter Indexierung versteht man die Zuteilung von inhaltscharakterisierenden Stich- oder Schlagworten zu Dokumenten. Bei den hier betrachteten Indexierungsystemen stehen für diese Zuteilung nur bestimmte, durch einen Thesaurus vorgegebene, Schlagworte zur Verfügung. Man spricht hier von einer Indexierung mit kontrolliertem Vokabular. Die zulässigen Schlagworte werden *Deskriptoren* genannt. Da diese nicht notwendig im Text des Dokuments (englischsprachige Titel und Referate) vorkommen, ist bei automatischen Verfahren ein Wörterbuch nötig, das möglichst viele Terme (Einzelworte und Mehrwortgruppen) der Dokumente über Relationen mit Deskriptoren verbindet. Das Indexierungssystem sucht in einem ersten, dem Beschreibungsschritt, solche Terme in einem zu indexierenden Dokument. Wird ein Term gefunden, der in Relation zu einem Deskriptor steht, bezeichnet man dies als Hinweis auf den entsprechenden Deskriptor. Die Beschreibung aller Hinweise aus einem Dokument auf einen Deskriptor bilden zusammen mit dokumentspezifischen Informationen die *Relevanzbeschreibung* des Deskriptors bezüglich des Dokuments. Diese wird in Form eines Vektors $\vec{x}$ reeller Zahlen, dem sogenannten *Beschreibungsvektor*, kodiert. Auf das Problem der Kodierung der Informationen wollen wir hier nicht weiter eingehen (siehe z.B. [Knorz 83]).

In einem zweiten, dem Entscheidungsschritt, wird durch eine *Indexierungsfunktion* der Relevanzbeschreibungsvektor auf eine reelle Zahl, das sogenannte Indexierungsgewicht abgebildet, das als Schätzung der Wahrscheinlichkeit interpretiert werden kann, daß die Zuteilung des Deskriptors korrekt ist. Diese Entscheidung über die Korrektheit einer Zuteilung kann z.B. aus Relevanzurteilen zu Retrievalergebnissen abgeleitet werden. Bei den hier durchgeführten Experimenten wird eine intellektuelle Indexierung als Vergleichsmaßstab benutzt. In einem Retrievaltest wurde gezeigt, daß Verbesserungen der Indexierungqualität gemessen an der intellektuellen Indexierung mit verbesserten Retrievalergebnissen korrespondieren (siehe z.B. [Fuhr 89]). Zur Entwicklung von Indexierungsfunktionen können verschiedene probabilistische Verfahren angewendet werden. Bei jedem dieser Verfahren (im folgenden auch Ansatz genannt) wird eine bestimmte Klasse von Funktionen zugrundegelegt, aus der dann durch Adaption auf einer sogenannten Lernstichprobe von Dokumenten eine optimale Funktion ausgewählt wird. Neben dem hier nicht weiter betrachten Booleschen Ansatz von Lustig (siehe [Beinke-Geiser et al. 86]) wurde bisher vorwiegend der Polynomansatz von Knorz (siehe [Knorz 83]) untersucht. Bei diesem werden lineare Funktionen der Form $\vec{b}^T \cdot \vec{x}$

---

*Neue Anschrift: Universität Dortmund, Lehrstuhl Informatik VI, W-4600 Dortmund 50.
E-mail: pfeifer@grete.informatik.uni-dortmund.de

betrachtet, wobei der Parametervektor $\vec{b}$ mit Hilfe der Methode der kleinsten Quadrate bestimmt wird.

In dieser Arbeit stellen wir Alternativen zu diesen linearen Funktionen vor. Dazu werden in Abschnitt 2 einige Bezeichnungen eingeführt. Anschließend werden die Kriterien, die hier zum Vergleich der verschiedenen Indexierungsfunktionen verwendet werden, beschrieben. In Abschnitt 4 stellen wir zwei iterative Varianten des linearen Ansatzes vor, die ausgehend von dem mehrstufigen Klassifikatorenkonzept von Knorz entwickelt wurden (siehe [Knorz 83] 183-189). Im darauffolgenden Abschnitt werden logistische Funktionen der Form $e^{\vec{b}^T \vec{x}}/(1 - e^{\vec{b}^T \vec{x}})$ vorgestellt, wobei der Parametervektor $\vec{b}$ mit Hilfe der Maximum-Likelihood-Methode bestimmt wird. Die Adaption aller Ansätze erfolgte jeweils auf einer Lernstichprobe D_L und wurde auf einer Teststichprobe D_T überprüft. Im Abschnitt 6 werden die verschiedenen Funktionen mit einem Signifikanztest auf einen weiteren Stichprobe D_H verglichen.

Alle Stichproben umfassen je 1000 Dokumente mit etwa 30000 Relevanzbeschreibungen. Als Beschreibungsvektor wurde der Vektor BV-FIZ verwendet, der derzeit bei der Inputproduktion des Fachinformationszentrums Karlsruhe eingesetzt wird (siehe [Knorz 86]).

Der letzte Abschnitt wertet die Ergebnisse und gibt einen kurzen Ausblick auf Erweiterungen der vorgestellten Ansätze.

2 Bezeichnungen

Gegeben sei eine Menge von Dokumenten D, eine Menge von Deskriptoren S und eine intellektuelle Indexierung der Dokumente, die wir als eine Funktion k auffassen:

$$k: \quad S \times D \;\to\; \{0,1\}$$
$$(s,d) \;\mapsto\; k(s,d) = \begin{cases} 0 & \text{Deskriptor nicht zugeteilt} \\ 1 & \text{Deskriptor zugeteilt} \end{cases}$$

Diese Funktion k soll durch eine Regressionsfunktion approximiert werden. Grundlage für die Regression sei eine Menge von Relevanzbeschreibungen in Form von Vektoren reeller Zahlen, die durch eine Beschreibungsfunktion x auf einer Teilmenge R von $S \times D$ erzeugt werden:

$$x: \quad R \subseteq S \times D \;\to\; \mathbb{R}^n$$
$$(s,d) \;\mapsto\; x(s,d)$$

Wir suchen eine (nach einem noch festzulegenden Kriterium) optimale Entscheidungsfunktion a aus einer Klasse von Funktionen, die den Vektoren die Indexierungsgewichte zuteilt.

$$a: \quad \mathbb{R}^n \;\to\; \mathbb{R}$$
$$x \;\mapsto\; a(x)$$

Die Hintereinanderausführung g von a und x nennen wir Indexierungsfunktion, wobei wir den Definitionsbereich auf beliebige Paare $(s,d) \in S \times D$ erweitern. Die Paare, für die keine Relevanzbeschreibung vorliegt erhalten das Indexierungsgewicht 0. Wir werden im Folgenden zwischen g und a nicht streng unterscheiden, da wir hier von einer festen Beschreibungsfunktion x ausgehen.

$$g: \quad S \times D \;\to\; \mathbb{R}$$
$$g(s,d) \;\mapsto\; \begin{cases} a \circ x(s,d) & (s,d) \in R \\ 0 & (s,d) \notin R \end{cases}$$

3 Vergleich von Indexierungen

Die Qualität von Indexierungsfunktionen sollte sinnvollerweise anhand ihrer Auswirkungen auf die Retrievalergebnisse beurteilt werden (siehe z.B. [Fuhr 89]). Aus Aufwandsgründen beschränken wir uns hier auf den Vergleich der automatischen mit der vorgegebenen intellektuelle Indexierung. Dabei ist zu beachten, daß die intellektuelle Indexierung mit Fehlern behaftet ist, da verschiedene Indexierer bezüglich der Zuteilung eines Deskriptors durchaus verschiedener Meinung sein können. Die intellektuelle Indexierung ist ungewichtet; unser automatisches Verfahren liefert aber reellwertige Indexierungsgewichte, die als Schätzungen für Wahrscheinlichkeiten interpretiert werden können. Wenn wir nun zwei Indexierungsfunktionen vergleichen wollen, können wir dies also nur anhand ihrer Übereinstimmung mit der intellektuellen Indexierung tun. Hierzu können wir für jede Indexierung diese Übereinstimmung messen und die Maße dann vergleichen, oder zwei Indexierungen direkt vergleichen.

3.1 Vergleich mithilfe von Maßen

Als Maß für die Übereinstimmung mit der intellektuellen Indexierung betrachten wir hier die Reststreuung $\triangle z$, also die mittlere quadratische Abweichung der automatischen von der intellektuellen Indexierung:

$$\triangle z(g, k, R_1) := \frac{1}{|R_1|} \sum_{(s,d)\in R_1} (k(s, d) - g(s, d))^2 \tag{1}$$

Der Wert dieses Maßes wird durch die Tatsache eingeschränkt, daß Indexierungsgewichte außerhalb des Intervalls $[0, 1]$, wie sie z.B. bei linearen Indexierungsfunktionen auftreten, in die Reststreuung nicht mit dem Wert 0 bzw. 1 eingehen, wie es vernünftig wäre. Wir verwenden deshalb auch die projezierte Reststreuung $\triangle z_{01}$. Dieses Maß sei definiert als die mittlere quadratische Abweichung der auf das Intervall $[0, 1]$ projezierten Indexierungsgewichte von den entsprechenden Werten der Funktion k:

$$\triangle z_{01}(g, k, R_1) := \frac{1}{|R_1|} \sum_{(s,d)\in R_1} [k(s, d) - \max\{0, \min\{1, g(s, d)\}\}]^2 \tag{2}$$

Die Aussagekraft der Reststreuung bleibt aber beschränkt, weil die Verteilung der Abweichungen ebenfalls von Bedeutung ist. Sicher ist z.B. eine Indexierungsfunktion, die für jeden Vektor eine Abweichung von 0.1 liefert, einer Funktion vorzuziehen, die 99% der Vektoren mit dem „richtigen" und 1% der Vektoren mit dem „falschen" Gewicht bewertet.

Dieses Problem können wir umgehen, wenn wir die automatische Indexierung zuerst auf eine ungewichtete Indexierung abbilden, um dann ihre Übereinstimmung mit der intellektuellen Indexierung zu messen.

Definieren wir die Schwellenwertabbildung s_p,

$$s_p : \quad \mathbb{R} \quad \rightarrow \{0, 1\}$$
$$x \quad \mapsto \begin{cases} 0 & x < p \\ 1 & p \leq x \end{cases}$$

so können wir eine Indexierungsfunktion g_p, die ungewichtete Indexierungen liefert, vereinbaren:

$$g_p : \quad S \times D \quad \rightarrow \{0, 1\}$$
$$(s, d) \quad \mapsto g_p(s, d) = s_p \circ g(s, d)$$

Die Mengen der Paare (s, d) mit Indexierungsgewicht 1 nennen wir A_p und K bezeichne die Menge der vorgegebenen korrekten Deskriptorenzuteilungen:

$$A_p \; := \; \{(s, d) \in S \times D | g_p(s, d) = 1\}$$
$$K \; := \; \{(s, d) \in S \times D | k(s, d) = 1\}$$

Dann haben wir mit

$$q_p := \frac{|A_p \cap K|}{|A_p \cup K|}$$

ein Maß für die Übereinstimmung der automatischen mit der intellektuellen Indexierung (Konsistenz). Abbildung 2 gibt den typischen Verlauf von q_p in Abhängigkeit von p an. Um ein vom Schwellenwert p unabhängiges Maß zu erhalten, definieren wir die maximale Konsistens q_{max}:

$$q_{max} := \max_{p \in [0,1]} (q_p)$$

3.2 Direkter Vergleich zweier Indexierungen

Wollen wir zwei automatische Indexierungen gemessen an der intellektuellen Indexierung vergleichen, so bietet sich der Vorzeichentest an. Es sollen zwei Verfahren verglichen werden, die den gleichen Relevanzbeschreibungen Indexierungsgewichte zuteilen. Für den Vergleich zweier Indexierungsfunktionen a_A und a_B bezüglich ihrer ungewichteten Indexierungen müßten eigentlich alle (sinnvollen) Kombinationen von zwei Schwellenwerten verglichen werden. Da bei der Anwendung jedoch der Schwellenwert durch Vorgabe einer Indexierungstiefe, d.h. gleicher mittlere Anzahl von Deskriptorzuteilungen pro Dokument, bestimmt wird, wählen wir für den Vergleich zwei Schwellenwerte p_A und p_B aus, die zu ungewichteten Indexierungsfunktionen a_{A, p_A} bzw. a_{B, p_B} mit gleicher Indexierungstiefe führen. Dann betrachten wir die Menge V_1 der Paare $(s, d) \in D_1$, für die die Indexierungsfunktion a_A ein von a_B verschiedenes Indexierungsgewicht liefert. Die Mächtigkeit $|V_1|$ von V_1 sei gleich n. B_1 sei die Menge der Paare $(s, d) \in V_1$, für die a_A ein Gewicht mit geringerer Abweichung von $k(s, d)$ liefert als a_B, also

$$B_1 = \{(s, d) \in V_1 \, | |k(s, d) - a_A(s, d)| < |k(s, d) - a_B(s, d)| \}$$

Für gewichtete Indexierungsfunktionen a_A und a_B seien V_1 und B_1 analog definiert. Unter der Nullhypothese H_0 „Die Indexierungen unterscheiden sich hinsichtlich ihrer Abweichung von k nicht signifikant" wäre für jedes Paar $(s, d) \in V_1$ die Wahrscheinlichkeit, zu B_1 zu gehören, gleich 1/2. Also wäre die Mächtigkeit K von B_1 eine $B\left(n, \frac{1}{2}\right)$ verteilte Zufallsvariable. Die Wahrscheinlichkeit, daß sich unter n Paaren aus V_1 mindestens k Paare befinden, denen a_A ein (gemessen an der Reststreuung) besseres Gewicht zuteilt, ergibt sich zu:

$$P(K \geq k) = 2^{-n} \cdot \sum_{i=k}^{n} \binom{n}{i}$$

Somit ist $1 - P(K \geq k)$ das Signifikanzniveau, auf dem H_0 bei einseitigem Test verworfen werden kann. Man erhält bei ungewichteten Indexierungen also für jede auftretende Indexierungstiefe ein Sicherheitsniveau, das zwischen verschiedenen Indexierungstiefen stark variieren kann. So sind meist nur Aussagen der Art „Die ungewichteten Indexierungen der Stichprobe D_1 mit der Funktion a_A sind im Bereich von 8.2 – 11.3 für die Indexierungstiefen mit weniger als 5% Wahrscheinlichkeit zufällig besser als die entsprechenden Indexierungen mit der Funktion a_B" möglich.

4 Linearer Ansatz

Beim einfachen linearen Verfahren wird durch Bestimmung eines Parametervektors $b \in \mathbb{R}^n$ die Indexierungsfunktion e aus der Klasse der Funktionen $a : x \mapsto b^T \cdot x$ so ausgewählt, daß die Reststreuung auf einer Dokumentstichprobe D_1 mit Relevanzbeschreibungen auf R_1 minimal ist. Dabei muß eine Minimierung der Reststreuung nicht notwendig gute Werte für q_{max} liefern.

4.1 Linear-iterativer Ansatz 1. Version

Ein wesentlicher Nachteil des einfachen linearen Verfahrens ist, daß Gewichte außerhalb des Intervalls $[0, 1]$ nicht mit 0 bzw. 1 in die Reststreuung eingehen; dadurch können diese Gewichte die Adaption überproportional beeinflussen. Dies wollten wir mit einer iterativen Variante des linearen Ansatzes kompensieren.

Betrachtet man die Indexierungsgewichte $g(s, d)$ zusammen mit den vorgegebenen Indexierungen

	$a(s, d) < 0$	$a(s, d) \in [0, 1]$	$a(s, d) > 1$
$k(s, d) = 1$	A	B	C
$k(s, d) = 0$	D	E	F

Abbildung 1: Klassen von Relevanzbeschreibungen

$k(s, d)$. so kann man die Relevanzbeschreibungen wie in Abbildung 1 in sechs Klassen A-F einteilen. Die Relevanzbeschreibungen der Klassen C und D tragen zur Reststreuung bei, obwohl für sie $g_p(s, d) = k(s, d)$ gilt (für alle $p \in [0, 1]$). Wir untersuchten nun, inwieweit sich die ungewichtete Indexierung verbessern läßt, wenn man diese Fälle bei der Adaption unberücksichtigt läßt. Hierzu bestimmten wir die Vektoren der Klassen A, B, E, F und adaptierten eine neue Funktion auf dieser eingeschränkten Stichprobe. Dies wurde solange wiederholt, bis entweder eine Iteration keine Veränderung mehr brachte, oder die Stichprobe zu klein geworden war.

Bei diesem Verfahren brach die Iteration nach dem fünften Schritt ab, weil kein neuer Vektor mehr in die Klassen C und D fiel. Beim letzten Iterationsschritt wurden 22257 von ursprünglich 27742 Vektoren für die Adaption verwendet. Es ergaben sich deutliche Verbesserungen gegenüber dem einfachen Verfahren (Zeile 1), wie Tabelle 1 zeigt. Sie gibt für D_L und D_T jeweils Reststreuung $\triangle z$, projezierte Reststreuung $\triangle z_{01}$ und maximale Konsistenz q_{max} nach jeder Iterationsstufe an.

Iteration	D_L			D_T		
	$\triangle z$	$\triangle z_{01}$	q_{max}	$\triangle z$	$\triangle z_{01}$	q_{max}
1	0.117539	0.115703	0.44583	0.118906	0.116699	0.45155
2	0.119233	0.113999	0.45185	0.120775	0.114936	0.45619
3	0.119977	0.113789	0.45193	0.121539	0.114709	0.45716
4	0.120003	0.113783	0.45189	0.121564	0.114702	0.45730
5	0.120003	0.113783	0.45189	0.121564	0.114702	0.45730

Tabelle 1: Linear-iterativer Ansatz Version 1

Die Tabelle zeigt, daß sich die Reststreuung im Laufe der Iteration naturgemäß verschlechterte, während die projezierte Reststreuung geringer wurde. Auch die maximale Konsistenz nahm zu. Abbildung 2 gibt den Verlauf der Konsistenz q in Abhängigkeit von der Indexierungstiefe t für die Indexierungen der verschiedenen Stufen an. Man kann erkennen, daß sich die Konsistenz mit

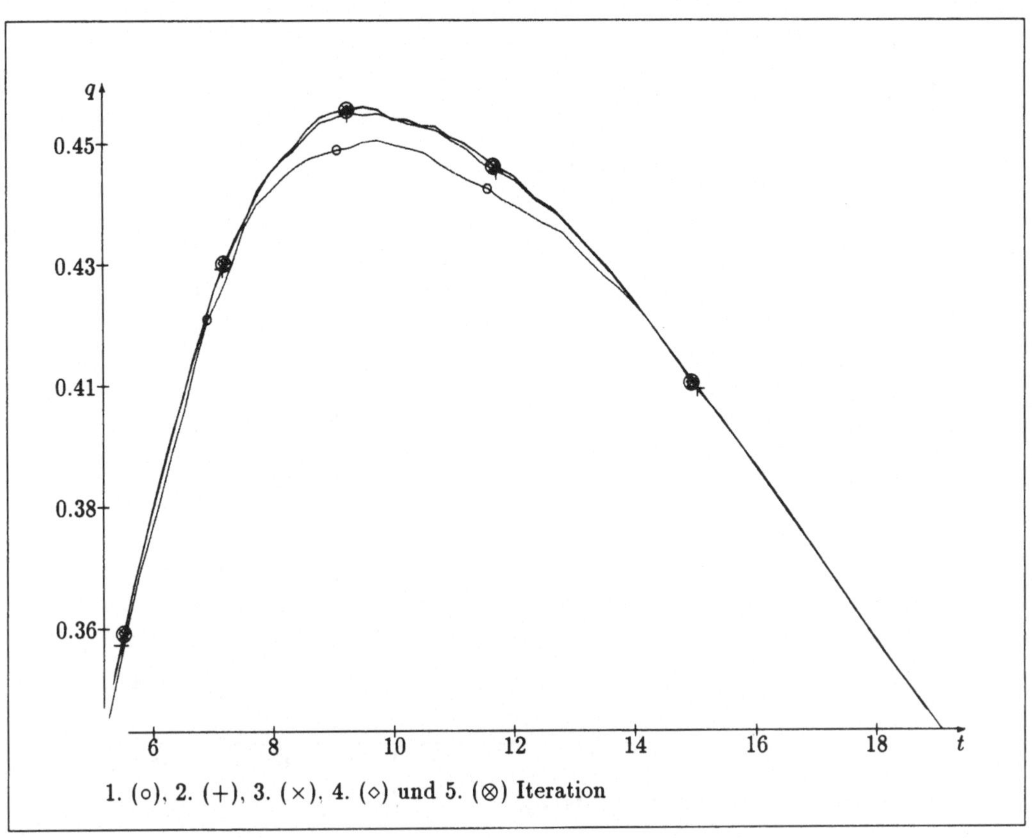

Abbildung 2: Linear-iterativer Ansatz Version 1

der intellektuellen Indexierung für alle wiedergegebenen Schwellenwerte gegenüber dem einfachen
Verfahren (1. Graph) verbesserte.

4.2 Linear-iterativer Ansatz Version 2

Zu einer zweiten Variante führte uns die Hypothese, daß die Vektoren der Klassen A und F statistische Ausreißer seien. Folglich schlossen wir bei dieser Variante alle vier Klassen mit Indexierungs-
gewichten außerhalb des Intervalls $[0, 1]$ vom nächsten Iterationsschritt aus.
Bei dem linear-iterativen Verfahren Version 2 konvergierte die Iteration nach 15 Schritten auf einer
Reststichprobe von 18976 Vektoren. Tabelle 2 gibt die Reststreuung und Konsistenz für die verschiedenen Iterationsstufen an. Abbildung 3 zeigt den Verlauf der Konsistenz für die Funktionen
der verschiedenen Stufen. Wir sehen, daß sich auch bei diesem Verfahren die projezierte Reststreuung verringerte und die Konsistenz erhöhte, wobei beide Kennzahlen bessere Werte erreichten
als bei der Iteration nach Version 1. Beim letzten Adaptionsschritt fielen nur 137 Vektoren in die
Klassen A und F. Trotzdem ergaben sich bei Verwendung der zweiten Version der Iteration, die
sich nur in der Behandlung dieser Klassen von der ersten Version unterscheidet, deutlich bessere
Indexierungsfunktionen.

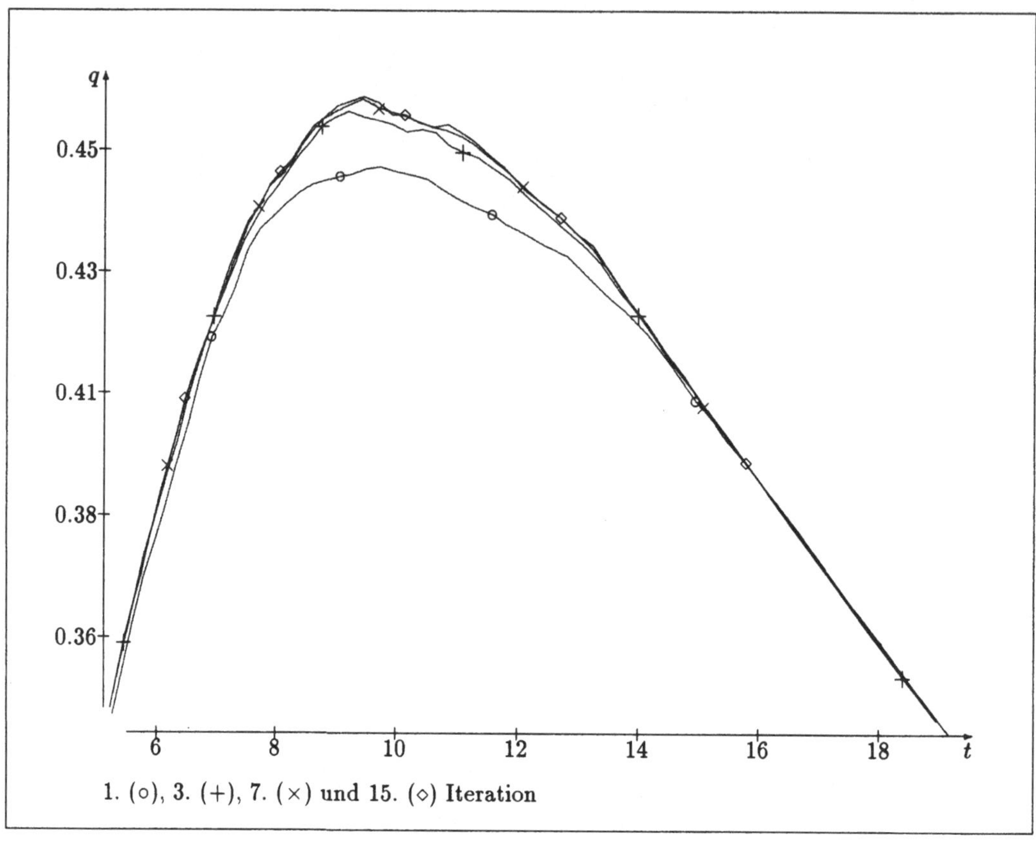

Abbildung 3: Linear-iterativer Ansatz Version 2

Bei allen durchgeführten Adaptionen dieser Art konvergierte das Verfahren, d.h. nach einigen Schritten blieb die Aufteilung der Stichprobe auf die Klassen $A \cup B \cup E \cup F$ und $C \cup D$ bzw. $B \cup E$ und $A \cup C \cup D \cup F$ gleich.

5 Der logistische Ansatz

Als zweiter Ansatz, Indexierungsgewichte außerhalb des Intervalls $[0, 1]$ zu vermeiden, wurden sogenannten logistische Funktionen (siehe [Freeman 87][Fienberg 80]) der Klasse $a : x \mapsto e^{b^T x}/(1 - e^{b^T x})$ mit $b \in \mathbb{R}^n$ untersucht. Als Adaptionskriterium wurde die Likelihoodfunktion gewählt (siehe [Bookstein 88]):

$$p(s, d) := P\left(k(s, d) = 1 | x(s, d)\right)$$
$$L(a_b, k, R_1) := \prod_{(s,d) \in R_1} p(s, d)^{k(s,d)} (1 - p(s, d))^{1 - k(s,d)}$$

Ein Minimum dieser Funktion läßt sich mit einem iterativen Verfahren (Newton-Iteration) näherungsweise berechnen.

Iteration	D_L			D_T		
	$\triangle z$	$\triangle z_{01}$	q_{max}	$\triangle z$	$\triangle z_{01}$	q_{max}
1	0.117539	0.115703	0.44583	0.118906	0.116699	0.45155
2	0.120762	0.113529	0.45252	0.122257	0.114333	0.45746
3	0.126464	0.112902	0.45362	0.127796	0.113546	0.46150
4	0.130395	0.112761	0.45482	0.131668	0.113322	0.46256
5	0.132742	0.112717	0.45560	0.133930	0.113195	0.46316
6	0.133761	0.112699	0.45579	0.134880	0.113152	0.46292
7	0.134760	0.112672	0.45569	0.135781	0.113115	0.46366
8	0.135784	0.112660	0.45551	0.136714	0.113087	0.46371
9	0.136351	0.112657	0.45539	0.137264	0.113081	0.46400
10	0.136883	0.112653	0.45545	0.137752	0.113078	0.46410
11	0.137222	0.112651	0.45548	0.138041	0.113067	0.46400
12	0.137436	0.112650	0.45564	0.138239	0.113057	0.46421
13	0.137460	0.112650	0.45570	0.138263	0.113058	0.46414
14	0.137460	0.112650	0.45570	0.138264	0.113058	0.46414
15	0.137460	0.112650	0.45570	0.138264	0.113058	0.46414

Tabelle 2: Linear-iterativer Ansatz Version 2

Die iterative Lösung des logistischen Ansatzes wurde nach 6 Iterationen abgebrochen, weil die
Änderung des Koeffizientenvektors eine vorgegebene Schranke unterschritt. Die Tabelle 3 enthält

Lösungs-iteration	D_L		D_T	
	$\triangle z$	q_{max}	$\triangle z$	q_{max}
1	0.121243	0.44571	0.121876	0.45120
2	0.114224	0.45130	0.114981	0.45656
3	0.113619	0.45197	0.114314	0.45887
4	0.113601	0.45248	0.114283	0.45876
5	0.113601	0.45244	0.114282	0.45872
6	0.113601	0.45244	0.114282	0.45872

Tabelle 3: Lösungsiterationen beim Logistischen Ansatz

die Reststreuung und die maximale Konsistenz für die Indexierungsfunktionen, die während des
Lösungsverfahrens berechnet wurden.
Wir sehen, daß die Werte besser als die der ersten, aber schlechter als die der zweiten linear-iterativen
Funktion sind. Das ist insoweit nicht überraschend, als mit der ersten linear-iterativen Version eine
Adaption einer Funktion angestrebt wurde, die ähnlich wie die logistische Funktion nur Werte aus
dem Intervall [0, 1] liefert. Die Elimination der statistischen Ausreißer kann die logistische Funktion
aber nicht simulieren.

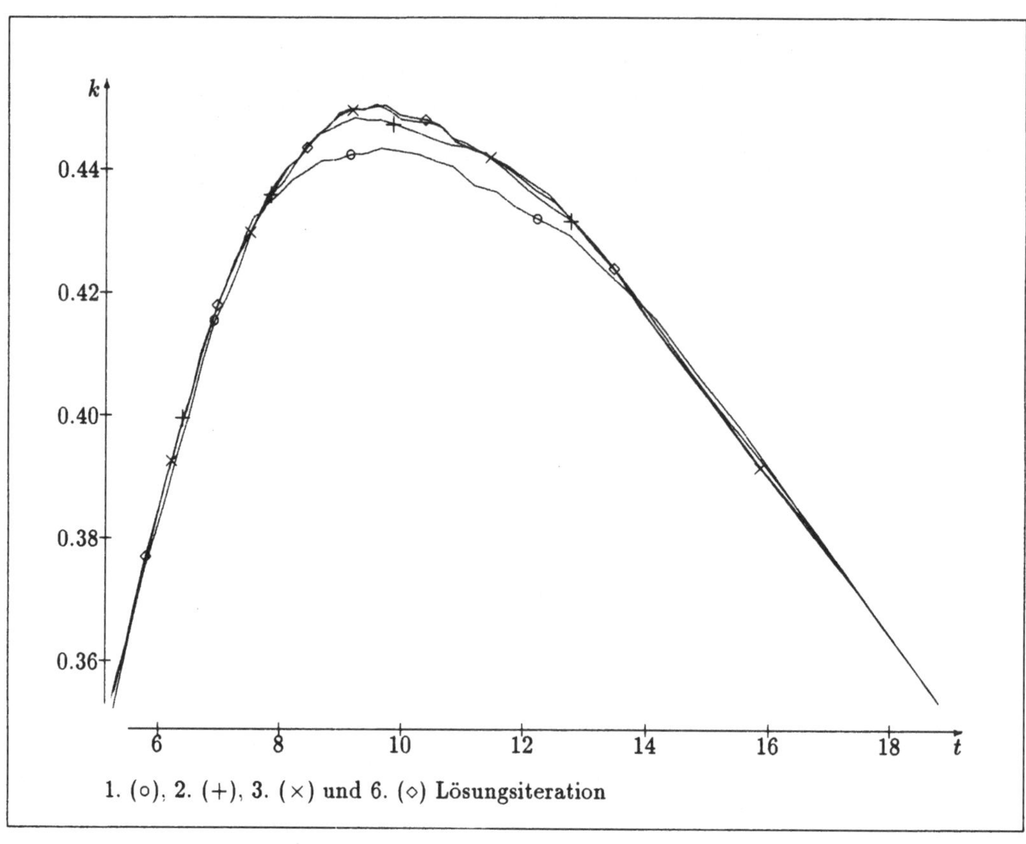

Abbildung 4: Logistischer Ansatz: Lösungsiteration

6 Vergleich der Varianten

Wir wollen nun die im vorangegangenen Abschnitt wiedergegebenen Ergebnisse mithilfe des Vorzeichentests auf einer weiteren Stichproben auf ihre Signifikanz untersuchen.

Die Tabellen dieses Abschnitts geben jeweils projezierte Reststreuung und maximale Konsistenz auf der neuen Stichprobe wieder. Weiter wird die Wahrscheinlichkeit eines Fehlers erster Art, also des fälschlichen einseitigen Verwerfens der Nullhypothese, für die gewichtete Indexierung wiedergegeben. Auf dem Rechner nicht mehr darstellbare Abweichungen von 0 oder 1 werden mit ε wiedergegeben. Für die ungewichtete Indexierung wurden die Funktionen bei Indexierungstiefen von 0 bis zum Maximum bei einer Schrittweite von 0.1 verglichen. Die jeweils letzte Zeile der Tabellen gibt die Indexierungstiefen an, bei denen die Gegenhypothese auf einem Sicherheitsniveau von 0.99 verworfen werden kann. Hierbei werden benachbarte Werte als Intervall dargestellt.

Wir vermuten, daß alle drei neuen Ansätze dem einfachen linearen Verfahren überlegen sind, und formulieren die Hypothese 1:

Hypothese 1 *Die iterativen Versionen des linearen Ansatzes und der logistische Ansatz sind dem einfachen linearen Ansatz überlegen.*

	Linear	Linear-iterativ Version 1
$\triangle z_{01}$	0.11510	0.11301
q_{max}	0.44519	0.45146
gewichtet	ε	
ungewichtet	3.9 [5.5, 5.8] [6.3, 7.9] [8.1, 13.4] 13.9	

	Linear	Linear-iterativ Version 2
$\triangle z_{01}$	0.11510	0.11141
q_{max}	0.44519	0.45826
gewichtet	ε	
ungewichtet	[4.8, 5.0] 5.2 [5.5, 14.9]	

	Linear	Logistisch
$\triangle z_{01}$	0.11510	0.11238
q_{max}	0.44519	0.45327
gewichtet	ε	
ungewichtet	[5.7, 5.8] 6.0 [6.3, 7.6] [7.8, 12.8] [13.1, 13.4] 13.6	

Die Hypothese kann für die gewichtete Indexierung als bestätigt gelten. Bei der ungewichteten Indexierung ist die Überlegenheit nicht für alle Indexierungstiefen nachgewiesen. Doch kann die Hypothese für den wichtigen Bereich [7.8, 12.8], in dem auch die maximale Konsistenz liegt, angenommen werden. Die Gegenhypothese wird nur bei dem Vergleich mit Version 2 bei einer uninteressanten Indexierungstiefe von 0.7 bestätigt.

Abbildung 6 zeigt die jeweils letzten Indexierungsfunktionen der drei Verfahren zusammen. Wir erkennen, daß der Graph des iterativen Ansatzes Version 2 im ganzen dargestellten Bereich über dem des Ansatzes Version 1 liegt. Wir vermuten also, daß ersteres letzterem überlegen ist.

Hypothese 2 *Die zweite Version des linear-iterativen Ansatzes ist der ersten Version überlegen.*

	Linear-iterativ Version 1	Linear-iterativ Version 2
$\triangle z_{01}$	0.11301	0.11141
q_{max}	0.45146	0.45826
gewichtet	ε	
ungewichtet	5.2 5.7 [5.9, 6.2] [6.5, 14.4] [14.7, 14.8]	

Wieder kann die Hypothese für die gewichtete Indexierung und im wichtigen Bereich der Indexierungstiefen für die ungewichteten Indexierungen als bestätigt angesehen werden.

Schwieriger ist es, den Verlauf des Graphen der logistischen Funktion zu interpretieren, da er die Graphen der beiden anderen Funktionen schneidet.

Hypothese 3 *Der logistische Ansatz ist der ersten Version des linear-iterativen Ansatzes überlegen.*

	Linear-iterativ Version 1	Logistisch
$\triangle z_{01}$	0.11301	0.11238
q_{max}	0.45146	0.45327
gewichtet	0.999770	
ungewichtet	11.7 11.9 12.1	

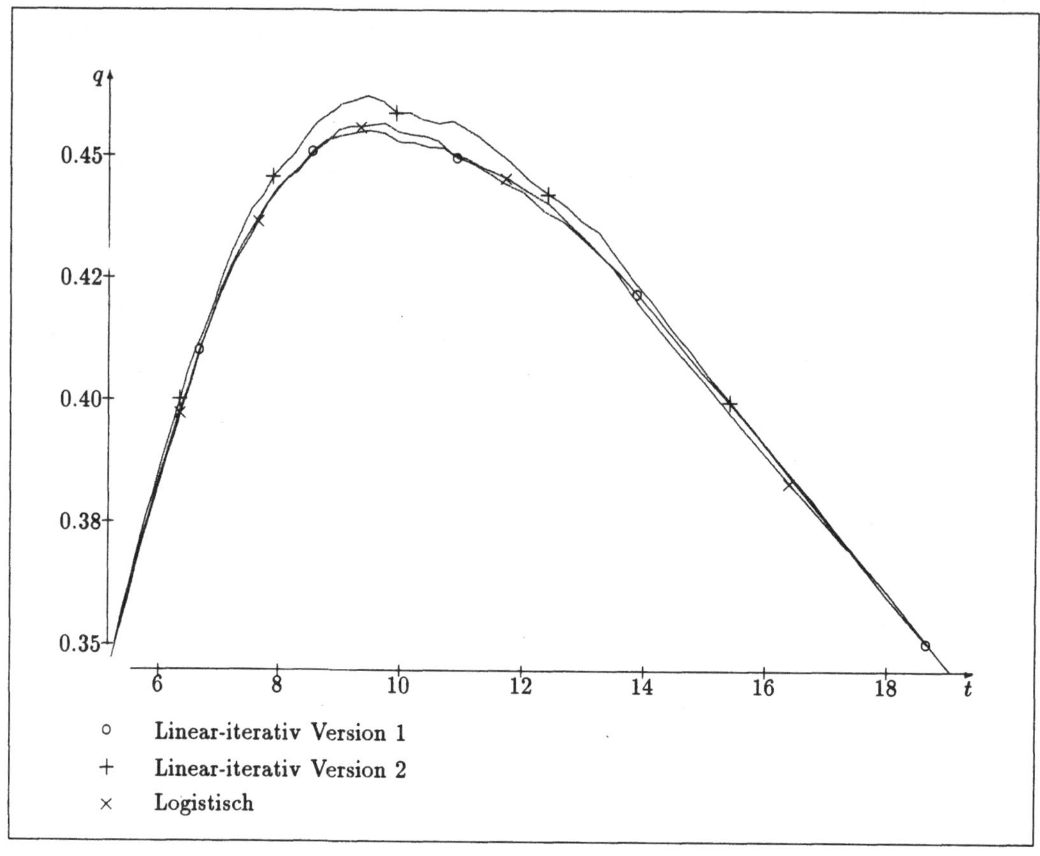

Abbildung 5: Vergleich der Varianten

	Logistisch	Linear-iterativ Version 1
$\triangle z_{01}$	0.11238	0.11301
q_{max}	0.45327	0.45146
gewichtet	0.00023	
ungewichtet	17.0	

Die Hypothese 3 ist für die gewichtete Indexierung sicher falsch. Bei der ungewichteten Indexierung ist ein Überlegenheit auf einem Signifikanzniveau von 0.99 nur an drei Punkten, allerdings im interessantesten Bereich, nachzuweisen. Auf einem Signifikanzniveau von 0.9 kann man die Gegenhypothese für die Bereiche von [8.9, 10.7] und [10.9, 12.7] verwerfen.
Dagegen ist der logistische Ansatz dem linear-iterativen Ansatz Version 2 sicher unterlegen.

Hypothese 4 *Die zweite Version des linear-iterativen Ansatzes ist dem logistische Ansatzes überlegen.*

	Logistisch	Linear-iterativ Version 2
$\triangle z_{01}$	0.11238	0.11141
q_{max}	0.45327	0.45826
gewichtet		ε
ungewichtet		[4.9, 5.0] 5.2 6.5 [6.8, 7.8] [8.2, 11.3] [11.7, 14.0] [14.4, 14.7] [14.9, 15.3]

Die Hypothese kann für die gewichtete Indexierung als bestätigt gelten. Auch bei den ungewichteten Indexierungen ist der lineare Ansatz bei vielen Indexierungstiefen, insbesondere bei der maximalen Konsistenz (Tiefe = 9.512 bzw. 9.832 Deskriptoren/Dokument) signifikant besser. Zu beachten ist bei dem Vergleich mit dem logistische Ansatz, daß der verwendete Beschreibungsvektor für den linearen Ansatz entwickelt wurde, also für diesen Ansatz nicht optimal kodiert war. Experimente mit Vektoren, die für den logistische Ansatz entwickelt wurden, sind in [Pfeifer 90] und [Fuhr & Pfeifer 91] beschrieben. Es zeigte sich, daß sich der Abstand zu linear-iterativen Funktionen durch geeignete Kodierung des Vektors zumindest verringern läßt.

7 Ausblick

Die oben wiedergegeben Experimente zeigen, daß die Suche nach neuen Regressionsfunktionen durchaus ein erfolgversprechender Weg zu besseren automatischen Indexierungsfunktionen ist. Insbesondere die Elimination von statistische Ausreißern scheint signifikante Verbesserungen möglich zu machen. Eine weitere Möglichkeit zur Homogenisierung der Stichproben ist eine Aufteilung in homogene Unterklassen, auf denen getrennt Funktionen adaptiert werden können. In [Pfeifer 90] wurde für verschiedene Beschreibungsvektoren nachgewiesen, daß eine Aufteilung in 3 bzw. 5 Unterklassen zu signifikanten Verbesserungen der Indexierungsqualität führen kann. Die homogenisierenden Eigenschaften der linear-iterativen Ansätze könnten auch in Kombinationen von linear-iterativen und logistischen Verfahren ausgenutzt werden, indem der linear-iterative Ansatz zu Elimination von statistische Ausreißern benutzt wird, und dann der logistische Ansatz auf der reduzierten Stichprobe adaptiert wird. Mit diesem kombinierten Verfahren konnten bei dem hier verwendeten Beschreibungsvektor zwar bessere Ergebnisse erzielt werden als mit dem logistischen Verfahren, die Ergebnisse des linear-iterativen Verfahrens wurden aber nicht erreicht.

Danksagung

Ich möchte Norbert Fuhr für die fachkundige und geduldige Betreuung meiner Diplomarbeit danken, aus der der größte Teil der hier vorgestellten Ergebnisse entnommen ist. Auch für kritische Anmerkungen und Anregungen bei der Erstellung dieses Beitrags schulde ich ihm Dank.

Literatur

Beinke-Geiser, U.; Lustig, G.; Putze-Meier, G. (1986). Indexieren mit dem System DAISY. In: Lustig, G. (Hrsg.): *Automatische Indexierung zwischen Forschung und Anwendung*, S. 73–97. Olms, Hildesheim.

Biebricher, P.; Fuhr, N.; Knorz, G.; Lustig, G.; Schwantner, M. (1988). Entwicklung und Anwendung des automatischen Indexierungssystems AIR/PHYS. *Nachrichten fuer Dokumentation 39*, S. 135–143.

Bookstein, A. (1988). *Loglinear Analysis of Library Data.* Research report, OCLC, Office of Research.

Fienberg, S. (1980). *The Analysis of Cross-Classified Categorial Data.* MIT Press, Cambridge, Mass., 2. Auflage.

Freeman, D. (1987). *Applied Categorial Data Analysis.* Dekker, New York.

Fuhr, N.; Pfeifer, U. (1991). Combining Model-Oriented and Description-Oriented Approaches for Probabilistic Indexing. In: *Proceedings of the 16th Annual International ACMSIGIR Conference on Research and Development in Information Retrieval.* ACM, New York.

Fuhr, N. (1989). Models for Retrieval with Probabilistic Indexing. *Information Processing and Management 25(1)*, S. 55–72.

Knorz, G. (1983). *Automatisches Indexieren als Erkennen abstrakter Objekte.* Niemeyer, Tübingen.

Knorz, G. (1986). Die Anwendung von Polynomklassifikatoren für die automatische Indexierung. In: Lustig, G. (Hrsg.): *Automatische Indexierung zwischen Forschung und Anwendung,* S. 98–126. Olms, Hildesheim.

Lustig, G. (Hrsg.) (1986). *Automatische Indexierung zwischen Forschung und Anwendung.* Olms, Hildesheim.

Pfeifer, U. (1990). *Entwicklung log-linearer und linear-iterativer Indexierungsfunktionen.* Diplomarbeit, TH Darmstadt, FB Informatik, Datenverwaltungssysteme II.

ATLAS-PfleSaurus:

Ein objektorientiertes System zur Unterstützung der Thesauruspflege

Josef Willenborg
Technische Universität Berlin, IFP ATLAS, Hardenbergstr. 28, 1000 Berlin 12
(Tel.: 49-30-31425400, E-mail: willenbo@db0tui11.bitnet)

Zusammenfassung:
ATLAS-PfleSaurus ist ein objektorientiertes System zur Unterstützung der Erstellung und Weiterentwicklung von (Teil)-Thesauri, das insbesondere übersichtliche Darstellungen von Thesauri und den redaktionellen Charakter der Thesauruspflege berücksichtigt. Die Systementwicklung wird in partizipativem Rahmen durchgeführt.

Abstract:
ATLAS-PfleSaurus, an object-oriented computer system to support the establishment and development of (partial)-thesauri is presented. Especially the desire for clearly arranged displays of thesauri and the editorial character of thesaurus cultivation is pointed out. The system development is realized in a participative working group.

0. Einführung:

Thesauri erleichtern den Zugriff auf Informationen. Sie verbessern i.A. Retrievalergebnisse. Weiterhin tragen sie dazu bei, die Bezeichnungsvielfalt für die beabsichtigte Anwendung zu ordnen und an dieser Stelle so mehr Sprachklarheit zu schaffen.

Auf der anderen Seite ist die Pflege von Thesauri mit hohem Aufwand verbunden und zudem kompliziert und unüberschaubar. Hinzu kommt, daß Thesauri in einem sinnvollerweise oft interdisziplinär zusammengesetztem Team (von Vielen für Viele) erstellt werden, und so Thesauruspflege durch den zusätzlichen organisatorischen Aufwand erschwert wird bzw. ganz außer Kontrolle gerät.

Um diesen Schwierigkeiten zu begegnen, werden zunehmend maschinelle Systeme zur Unterstützung der Thesauruspflege eingesetzt.

In diesem Beitrag werden Prinzipien und die technische Realisierung einer maschinellen Unterstützung der Mehrbenutzer-Thesauruspflege erläutert. Rollen und Authorisierungen der Mitglieder der Thesaurusredaktion werden spezifiziert (siehe Kap. 1). ATLAS-PfleSaurus (**Pflege den Thesaurus!**), ein System zur Unterstützung der Erstellung und Weiterentwicklung von Thesauri, das neuere objektorientierte Softwarekonzepte berücksichtigt, wird hinsichtlich seiner Funktionalität und Implementierung vorgestellt (siehe Kap. 2.).

1. Redaktionelle Thesauruspflege

Die Thesaurusredaktion bestimmt die Qualität von Thesauri in ihren Anwendungsgebieten. Thesaursredaktionen sind sinnvollerweise oft aus Mitgliedern unterschiedlicher Bereiche zusammengesetzt. Durch heterogen zusammengesetzte Thesaurusredaktionen wird
1. der Thesaurus vielseitiger, vielschichtiger aufgebaut.
2. die Blickrichtung mehr auf die beabsichtigte Anwendung, zum Thesaurusnutzer hin verschoben (Vermeidung von Expertenblindheit).

Thesaurusredaktionen sind niemals "fest auf alle Zeit". Die Mitglieder wechseln von Zeit zu Zeit; die erforderlichen Treffen sind oft nur schwer organisierbar.
Die Kommunikation der Mitglieder der Thesaurusredaktion verbessert sich zwar im Lauf der Zeit, was jedoch den negativen Effekt einer starken Sprachangleichung zur Folge haben kann.

Weiterhin ist zu beachten, daß:
1. durch eine zu schwach besetzte Thesaurusredaktion, die Mitglieder überfordert und das Thesaurusvokabular von zu wenigen Thesauruspflegern abhängig wird und andererseits
2. durch zu viele Thesauruspfleger die Thesauruspflege unüberschaubar wird und die Konsistenz des Thesaurus beeinträchtigt wird.

Um die Arbeit der Thesaurusredaktion nicht chon frühzeitig zum Scheitern zu verurteilen, empfiehlt sich die Verfügung von **Rollen** mit entsprechenden **Authorisierungen**. Folgende Rollen bzw. Authorisierungen der Mitglieder der Thesaurusredaktion haben sich in unserer interdisziplinären Arbeitsgruppe herausgebildet:

Der Fachgebietsspezialist: Der Fachgebietsspezialist ist meistens mit vielen Dingen beschäftigt und will deswegen nur wenig Zeit für die eigentliche, oft mühsame Thesauruspflege aufbringen. Er hat zudem oft einen speziellen Wortschatz entwickelt, der für Außenstehende schwer verständlich ist. Deswegen ist eine Aufgabe des Fachgebietsspezialisten bei der Thesauruspflege darin zu sehen, im Konfliktfall allein oder im Dialog mit anderen Redaktionsmitgliedern zweifelhafte Begriffsstrukturen im Thesaurus zu klären. Zu Beginn der Thesauruserstellung kann die Aufgabe des Fachgebietsspezialisten darin bestehen, einen Überblick über das Fachgebiet zu geben.

Authorisierung: Dem Fachgebietsspezialisten werden umfassende Vollmachten zur Thesaurusmodifikation gegeben (eingeschränkt auf die von ihm zu bearbeitetenden Thesauri):
Lesen, Suchen nach, Erzeugen, Ändern und Löschen von Thesauruseinträgen (Knoten und Beziehungen).

Der Fachgebietskenner: Die Aufgabe des Fachgebietskenners besteht darin, im Dialog mit den Redaktionsmitgliedern den Thesaurus zu erstellen und weiterzuentwikkeln.

Zu Beginn der Thesauruserstellung sind Experten auf dem Gebiet der Thesauruspflege, Fachgebietsspezialisten und bei Bedarf die Systementwickler zu Rate zu ziehen. Während der Thesauruspflege sind zweifelhafte Begriffsstrukturen im Dialog mit Fachgebietskennern und -spezialisten aufzulösen.

Authorisierung: Dem Fachgebietskenner werden wie dem Fachgebietsspezialisten umfassende Vollmachten zur Thesaurusmodifikation gegeben (eingeschränkt auf die von ihm zu bearbeitenden Thesauri):
Lesen, Suchen nach, Erzeugen, Ändern und Löschen von Thesauruseinträgen (Knoten und Beziehungen).

Der Fachgebietsnovize: Die Aufgabe des Fachgebietsnovizen besteht einerseits darin, im dauernden Dialog mit den Redaktionsmitgliedern seine eigenen Kenntnisse zu erweitern, andererseits darin, durch seine nicht immer fachbezogenen Hinweise, Einwände und Fragen weitere Klarheit in das Fachgebiet und darüber hinaus zu bringen (Spezialistenblindheit vermindern, alltäglichere Sprache verwenden).

Authorisierung: Nur im Ausnahmefall ist ihm die Modifikation von Thesauri gestattet. Das Lesen und Suchen nach Thesauruseinträgen (Knoten und Beziehungen) ist ihm erlaubt.

Der Indexierer: Die Aufgabe des Indexierers besteht darin, auf die Probleme der Adäquatheit von Thesaurusbegriffen für die Beschreibbarkeit von Dokumenten hinzuweisen. Seine Blickrichtung ist immer auf die mit dem Thesaurus zu verwaltenden Dokumentenmengen gerichtet.
Oft sind Indexierer und Fachgebietskenner dieselbe Person.

Authorisierung: Nur im Ausnahmefall ist ihm die Modifikation von Thesauri gestattet. Das Lesen und Suchen nach Thesauruseinträgen (Knoten und Beziehungen) ist ihm erlaubt.

Ihm kann das Erzeugen neuer Thesauruseinträge (kein Löschen s.u.) während der Indexierung gestattet werden (z.B. wenn sich herausstellt, daß ein Begriff, der nicht im Thesaurus enthalten ist, für die Beschreibung eines Dokuments geeignet ist und der Indexierer Fachgebietskenntnisse nachweisen kann). Oder noch eingeschränkter: Ihm kann das Erzeugen von Synonymen (Thesaurusbezeichnungen) gestattet werden.

Der Experte auf dem Gebiet der Thesauruspflege: Die Aufgabe des Experten auf dem Gebiet der Thesauruspflege besteht darin, allen Redaktionsmitgliedern Theorie, Methodik und Aufgabe der Thesauruspflege zu erläutern.

Authorisierung: Die Modifikation von Thesauri ist ihm nicht gestattet. Das Lesen und Suchen nach Thesauruseinträgen (Knoten und Beziehungen) kann ihm im Ausnahmefall gestattet werden.

Der Systementwickler: Wenn parallel zur Thesauruspflege ein System zur Thesauruspflege entwickelt wird (partizipative Systementwicklung, Prototyping), besteht die Aufgabe des Systementwicklers darin, im Dialog mit den Redaktionsmitgliedern Bedarfsanalysen und die Entwicklung des Systems durchzuführen. Weiterhin weist der Systementwickler auf Möglichkeiten und Restriktionen hin, die sich aus dem Einsatz konkreter Systeme ergeben.

Authorisierung: Die Modifikation von Thesauri ist ihm nicht gestattet. Das Lesen und Suchen nach Thesauruseinträgen (Knoten und Beziehungen) kann ihm im Ausnahmefall gestattet werden.

Von den Mitgliedern der Thesaurusredaktion ist über alle Modifikationen der Thesauri Buch zu führen:

- Name
- Zeitpunkt der Modifikation
- Zweck der Modifikation
- Bemerkungen

Die Thesaurusredaktion trifft sich regelmäßig und ist mindestens aus folgenden Mitgliedern zusammengesetzt:

a.) ein Experte auf dem Gebiet der Thesauruspflege
b.) für jedes Fachgebiet ein Fachgebietsspezialist, der nur bei Bedarf herangezogen wird
c.) für jedes Fachgebiet zwei Fachgebietskenner
d.) ein Fachgebietsnovize
e.) eventuell ein Indexierer
f.) eventuell ein Systementwickler

Neue Mitglieder für die Thesaurusredaktion werden nur für einen "längeren Zeitraum" aufgenommen.

Bildlich kann die Arbeit der Thesaurusredaktion als ein dauernder Wechsel zweier Phasen dargestellt werden:

1. Diskussions –und Klärungssphase:

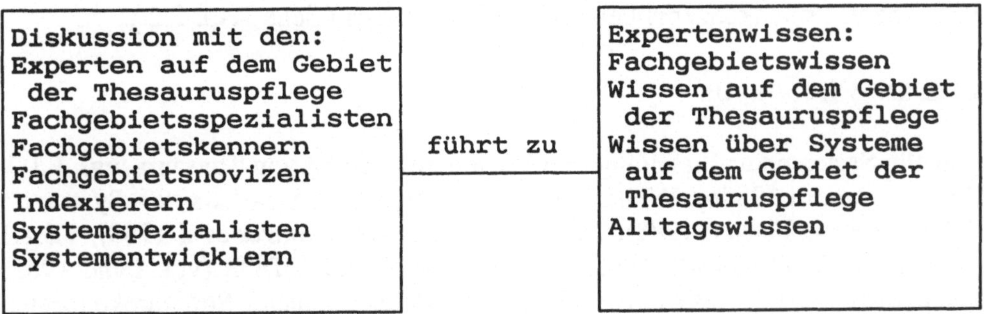

2. Thesauruspflege:

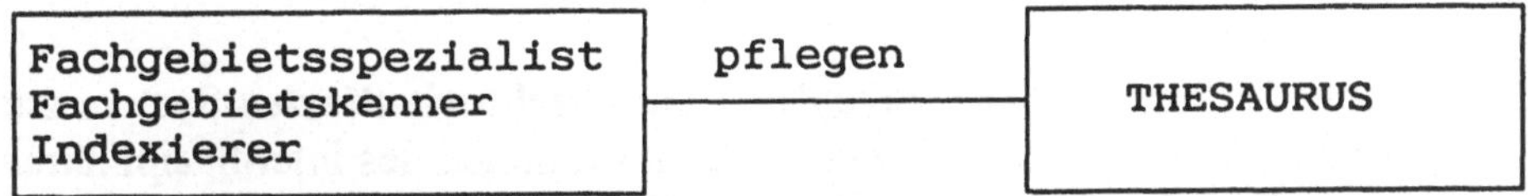

Abb. 1: Phasenmodell der Thesaurusredaktion

Jo Redejohann schlägt als Ansatz zur Verringerung der Abhängigkeit des Thesaurus von der Thesaurusredaktion vor, die in DIN 1463 angeführte Möglichkeit der Indexierung mit frei gewählten Benennungen zu verwenden und sie so zu erweitern, daß in einem der Indexierung nachfolgendem Schritt die Zusammenführung der einem Begriff zugeordneten Bezeichnungen in Äquivalenzklassen ermöglicht wird (vgl. Redejohann 1987 376).

Das Modell der Indexierung mit ausschließlich verbindlichem Vokabular wird zu einem Modell der Indexierung mit teilweise freiem, teilweise verbindlichem Vokabular erweitert, wobei das freie Vokabular während der Indexierung in den Thesaurus übernommen wird.

Die uneingeschränkte Übernahme von freiem Vokabular in den Thesaurus durch den Indexierer hieße jedoch, daß die durch Prinzipien festgelegte Arbeit der Thesaurusredaktion, die bisher erreichte inhaltliche Konsistenz des Thesaurus zerstören könnte. Für eine Übernahme sind also geeignete Vorsichtsmaßnahmen zu treffen:

1. Jeder vom Indexierer neu erzeugte Thesauruseintrag (Begriff oder Bezeichnung) enthält mindestens den Indexierernamen, den Zeitpunkt der Erzeugung (Datum, Uhrzeit) und eine geeignete Dokumentation dieses Eintrags.

2. Das Entfernen von Thesauruseinträgen durch den Indexierer verlangt entweder weitere komplexe Indexiererarbeiten (jeder geänderte Thesauruseintrag muß zusätzlich in der schon vorhandenen Dokument – Deskriptorzuordnung geändert werden) oder ist ganz zu verbieten, was als die natürlichere Lösung erscheint.

Zur Unterstützung redaktioneller Thesauruspflege sind maschinelle Systeme heranzuziehen: ATLAS–PfleSaurus berücksichtigt Maßnahmen zur Unterstützung des Mehr-
benutzer –bzw. Rollenkonzepts bei der Thesauruspflege (siehe Kap. 2.2.).

2. ATLAS–PfleSaurus

Maschinelle Systeme zur Erstellung und Weiterentwicklung von Thesauri (vgl. PRO-
TERM (vgl. Burkart 1988b),.INDEX (vgl. Lukas 1988), das Smalltalk–80–System der
GMD (vgl. Rostek, Fischer 1988), TEGEN (vgl. Felsner, Güntzer et al 1988), CBAIR
(vgl. Giger 1989), TERM–PC (vgl. Hohnhold 1990) und LIDOS (vgl. Land 1989))
berücksichtigen nur teilweise Entwicklungen im Bereich neuerer Softwarekonzepte:
Schlagworte sind hier: Partizipative und evolutionäre Softwareentwicklung, Gestal-
tungsmöglichkeiten im Bereich der Benutzeroberflächen, Mehrbenutzerkonzept, Einsatz
von (objektorientierten) Datenbanken.

ATLAS-PfleSaurus (Pflege den The**saurus**!) ist ein **objektorientiertes** System zur
Erstellung und Weiterentwicklung von Thesauri, das im Rahmen des interdisziplinären
Forschungsprojekts ATLAS partizipativ unter Beteiligung der Institute: Psychologie,
Linguistik und Informatik entwickelt wird.

ATLAS–PfleSaurus bietet insbesondere übersichtlichere Darstellungen von (Teil)–
Thesauri an: **alphabetische, polyhierarchische und graphische Darstellungen.**

Weiterhin ist ATLAS–PfleSaurus für den Einsatz im **Mehrbenutzerbetrieb** konzipiert
(siehe Kap. 1 und 2.2).

Die Systementwicklung wird bei ATLAS in einem **partizipativen** Rahmen durchgeführt (vgl. Coad, Yourdan 1990): Es besteht der Wunsch der Anwender und Systementwickler, in interdisziplinärer Zusammenarbeit Ideen und Wünsche bzw. Anforderungen zu verwirklichen (und zu verwerfen).
Die Implementierung ist auf Nutzung und Schaffung **wiederverwendbarer Software**
hin ausgerichtet. Beispielsweise ist die polyhierarchische Darstellung in allen diesbezüglichen Anwendungen einsetzbar.
Durch die Wahl der objektorientierten Programmiersprache Smalltalk V 286 bzw.
Smalltalk V Windows sind die Voraussetzungen gegeben, die implementierten Anwendungen einer großen Öffentlichkeit zukommen zu lassen.

ATLAS–PfleSaurus wird in das bei ATLAS entwickelte Information Retrieval System
bzw. in das textinterpretationsunterstützende System ATLAS/ti eingegliedert (vgl.
Muhr 1990).

2.1. Darstellungen von Thesauri

ATLAS–PfleSaurus bietet alphabetische, polyhierarchische und graphische Darstellungen von (Teil)–Thesauri an.

Die **alphabetische Darstellung** zeigt Thesaurusbegriffe alphabetisch geordnet, zusätzlich zu jedem Begriff dessen Kontext, also alle Nachbarbegriffe mit der jeweiligen Beziehungsart, dessen Definition bzw. Erläuterung, dessen Einfügungszeitpunkt (Datum, Uhrzeit) und dessen zuständigen Thesauruspfleger.

Die **polyhierarchische Darstellung** zeigt Thesaurusbegriffe nach den im Thesaurus enthaltenen hierarchischen Relationen geordnet. Wenn für einen Begriff mehr als ein direkt übergeordneter Begriff angegeben ist (Polyhierarchie), erscheint dieser mehrfach in der Systematik (siehe Abb. 2).

"Begriffe, die in mehreren Begriffsleitern vorkommen, sind jeweils in diesen aufzuführen (erscheinen also mehrfach in der Systematik)."
(DIN 1463 Teil 1 8)

Die Sicht auf Unterbegriffe kann (auf Mausdruck) an –und ausgeblendet werden.

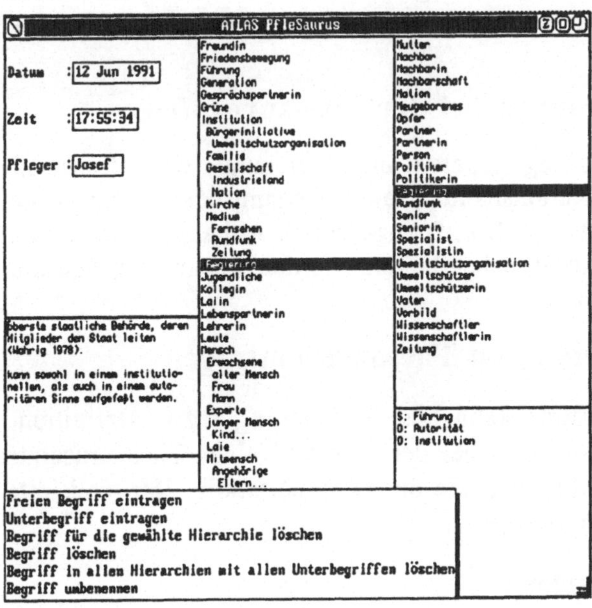

Abb. 2: Momentaufnahme einer alphabetisch, systematisch–polyhierarchischen Darstellung eines Beispiel–(teil)–thesaurus mit ATLAS–PfleSaurus (Erläuterung: O entspricht der Oberbegriffsbeziehung, U entspricht der Unterbegriffsbeziehung).

Die graphische Darstellung des Thesaurus zeigt eine Auswahl von Thesaurusbegriffen und deren Beziehungen als Beziehungsgraph:

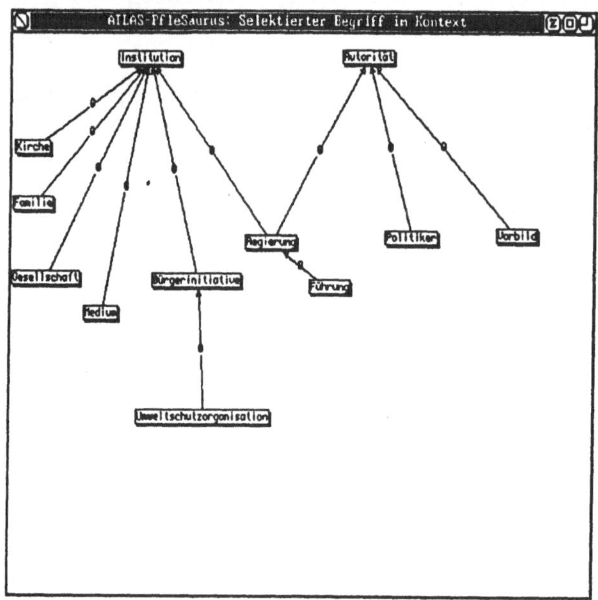

Abb. 3: Momentaufnahme einer graphischen Darstellung eines Beispiel–(teil)–thesaurus mit ATLAS–PfleSaurus (B entspricht der Benutze–Synonym–Beziehung hier bei Führung)

2.2. Authorisierungen bei der Thesauruspflege

Jedem Thesauruseintrag (Knoten und Beziehung) wird dessen zuständiger Thesauruspfleger (Identifikationsname, Name, Zugangsberechtigung) und dessen Zeitpunkt der Erzeugung (Datum, Uhrzeit) zugeordnet. Abhängig von der Zugangsberechtigung bzw. Rolle des Thesaurusbearbeiters werden bestimmte Thesaurusoperationen zugelassen (siehe Kap. 1).

2.3. Kommentieren von Thesauruseinträgen

Jedem Thesauruseintrag kann eine Erläuterung (bzw. Definition, Kommentar) zugeordnet werden. Sie wird bei der Auswahl eines Thesauruseintrags angezeigt und kann durch die Funktionen, die der in Smalltalk V 286 realisierte Texteditor bietet, geeignet modifiziert werden.

2.4. Beziehungsarten

ATLAS–PfleSaurus läßt grundsätzlich die freie Wahl bzw. Definition von Beziehungsarten zwischen Thesaurusbegriffen zu, unterstützt aber (vorgegebene, formal definierte) Beziehungen wie Oberbegriff, Unterbegriff, Synonym und verwandter Begriff.

2.5. Suche nach Thesauruseinträgen

Für die alphabetische und systematische Darstellung von Thesaurusbegriffen ist die inkrementelle Suche nach Thesaurusbegriffen realisiert. Inkrementelle Suche heißt, daß abhängig von nacheinander eingegebenen Zeichen einer Suchzeichenfolge die bis dahin treffende Zeichenfolge aus einer alphabetisch geordneten Menge von Zeichenfolgen angezeigt wird.

Weiterhin wird die einfache Navigation im Thesaurusgraphen ermöglicht, indem durch Mausklick im Kontextfenster der jeweilige Nachbarbegriff direkt angewählt werden kann.

2.6. Konsistenzüberprüfungen

ATLAS–PfleSaurus nimmt Zyklenüberprüfungen des Thesaurus bezüglich hierarchischer Beziehungen vor (cycle check).
Weiterhin wird beim Hinzufügen einer neuen Kante überprüft, ob diese Kante schon existiert (already exist check).

2.7. Thesaurusmodifizierende Operationen

Abhängig von den Darstellungen von Thesauri bietet ATLAS–PfleSaurus z.B. folgende thesaurusmodifizierende Operationen an:

1. Hinzufügen von Thesaurusbegriffen;
2. Hinzufügen von Beziehungen zwischen Thesaurusbegriffen;
3. Entfernen von Thesaurusbegriffen;
4. Entfernen von Beziehungen zwischen Thesaurusbegriffen;
5. Umbenennen von Thesaurusbegriffen;
6. Entfernen von Teilnetzen;

2.8. Ex –und Import von Thesauri

Thesauri können in/von maschinenlesbaren Dateien geschrieben/gelesen werden (auf Effizienz bedachte, systemorientierte Auslagerung). Das objektorientierte Anwendungsprogramm wird so von den Anwenderdaten getrennt.
Weiterhin können Thesauri in ein für den Benutzer lesbares, druckfertiges Dateiformat (die übliche alphabetische und sysstematische Darstellung, vgl. DIN 1463 Teil 1 1987 7) überführt werden.
Besonders hervorgehoben ist durch den Einsatz eines objektorientierten Parser-Generators (vgl. Rovira 1991) der Import beliebiger Thesaurusformate, die in BNF (Bakkus– Naur–Form) definiert werden, möglich.

2.9. Implementierung

Für die Entwicklung von ATLAS-PfleSaurus wird die Programmiersprache Small-talk/V 286 (vgl. Digitalk 1988) verwendet. Smalltalk/V 286 übernimmt größtenteils Konzepte und damit auch die Vorteile aus einer Smalltalk 80-Implementierung (vgl. Goldberg, Robson 1983), ist aber für PCs verfügbar.

3. Ausblick

Zukünftige Entwicklungsmöglichkeiten liegen für ATLAS-PfleSaurus u.a. in folgenden Bereichen an:

1. Verbesserte graphische Darstellungsmöglichkeiten, z.B. der fokussierten Darstellung eines Begriffs und seiner Nachbarbegriffe;

2. Weitere strukturtransformierende Operationen, z.B. das Verschmelzen mehrerer Begriffe zu einem Begriff oder das Trennen eines Begriffs in mehrere andere;

3. Ausbau des Authorisierungskonzepts: Authorisierung auf Sachgebietsebene, Authorisierung auf Beziehungsarten;

4. Verbesserte Suchmöglichkeiten im Thesaurus bzw. die Entwicklung einer eigenen Anfragesprache (vgl. Reiner 1988): beispielweise Anfragen mit beliebigen Thesaurusoperatoren, verbessertes Navigieren im Thesaurus, die Suche nach Relationsarten, Suche nach Mehrwortbegriffen (Wortgruppen, Phrasen);

5. Weitere Konsistenzüberprüfungen, z.B. Überprüfung der Existenz der jeweiligen inversen Beziehungen, Existenz genau einer Vorzugsbenennung, Cliquensuche hinsichtlich einer Beziehungsart;

6. Direkte Unterstützung bei der Behandlung von Homonymen (nach DIN 1463, Teil 1, 1987 Angabe von <...>) und der Kombination von Begriffen (Benutze Kombination);

7. Verbesserter Ex –und Import von (Teil)-Thesauri, Einsatz von objektorientierten Datenbanken, Verbindung von objektorientierten Programmiersprachen mit relationalen Datenbanken;

8. Einbindung anderer Anwendungen (z.B. eines Textverarbeitungssystems) z.B. durch das DDE Konzept (Dynamic Data Exchange) bei Windows 3.0.

4. Schluß

Die Erstellung und Weiterentwicklung von Thesauri ist mit enormen Arbeitsaufwand verbunden. Um diese Arbeit nicht schon frühzeitig in unkontrollierbare, nicht mehr durchschaubare Begriffsdschungel zu verwandeln, sind neuere Entwicklungen zur Unterstützung der Thesauruspflege heranzuziehen.

Insgesamt ist bei dem Einsatz von Information–Retrieval–Systemen zu beachten:

1. "Der Berg an Forschungsarbeiten nimmt ständig zu ... Der Wissenschaftler macht unter der Last neuer Erkenntnisse und Schlußfolgerungen von tausenden von Kollegen Schlußfolgerungen, für die er weder die Zeit findet, sie zu verstehen, geschweige denn, sich an sie zu erinnern. Die Summe menschlicher Erfahrung nimmt mit ungeheurer Geschwindigkeit zu (...)
(Bush 1945)

Durch den Einsatz neuerer Information–Retrieval–Techniken wird die Informationsflut insgesamt – und damit auch die relevante Information – weiter zunehmen.

2. Durch den Einsatz neuerer Information–Retrieval–Techniken wird es zu einem gewissen Grad gelingen, den Zugriff auf relevante Informationen zu verbessern.

Solange diese beiden Entwicklungen dazu beitragen, das Richtige zu tun und animalische Sprachspiele (vgl. auch Wittgenstein 1949) zu fördern, solange sind sie voranzutreiben.

Literatur

Burkart 1988a. Burkart, Margarete. Neue Thesaurusansätze – Frischer Wind in alten Segeln? In: NFD–Nachrichten für Dokumentation, Vol.39, Nr.4, August 1988 S. 207–208.

Burkart 1988b. Burkart Margarete. PROTERM – Ein Softwarepaket für Aufbau, Pflege, Handling von Thesauri und anderen Wortgutsammlungen. In: NFD–Nachrichten für Dokumentation, Vol.39, Nr. 4, August 1988 S. 249–252.

Bush 1945. Bush, V. As we may think. In: Atlantik Monthly, Vol 176, Nr.1, S. 101–108, 1945.

Coad, Yourdan 1990. Coad, Peter und Edward Yourdon. Object–Oriented–Analysis. Prentice–Hall, New Jersey, 1990.

Digitalk 1988. Digitalk Inc. Smalltalk/V 286, Object – Oriented Programming System (OOPS), Tutorial and Programming Handbook. Digitalk Inc. 1988.

DIN 1463, Teil 1, 1987. Erstellung und Weiterentwicklung von Thesauri. Berlin, Beuth Verlag, November 1987.

Felsner, Gützner et al 1988. Felsner G., Gützner U., Jüttner G., Sarre F. Die Thesaurus–Relationen des lernfähigen Information Retrieval Systems TEGEN. Dez. 1988 (andere Angaben leider nicht vorhanden: Sarre J. Postfach 202420, D–8000 München 2)

Giger 1989. Giger, Hanspeter. Konzeptbasiertes Recherchieren. Zürich, Verlag der Fachvereine Zürich (Vdf), 1989.

Goldberg, Robson 1983. Goldberg, Adele und David Robson. Smalltalk – 80: The language and its implementation. Addison Wesley, London, Amsterdam, 1983.

Hohnhold 1990. Hohnhold, I. Terminographie auf Term–PC. In: Mitteilungsblatt für Dolmetscher und Übersetzer, 4/1990.

Land 1989. Land, Doris. LIDOS 3 Arbeit–und Handbuch. Doris Land Softwareentwicklung PF 1126, 8507 Oberasbach, 1989.

Lukas 1988. Lukas, INDEX – Ein Programm zur Erstellung von Wörterbüchern und Dokumentationssprachen auf Personal–Computern. In: NFD–Nachrichten für Dokumentation, Vol.39, Nr. 4, August 1988 S. 253–256.

Muhr 1990. Muhr, Thomas. ATLAS/ti: Ein Prototyp zur Unterstützung der Textinterpretation – Konzepte und Funktionen. Forschungsbericht Nr. 90–10, Projekt ATLAS, TU Berlin 1990.

Panyr 1988. Panyr, Jiri. Thesaurus und wissensbasierte Systeme – Thesauri und Wissensbasen. In: Nachrichten für Dokumentation (NFD) 39, Nr.4, S. 209–215, 1988.

Reiner 1988. Reiner, Ulrike. Semantik von Anfragesprachen für Dokumenten-, Fakten –und Erklärungssuchsysteme. Dissertation am FB 20 Informatik der Technischen Universität Berlin, 1988.

Rostek, Fischer 1988. Objektorientierte Modellierung eines Thesaurus auf der Basis eines Frame–Systems mit graphischer Benutzerschnittstelle. In: Nachrichten für Dokumentation (NFD) 39, Nr.4, S. 217–226, 1988.

Rovira 1991. Rovira, Charles, A. A YACC and Lex type parser for Smalltalk. In: Smalltalk Magazine, Sept. 1991.

Salton 1987. Salton, Gerard und Michael McGill. Information Retrieval – Grundlegendes für Informationswissenschaftler. Hamburg, McGraw–Hill, 1987.

Samulowitz 1988. Samulowitz, H. 40 Jahre DGD und ein Plädoyer für Thesauri. In: Nachrichten für Dokumentation (NFD) 39, Nr.4, S. A26, 1988.

Wersig 1985. Wersig, Gernot. Thesaurus–Leitfaden, eine Einführung in das Thesaurus Prinzip in Theorie und Praxis. 2. erg. Auflage, München, Saur KG, 1985.

Willenborg 1991. Willenborg, Josef. PfleSaurus – ein System zur Erstellung und Weiterentwicklung von Thesauri. Unveröffentl. Diplomarbeit an der TU Berlin 1991.

Wittgenstein 1949. Wittgenstein, Ludwig. Über Gewißheit. 1949–1951. Erschienen in: Anscombe G.E.M. (Hrsg.). Über Gewißheit. Suhrkamp, Frankfurt/Main, S. 190–191, Paragraph 357–359, 1984.

ATLAS/ti – ein Interpretations–Unterstützungs–System

Thomas Muhr
Technische Universität Berlin, Fachbereich Informatik
Interdisziplinäres Forschungsprojekt ATLAS
Hardenbergstr. 28, D-1000 Berlin 12
e-mail: muhrth@db0tui11.bitnet

Zusammenfassung

Der vorliegende Beitrag stellt das Interpretations–Unterstützungs–System ATLAS/ti (ti = Textinterpretation) vor, das von Psychologen, Informatikern und Linguisten im Rahmen des interdisziplinären Forschungsprojekts ATLAS an der Technischen Universität Berlin entwickelt wird. Ausgangspunkt für die Entwicklung unseres Systems ist die Erfahrung von Sozialwissenschaftlern, in den bei qualitativ orientierten Untersuchungen anfallenden, großen Daten und Textmengen regelrecht zu ertrinken ("Zettels (Alb-) Traum").
Die dominierende Rolle des Computers in den Sozialwissenschaften ist immer noch die eines quantitativ–statistischen "Zahlenfressers". ATLAS/ti stellt dagegen einen neuartigen Typ von Informationssystem dar, zugeschnitten auf die spezifischen Bedürfnisse von Forschern mit qualitativ–hermeneutischer Ausrichtung. Systematische Auseinandersetzung mit textuellem Material definiert weitere mögliche Anwendungsfelder: Akquisition von Expertenwissen aus verbalen Protokollen, vergleichende Literaturanalyse, Kommentierung juristischer Fachtexte, Analyse von Argumentationsstrukturen in Round–Table–Diskussionen.

Textinterpretation und qualitative Methode

Qualitativ–hermeneutische Methoden waren lange Zeit als zu wenig wissenschaftlich verpönt; quantitativ–statistisch orientierte Methoden genossen dagegen den Vorteil der mathematisch–logischen Fundierung ihrer Verfahren und der effizienten und systematischen Verarbeitung großer Datenmengen durch den Computer. Sie scheiterten jedoch nicht selten an der Geltungsbegründung ihrer Aussagen (mangelnde Validität) und an gewagten Vorannahmen (Normalverteilung).

Wenig systematisches Vorgehen, kaum reproduzierbare und auf geringen Fallzahlen basierende Resultate, die zudem stark von der Person des Wissenschaftlers abhingen, sind die Vorwürfe positivistisch orientierter Kritiker gegenüber qualitativ–hermeneutischen Ansätzen. Gerade der letztgenannte Einwand, der Einfluß des Forschers selbst auf den Forschungsprozess, ist nicht unproblematisch; gehört er doch bei den hermeneutischen Ansätzen bewußt zum methodischen Inventar, während er in den sog. objektiven Verfahren zwar auch Wirkung zeigt, aber eher verleugnet wird.

Über die in letzter Zeit zu verzeichnende Renaissance hermeneutischer Ansätze und über die Methoden–Diskussion von Hermeneutik und Textinterpretation in Philosophie und Sozialwissenschaften siehe auch Flick et. al. (1991) Oevermann (1979) und Lamnek (1988).

Trotz teilweise erheblicher Unterschiede zwischen den von verschiedenen Schulen vertretenen hermeneutischen Methoden lassen sich Gemeinsamkeiten hermeneutischer Interpretationsverfahren feststellen (Böhm 1991), die wichtige Anhaltspunkte für die Konzeption unterstützender Werkzeuge für die Textinterpretation liefern:

- Der Auswertungsprozeß ist systematisch und geordnet, aber nicht starr; er enthält *spielerische* und *künstlerisch–kreative* Momente
- Die wichtigste intellektuelle Tätigkeit besteht im *Vergleichen* (von Texten), hier: Suche nach Ähnlichkeiten und Unterschieden
- Zu diesem Zweck wird der Text *kodiert*, d.h., in relevante Teiltexte zerlegt, die mit Hilfe von Stichworten und Anmerkungen geordnet und angereichert werden
- Der Bezug zum Ganzen (Text) wird beibehalten: Der Textteile und Kodes umgebende *Kon*text ist jederzeit rekonstruierbar
- Das Ergebnis der Auswertung ist eine Art *Synthese*. Resultat sind neue Textdaten, die der Forscher in "Memos" aufschreibt, ehe das endgültige Forschungsmanuskript daraus erstellt wird.

Ziel hermeneutischer Methoden ist nicht die Falsi– oder Verifikation von Hypothesen anhand von Rohdaten, sondern das *Verstehen* meist in textueller Form vorliegenden Ausgangsmaterials, z.B. historische Quellentexte, transkribierte psychologische Interviews oder Feldnotizen aus ethnologischen Untersuchungen.

Systeme, die zu interpretierende Texte in geeigneter Form, etwa für den direkten Vergleich, zur Verfügung stellen und die Referenzierung, Kommentierung, Kategorisierung und das Retrieval relevanter Textpassagen ermöglichen, werden von uns als *Interpretations–Unterstützungs–Systeme* (IUS) bezeichnet. Da Textinterpretation immer auch die Zuordnung von neuem Text zu vorhandenem Text einschließt, muß ein IUS auch für die Aufgaben der Textproduktion ausgelegt sein. Resultat einer Interpretation ist ohnehin ein – in der Regel zur Veröffentlichung anstehender – linearer Text. Die sich aus dem (linearen) Text entwickelnden komplexen Strukturen, die während der computerunterstützten Textinterpretation entstehen, erfüllen ihre Funktion als eine Art Zwischenprodukt *im Verlauf* der Interpretation.

Ausgehend vom Theoretischen Kodieren nach Glaser und Strauss (1967) (siehe auch Corbin & Strauss 1990), eine aus der Soziologie stammende Methode des qualitativen Umgangs mit Texten, lassen sich als grundlegende materiale Teilaktivitäten der Textinterpretation darstellen (vgl. auch Böhm 1991, Böhm & Muhr 1990 und Muhr 1990a):

- Auswählen der für die Fragestellung relevanten Dokumente *(Primärtexte)*
- Sichten, Lesen und *Vergleichen* von Dokumenten
- die zentralen, annotativen Aktivitäten des *Kodierens* und *Kommentierens* und
- Extraktion und Zusammenstellung von Textpassagen zu einem (oder mehreren logisch verknüpften) Kode(s)

- Umbenennen, Zusammenfassen oder Zerlegen von Kodes und Memos
- In–Beziehung–Setzen, *Vernetzen* von Textpassagen, Kodes und Kommentaren
- Bilden von *Sekundärtexten* als eigentlichen Resultaten der Textinterpretation

Der Verlauf der Textinterpretation läßt sich also grob wie folgt skizzieren: Ausgehend von linearen Texten wird eine Struktur auf dem Textmaterial erzeugt. Aus dem delinearisierten Text und den Kode–Strukturen entsteht ein wiederum linearer Text, der zur Veröffentlichung aufbereitet wird (Abb. 1)

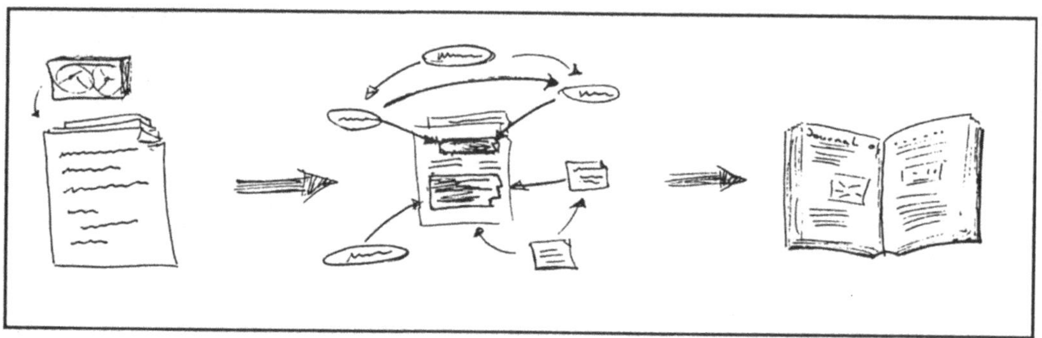

Abb. 1 Textinterpretation als Textproduktion: Vom Primärtext zur Struktur zum Sekundärtext

Für Systeme, die die obigen Operationen unterstützen und somit zu einer Systematisierung der Textinterpretation beitragen, besteht gerade im Bereich der Sozialwissenschaften großer Bedarf (Tesch 1989, Brent & Spencer 1987). Dies wurde durch eine von uns durchgeführte Erhebung (Böhm 1989), als auch durch die Resonanz auf verschiedenen Kongressen (vgl. Muhr 1989, 1990b) bestätigt.

Die Konzeption unseres Systems war von Beginn an nicht auf die *Ersetzung* der für die Textinterpretation notwendigen intellektuellen Leistungen ausgerichtet. Unserer Ansicht nach gibt es für das Verstehen, vor allem von alltagssprachlichen Texten, keine theoretischen Ansätze, geschweige denn technischen Realisierungen. Wir teilen den Standpunkt, daß eine automatische Interpretation von Texten an dem Problem der Komplexität, Nicht–Explizitheit und Kontextualität von Alltagswissen scheitern muß (Dreyfus 1990, Konrad 1990).

ATLAS/ti soll daher Forschern in der qualitativen Sozialforschung optimale *Unterstützung* für Tätigkeiten im Rahmen der Textinterpretation anbieten. Unter anderem beinhaltet dies den oben skizzierten Umgang mit *großen* Textmengen und die Verwaltung der sich bei der Interpretation bildenden Annotationen, Begriffsbildungen und Verweisstrukturen. Unsere Konzeption beinhaltet ferner eine ergonomisch sinnvolle Aufteilung der Interpretations–Tätigkeiten in solche, die direkt am Computer stattfinden und andere, wie bspw. die Rezeption der Texte, die abseits des Computers mit traditionellem "Zeug" – Papier und Bleistift – durchgeführt werden sollten. Auch dafür kann das System Unterstützung anbieten, etwa in Form ausgedruckter Referenzlisten, Netzwerkgrafiken, etc., als Beilage zum ausgedruckten Originaltext.

Anwendungsgebiete

Im Frühjahr 1991 stellten wir ATLAS/ti im Rahmen des Forschungsmarktes Berlin auf der CeBIT 91 vor. Auch dort wie schon in Diskussionen im Umfeld unseres Projektes zeichneten sich weitere Anwendungsgebiete neben den Sozialwissenschaften ab, die von einer computerunterstützten Textinterpretation profitieren könnten:

- Wissenselizitation anhand von Experten-Protokollen
- Analyse von Argumentationsstrukturen
- Ausbildung von Indexierern
- Literaturwissenschaften
- Linguistische Textanalyse
- Auslegung historischer, juristischer und religiöser Texte
- Softwaredokumentation
- Analyse klinischer Gespräche, Exploration, Anamnese

Zur Zeit erfolgt eine Evaluation des Systems mit "Beta-Testern" aus unterschiedlichen Anwendungsbereichen, die sich in regelmäßig stattfindenden User-Entwickler-Treffs zum Erfahrungsaustausch einfinden. Zudem finden Seminare zur Textinterpretation unter Einsatz von ATLAS/ti statt.

Textinterpretation mit ATLAS/ti

Computergestützte Systeme, die im Bereich qualitativer Methoden zur Analyse von Textmaterial eingesetzt werden, lassen sich hinsichtlich bestimmter Funktionsbereiche als "Kode-and-Retrieve"-Systeme einordnen (Richards & Richards 1990). Dazu gehört das Markieren von Textteilen, die Zuordnung von Begriffen (Kodes) und das Retrieval von Textpassagen über die Kodes. Auch ATLAS/ti realisiert diese Kernfunktionen.

ATLAS/ti beinhaltet darüber hinaus:

- die Integration von Dokumenten, Zitaten, Kodes und Memos zu **hermeneutischen Einheiten**
- die **Formulierung von Theorien** durch Konstruktion von Begriffsnetzwerken
- **komplexe Suchoperationen**, z.B. für die Identifikation *Bedingungen* anzeigender Textteilen wie *"weil"*, *"seit"* und *"wegen"*. (vgl. *Kodierungs-Paradigma* der Grounded Theory)
- **Semi-Automatische Kodierung**: Nach Spezifikation von Volltext-Suchbedingungen und Zielkode erfolgt die Zuordnung der Fundstellen
- **Tutorialkomponente** zur Textinterpretation

- eine **kooperative Arbeitsweise**: mehrere Autoren arbeiten am gleichen Projekt
- die **Evaluation** verschiedener Strategien der Textinterpretation
- eine **interaktive Arbeitsweise**

Textinterpretation mit ATLAS/ti läßt sich folgendermaßen beschreiben:

Zu Beginn einer Bearbeitung wird vom Textinterpreten ein kontextueller Rahmen, die sog. *hermeneutische Einheit* definiert, die mit der Fragestellung der aktuellen Analyse betitelt wird. Aus Sicht der Informatik ist eine hermeneutische Einheit ein *Container* für die unterschiedlichen Informationsarten, die im Prozess der Textinterpretation kreiert und verwendet werden. Der nächste Schritt besteht in der *Zuordnung* der zu interpretierenden Dokumente (*Primärtexte*) zu der hermeneutischen Einheit. Ganz im Sinne einer hypothesengeleiteten Datenerhebung (Theoretical Sampling der Grounded Theory, Strauss 1987) ist die Zuordnung weiterer Primärtexte zu hermeneutischen Einheiten auch noch im späteren Verlauf der Interpretation möglich. Für den Zugriff auf die in einer *Textbank* abgelegten Primärtexte ist mittelfristig der Einsatz eines Information–Retrieval–Systems geplant.

Die der Zusammenstellung des Arbeitskorpus folgende intellektuelle Auseinandersetzung mit den Texten (Lesen und Vergleichen) führt zu als inhaltlich relevant erachteten Textpassagen *(Zitate)*, die mit Hilfe des Systems markiert werden. Diese Zerlegung der Primärtexte in Zitate ist Bestandteil des *Kodierens,* hier: der Zuordnung von Zitaten zu *Kodes.* Kodes können dabei vereinfacht als Schlagworte verstanden werden. Ein Zitat kann mehreren Kodes und, vice versa, mehrere Zitate einem Kode zugeordnet werden, wobei zusätzliche Annotationen (Memos) erstellt werden können.

*Exkurs:*In Anlehnung an Glaser & Strauss unterscheiden wir das *offene, axiale* Kodieren und *selektive* Kodieren. Beim offenen Kodieren entstehen die fürs Kodieren verwendeten Begriffe direkt aus der Arbeit am vorliegenden Text; in–vivo–Kodes werden direkt dem Text entnommen. Das axiale Kodieren geht von der Menge schon vorhandener Kodes aus, um zusätzliche Textstellen zu kodieren. Kodes werden weiter differenziert. Beim selektiven Kodieren werden Kodes einer zentralen Kategorie zugeordnet und untereinander in Beziehung gesetzt.

Da für jede neue Textzerlegung, jeden Kode und jedes Memo der Zeitpunkt der Erstellung und das Signum des Interpreten registriert wird, ergeben sich Möglichkeiten zur Evaluation: Die explizite Autorenschaft schafft Voraussetzungen für einen Vergleich von Interpretationsstilen; die chronologische Ordnung unterstützt die Rekonstruktion des *Prozesses* der Textinterpretation. Durch die Autorenschaft wird zudem eine *kollaborative* Arbeitsweise unterstützt: Mehrere Autoren arbeiten gemeinsam an einer hermeneutischen Einheit (zur Zeit leider nur asynchron).

Im Hinblick auf sprachwissenschaftliche und andere eng am manifesten Text orientierte Untersuchungen haben wir eine *semi–automatische* Kodierung ("Auto-

Koding") realisiert, die über eine erweiterte Freitextsuche eine automatische Segmentierung der Fundstellen mit einstellbarer Begrenzung (Wort, Satz, Absatz) durchführt. Die so extrahierten Zitate werden automatisch einem vorher ausgewählten Kode zugeordnet. Als Suchspezifikation sind sowohl "Wildcards" zur Maskierung von Suchbegriffen als auch deren disjunktive Verknüpfung zu Suchschwärmen möglich. Ferner können Suchschwärme benannt und mit dem Namen dieses "Makros" für eine zu einem späteren Zeitpunkt erfolgende Suche wiederverwendet werden.

Während dieser Phase der *textuellen* Bearbeitung werden verschiedene Retrieval-Operationen durchgeführt: Zitate können über die sie repräsentierenden Kodes (in diesem Sinne sind Kodes mit Deskriptoren vergleichbar) wiedergefunden, im Kontext dargestellt, ausgedruckt oder zu einem neuen Text zusammengeführt werden, jedoch kann auch die Menge der zu einem Zitat gehörenden Kodes das Resultat einer Anfrage sein. Das *Anklicken* eines Kodes führt direkt zur Anzeige zugeordneter Zitate, es können mit Hilfe der Klicktechnik mehrere Kodes disjunktiv oder konjunktiv verknüpft werden. Eine Komponente für komplexere Anfragen ist in Vorbereitung (Muhr 1991).

Alle dem Benutzer am Bildschirm und im Ausdruck präsentierten Listen können mit Hilfe von Sortier- und Filterfunktionen variiert werden. So können Kodes bspw. alphabetisch, zeitlich und gemäß der Zahl ihrer Zitate und vernetzten Kodes sortiert werden.

Geltungsbereich von Zitaten, Kodes und Kommentaren und aller auf diesen Komponenten basierenden Operationen ist die einbettende hermeneutische Einheit: der Begriff "Angst" hat also je nach Kontext eine möglicherweise andere Bedeutung. Neben einem "ideosynkratischen" Umgang mit Begriffen ist aber auch die Nutzung eines "kontrollierten Vokabulars" möglich, bspw. aller für das Thema "Stress" wichtigen Begriffe. In diesem Zusammenhang sei auf eine weitere Entwicklung im Rahmen des ATLAS-Projekts hingewiesen, einem Thesaurus-Erstellungs- und Pflegesystem, welches über eine Zwischenrepräsentation Ergebnisse der Arbeit mit ATLAS/ti übernehmen können wird (Siehe auch *Kopplung zu anderen Systemen*).

Hypertextfunktionalität

Auf der Menge der Zitate kann unabhängig von ihrer indirekten Ordnung durch die ihnen zugeordneten Kodes eine Ordnung mit Hilfe benannter Relationen definiert werden. Eine Textstelle kann bspw. mit anderen Textstellen in eine *folgt–inhaltlich*–Relation gebracht werden. Durch diese *Hypertext*-Funktionalität ergeben sich für das Retrieval von Zitaten weitergehende Möglichkeiten, als durch boolesche Dokumenten- und Freitextsuchsysteme. Die Integration inhalts–bezogener und assoziativ–navigierender Suche wird zur Zeit erforscht (Coombs 1990, Fuhr 1990). Beim "Stöbern" in Hypertexten tritt der Serendipity-Effekt auf (Kuhlen 1990), also die Möglichkeit, ohne explizite Suchanfrage auf (relevante!) Informationen zu stoßen.

Der subsymbolische, assoziative Charakter der Verbindungen kann jedoch auch zu einer gewissen Desorientierung bei der Navigation in umfangreichen Hypertexten führen. Einem "getting-lost-in-hyperspace" wird in ATLAS/ti durch zwei Komplexität reduzierende Maßnahmen gegengesteuert: zum einen durch die Partitionierung in hermeneutische Einheiten, zum anderen durch die Benennung der zwischen den Zitaten etablierten Verbindungen.

Für das Retrieval der informationstragenden Einheiten (Primärtexte, Zitate, Memos und Kodes) in ATLAS/ti wird zur Zeit vom Autor eine auf dem *Reinerschen* Ansatz (Reiner 1988) basierende Anfragesprache AQL (Atlas Query Language) entwickelt, die u.a. die Auswertung von Hypertext- und Kode-Kode-Links beinhaltet.

Konzeptuelle Bearbeitungsebene

Wir unterscheiden zwei Ebenen beim Arbeiten mit ATLAS/ti. Neben der oben skizzierten *textuellen* Bearbeitungsebene, mit ihrem unmittelbaren Bezug auf die Primärtexte, werden Tätigkeiten, die die Theoriebildung unterstützen, als *konzeptuelle* Ebene bezeichnet. Textuelle und konzeptuelle Bearbeitung folgen nicht notwendigerweise streng aufeinander – zwischen beiden Ebenen kann beliebig gewechselt werden. Analyseobjekt für die konzeptuelle Bearbeitungsphase ist nun die Menge der bisher gefundenen Kodes, die mit *benannten Kode-Kode-Relationen* zu komplexen *Kodenetzen* verknüpft werden; vergleichbar etwa semantischen Netzen oder Thesaurusstrukturen.

Die verwendeten Relationen sind im allgemeinen abhängig vom Anwendungsbereich. Wir haben zunächst einige allgemeine Relationen fest ins System integriert, mit der Option, eigene Relationsarten definieren zu können. Folgende Relationen stehen zur Verfügung (k1, k2 sind Kodes):

k1 *ist-assoziiert-mit* k2 (reflexiv, symmetrisch)
k1 *steht-in-Widerspruch-zu* k2 (symmetrisch)
k1 *ist-ein* k2 (transitiv)
k1 *ist-Ursache-von* k2 (transitiv)
k1 *ist-Eigenschaft-von* k2 (transitiv)
k1 *ist-Teil-von* k2 (transitiv)

Die Herausarbeitung von Strukturen mit Hilfe grafischer Editions-Werkzeuge (vgl. Abb. 2) fördert eine *explorierende* Bildung von Theorien. Abb. 2 zeigt eine hermeneutische Einheit mit geöffnetem Netz-Editor auf der Netz-Sicht "Terminology". Gerade aktiv ist das Auswahlmenü für die Beziehungsarten; am oberen Rand des Menüs erscheinen die beiden Kodes die im nächsten Schritt verknüpft werden sollen. Der Benutzer kann sich durch beliebiges Ein- und Auslagern von Kodes (Teil-) Ansichten des Konzept-Netzwerks generieren, die sich u.a. durch die räumliche

Plazierung der Knoten unterscheiden. Im Netzwerk-Editor stehen dem Benutzer eine ganze Reihe von Manipulationsmöglichkeiten zur Verfügung, etwa das Erzeugen, Löschen und die Verknüpfung mehrerer Kodes mit Hilfe direktmanipulativer Techniken. Beim Anklicken von Objekten werden vom Objekttyp abhängige Spezialwerkzeuge aktiviert, z.B. Anmerkungs-Editoren für Kodes und Memos.

Oben rechts in der Abbildung ist die Liste der Kodes zu sehen. Hinter jedem Eintrag wird in geschweiften Klammern die Anzahl der Textbelege (Zitate) und – rechts vom Strich – die Anzahl der schon verknüpften Nachbarkodes angezeigt. Das Tilde-Zeichen ˜ markiert all jene Kodes, zu denen bereits eine Anmerkung erstellt wurde.

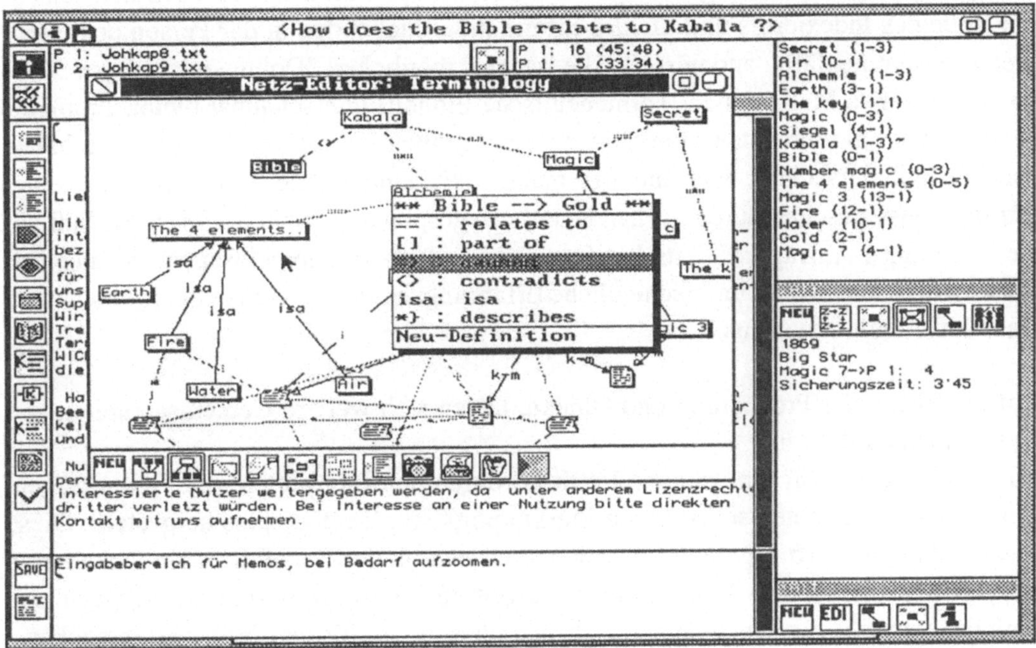

Abb. 2 Bildschirmansicht einer hermeneutischen Einheit mit Netz-Editor

Wie bei den schon erwähnten Hypertext-Links zwischen Zitaten kann der Interpret das Netz von Kodes traversieren und sich u.a. Textbelege zu Konzepten ausgeben lassen. Für die Ausgabe von Textbelegen können rekursiv alle transitiv mit einem Kode verbundenen Unter-Kodes traversiert und deren Belegstellen in die Ausgabe eingebunden werden.

Kopplung zu anderen Systemen

Geplant ist die Kopplung von ATLAS/ti mit dem in Entwicklung befindlichen Thesauruspflegesystems ATLAS/PfleSaurus (Willenborg 1991). Die mit Hilfe des grafischen Netzwerk-Editors konstruierten Kodenetze können in Prolog-Notation aus der hermeneutischen Einheit exportiert und als Teil-Thesauri "entprivatisiert" werden.

Dazu wird ATLAS/PfleSaurus mit einer entsprechenden Import–Schnittstelle ausge-
stattet. In dieser universellen Repräsentation kann das terminologische Wissen eines
Gegenstandsbereichs auch als Grundstock einer Wissensbasis verwendet, und somit
ATLAS/ti als *Wissenselizitations–Werkzeug* betrachtet werden.

Vergleich mit dem klassischen Information Retrieval

Die dem klassischen Information–Retrieval eigenen Precision–Recall–Probleme
kommen weniger zum Tragen, da bei der Textinterpretation mit ATLAS/ti einerseits
die Rolle des Indexierers und die des Information Suchenden in der Person des Interpreten zusammenfällt, andererseits die Menge möglicher "Dokumente" durch kon-
textbegrenzende Maßnahmen (hermeneutische Einheit) überschaubar bleibt. Probleme
bei der Auswahl relevanten Materials aus einer großen Menge von Dokumenten haben
verschiedene Ursachen, wie die oft mangelhaft unterstützte Repräsentation eines
Informationswunsches durch vorhandene Anfragesprachen (Salton 1987). Einfluß auf
die Güte eines Anfrageresultats hat ferner der – trotz oft gemeinsamer sozialer und
kultureller Lebenswelt – unterschiedliche Erfahrungskontext von Indexierer und Nutzer
eines Informationssystems.

Auf der Ebene der Prozeduren und Objekte lassen sich weitere Gemeinsamkeiten und
Unterschiede anführen:

Die Kandidaten für ein späteres Retrieval durch den Interpreten, die Textpassagen,
werden vom Interpreten selbst durch Markierung eines Textbereichs hergestellt. Diese
"Personalunion" trifft für das Information–Retrieval in der Regel nicht zu: Dokumente
sind, wie oft auch die Deskriptoren (soweit in Thesauri normiert), vorgegebene
Entitäten, sowohl für den Indexierer als auch besonders für den Informationssuchenden.

Das *Kodieren* einer Textpassage mit einer Menge von Kodes entspricht in etwa dem
Indexieren eines Dokuments mit einer Menge von Deskriptoren. Anzeige bzw. Ausdruck von Textpassagen bei Aktivierung (Anklicken) eines Kodes (ANGST) entspricht
einer einfachen Retrieval–Anfrage: Liefere alle Textpassagen, die mit ANGST kodiert
wurden.

Kodes haben jedoch im Kontext der Textinterpretation eine weitergehende Bedeutung:

"Codes bilden nicht nur die farbig–schillernden individuellen Formulierungen auf ein weniger komplexes und vieldeutiges Notationssystem als die Alltagssprache ab, sondern sie repräsentieren gleichzeitig die interpretativen oder explanativen Leistungen des Forschers." (Huber 1990, S. 12).

Unterschiede bestehen zwischen Dokumenten und Textpassagen: Dokumente sind
disjunkte Einheiten, Textpassagen sind dagegen immer in einem umgebenden (Kon)-
Text eingebettet und stehen in verschiedenen Ordnungsrelationen zueinander:

Implizit (Vorkommen im Dokument): t_1 folgt t_2, t_1 ist in t_2 eingebettet, t_1 überlappt t_2. Explizit (per Hypertext-Verbindung): t_1 steht–in–Widerspruch–zu t_2, t_1 folgt–inhaltlich–auf t_2.

Weder Kodes noch Textpassagen sind demnach homogene Mengen disjunkter Elemente, sondern können in komplexer Weise aufeinander bezogen sein. Deskriptoren dienen der Reduktion umfangreicher Informationen. Für Kodes gilt dies eingeschränkt; sie haben aber über die klassifikatorische Funktion hinaus den Status theoretischer Konstrukte. Kodierung kann so als eine Art Indexierung, letztere jedoch auch als interpretativer Akt interpretiert (!) werden.

Erweiterte Anfragemöglichkeiten

Diese zusätzliche Struktur auf Textpassagen ermöglicht Anfragen und (navigierende) Operationen, die auf herkömmlichen, unstrukturierten Dokumentenbeständen nicht möglich sind. Als Suchergebnis mag etwa nicht ein bestimmtes Zitat z_i interessieren, sondern die zu diesem in–Widerspruch–stehenden, oder z_i und die im Textverlauf auf z_i folgenden weiteren 3 Zitate. Eine genauere Analyse der Eigenschaften und der Beziehungen zwischen Textpassagen ist für den Aufbau einer Anfragesprache notwendig; bei deren Nichtberücksichtigung würde wertvolle Information ignoriert.

Auswirkungen des Einsatzes eines IUS

Wir versuchen, uns die möglichen Auswirkungen zu vergegenwärtigen, die sich mit der Einführung einer neuen Technologie für die Lebenswelten der unmittelbar und mittelbar davon Betroffenen ergeben. Unser Interesse richtet sich deshalb zunächst auf mögliche Veränderungen von Arbeits- und Denkweisen bei den *unmittelbar* Betroffenen, d.h., den Benutzern des neuen Werkzeugs. Eco, Vertreter eines semiotischen Zugangs zur Textinterpretation (Eco 1990), schildert recht pointiert, wie sich Denken und Fühlen durch die Verwendung eines Werkzeugs verändern können:

"Doch Abu *(ein Textsystem, d.A.)* erlaubt nun kleine lokale Selbstmorde, provisorische Amnesien, schmerzlose Sprachverluste....Es genügte ein Befehl, ein milchiges Licht ergoß sich über den fatalen und deplacierten Absatz, ich drückte die Löschtaste und pffft war alles verschwunden....ich könnte meinen gelöschten Text wiederhaben, wenn ich mich nur rechtzeitig entschlösse, die Rückholtaste zu drücken. Welche Erleichterung! Im bloßen Wissen, daß ich, wenn ich wollte, mich erinnern könnte, vergesse ich sofort." (Eco, Das Foucaultsche Pendel, S. 37)

In seiner kritischen Betrachtung zum Computereinsatz bei der Textinterpretation zitiert Münch (1991) aus Husserls *Philosophie der Arithmetik*:

"selbst scheinbar so nichtige Unterschiede wie die, ob man mit Tinte und Feder auf Papier oder mit

Griffel auf staubbedeckten Täfelchen schreibt, können den Gang arithmetischer Methoden wesentlich beeinflussen"

Stimmt man dem zu, sollte der Übergang von Papier plus Bleistift zu Computertechnologie den "Gang der Textinterpretation" erheblich verändern.

Benutzeroberfläche

Bei der Gestaltung der Mensch–Maschine–Schnittstelle liegt der Schwerpunkt neben grundlegenden Problemen wie der Konzeption des Bildschirms vor allem auf der Gestaltung des Dialogs und einer möglichst adäquaten Präsentation der Objekte (Texte, Kodes, Memos). Ein interaktives Werkzeug soll funktional korrekt und möglichst vollständig sein; darüber hinaus sollte es die Besonderheiten menschlicher intellektueller Arbeitsformen berücksichtigen. Vor allem bei kreativen Tätigkeiten neigen Menschen zu einer *nichtsequentiellen* und durch viele Unterbrechungen des Ablaufs charakterisierbaren Vorgehensweise (Miyata & Norman 1986):

Beim Kodieren fällt mir ein, daß ein Memo zum Vorgang geschrieben werden sollte, jetzt erst wird mir einiges klarer, also könnte der Kode natürlich gleich umbenannt und in zwei Teilkodes zerlegt werden, usw.

Ein solches Vorgehen erfordert einen raschen, unkomplizierten Wechsel zwischen verschiedenen Arbeitskontexten und die Möglichkeit der Wiederaufnahme unterbrochener Handlungen. Die in ATLAS/ti verwendete *modusarme Fenstertechnik* unterstützt diesen Arbeitsstil.

Mittelfristige Vorhaben

- Die Weiterentwicklung der Anfragekomponente für die Suche innerhalb der hermeneutischen Einheit.
- Entwicklung einer wissensbasierten Tutorialkomponente für Methoden der Textinterpretation.
- Integration eines Information–Retrieval–Systems für den Zugriff auf Primärtexte
- Adaptation des Systems an weitere methodische Ansätze, wie bspw. akteursorientierten Forschungsansätzen (Legewie, 1991)
- Die Vervollständigung der oben skizzierten Hypertextfunktionalität.
- Kopplung zum Thesaurus-Pflegesystem ATLAS/PfleSaurus
- Ausbau der für eine kollaborative Arbeitsweise wichtigen Komponenten (LAN-Integration, Kommunikation, Transaktion)
- Portierung in Windows, OS/2, MacOS

Implementierung

Der Prototyp ATLAS/ti ist auf Grundlage eines partizipativen, objektorientierten Softwareentwicklungs-Ansatzes entworfen und in Smalltalk/V der Fa. Digitalk implementiert. Es läuft unter DOS auf PCs des Industriestandards (Prozessor: Intel 80286, 80386, 80486) mit mind. 4MB RAM.

Literatur

Böhm, A. (1989). Bedarfserhebung für eine EDV-Unterstützung bei der Archivierung und Interpretation von Texten (Bericht aus dem Interdisziplinären Forschungsprojekt ATLAS 89-1).

Böhm, A. (1991). Arbeitsmaterialien zur Textinterpretation (Bericht aus dem Interdisziplinären Forschungsprojekt ATLAS, TU Berlin, in Vorb.).

Böhm, A. & Muhr, T. (1990). ATLAS – Dokumentation und Interpretation von Technikdiskursen. Forschung Aktuell, TU Berlin (Sonderheft zur Tagung "Technik und Gesellschaft" an der TU Berlin).

Brent, E., Scott, J. & Spencer, J. (1987). The use of computers by qualitative researchers. Qualitative Sociology, 10, 309-313.

Coombs, J.H. (1990). Hypertext, Full Text and Automatic Linking. In: 13th International Conference on Research and Development in Information Retrieval. 5-7 September 1990. Organized by Universite Libre de Bruxelles, (Jean-Luc Vidick, ed.) Presses Universitaires de Bruxelles, 1990

Corbin, J., Strauss, A. (1990). Grounded Theory Research: Procedures, Canons and Evaluative Criteria. Qualitative Sociology. New York: Human Sciences Press, 13, 3-21.

Dreyfus, H.L. (1990). Hermeneutics and Artificial Intelligence (Vortrag im Rahmen des ATLAS-Projekts, TU Berlin).

Eco, U. (1987). Das Foucaultsche Pendel.

Eco, U. (1990). Lector in fabula. dtv Wissenschaft. München: Deutscher Taschenbuch Verlag

Flick, U., v. Kardoff, E., Keupp, H., v. Rosenstiel, L., Wolff, S. (Hrsg.) (1991). Handbuch Qualitative Sozialforschung. München: Psychologie Verlags Union

Fuhr, N. (1990). Hypertext und Information Retrieval. In: Gloor & Streitz (Hrsg.) Hypertext und Hypermedia. Informatik Fachberichte 249. Berlin: Springer

Glaser, B. G., & Strauss, A. L. (1967). The discovery of grounded theory. Strategies for qualitative research. Chicago: Aldine Publ.

Huber, G. (1990). AQUAD 3.0 – Das Programmpaket für die computerunterstützte Analyse qualitativer Daten (Programmbeschreibung und Manual).

Konrad, E. (1990). Phänomenologie und Künstliche Intelligenz (ATLAS–Bericht 2/90). Berlin: IFP ATLAS – Technische Universität Berlin.

Kuhlen, R. (1990). Informationswissenschaft und ATLAS (Vortrag gehalten im ATLAS–Kolloquium – Januar 1990).

Lamnek, S. (1988). Qualitative Sozialforschung (Vol. Bd. 1). München: Psychologie Verlags Union.

Legewie, H. (1991). Konfliktanalyse. Beitrag zum ATLAS–Kolloquium. Berlin, Juni 1991

Miyata, Y., Norman, D.A. (1986). Psychological Issues in Support of Multiple Activities. In D.A. Norman & St. W. Draper (Eds.), User Centered System Design (pp. 265–284). Hillsdale: Lawrence Earlbaum.

Münch, D. (1991). Zur Semiotik der Textinterpretation. (Vortrag gehalten im ATLAS–Kolloquium). Berlin, Juni 1991.

Muhr, T. (1989). A Computer Aided Textbank– and Textinterpretation System for Qualitative Research in Technology Assessment (ATLAS). 8th International Human Science Research Conference. Aarhus:.

Muhr, T. (1990a). ATLAS/ti Ein Prototyp zur Unterstützung der Textinterpretation – Konzepte und Funktionen (Bericht aus dem Interdisziplinären Forschungsprojekt ATLAS 90–10, TU Berlin).

Muhr, T. (1990b). Technikgestaltung für den Alltag am Beispiel der Softwareentwicklung für die sozialwissenschaftliche Technikforschung. In Frey, D. (Ed.), Bericht über den 37. Kongreß der Deutschen Gesellschaft für Psychologie in Kiel 1990 (Vol. 1, pp. 368–369). Göttingen: Hogrefe.

Muhr, T. (1991). AQL – Eine Anfragesprache für ATLAS/ti. Interner ATLAS–Arbeitsbericht.

Oevermann, U., Allert, T., Konau, E., & Krambeck, J. (1979). Die Methodologie einer "objektiven Hermeneutik" und ihre allgemeine forschungslogische Bedeutung in den Sozialwissenschaften. In H. G. Soeffner (Ed.), Interpretative Verfahren in den Sozial- und Textwissenschaften (pp. 352–434). Stuttgart: Metzler.

Reiner, U. (1988). Semantik von Anfragesprachen für Dokumenten-, Fakten- und Erklärungssuchsysteme (Dissertation, TU Berlin, FB Informatik).

Richards, L.; Richards, T. (1990). Old Goals, New Goals: Toward the Next Generation of Qualitative Analysis Programs. La Trobe University, Bundoora, Australia. Interner Bericht

Salton, G. (1987). Information–Retrieval – Grundlegendes für Informationswissenschaftler. Hamburg: McGraw Hill, 1987

Strauss, A. (1987). Qualitative analysis for social scientists. Cambridge: Cambridge University Press.

Tesch, R. (1989). Qualitative research. Analysis types and software tools (Kongreß–vortrag).

Willenborg, J. (1991). PfleSaurus – ein System zur Erstellung und Weiterentwicklung von Thesauri. Unveröff. Diplomarbeit. TU Berlin – Institut für Angewandte Informatik. 1991.

Elektronische Ablage und Archivierung auf der Basis
eines Database Management Information Retrieval Systems:
- Die Bedürfnisse - Das Angebot - Die Realität
(Projekterfahrungen und -aussichten einer Schweizerischen
Grossbank)

Hans Amstutz, Barbara Holländer-Thönssen
Schweizerischer Bankverein
Systemplanung
Hochstrasse 16
CH - 4053 Basel

1.   Einleitung

In unserem Vortrag möchten wir Ihnen aufzeigen, welche praktischen Erfahrungen beim Schweizerischen Bankverein (SBV) im
Bereich "Data Base Management Information Retrieval System"
(DBM[IR]S) gemacht wurden. Wir beziehen uns auf die bisher
erfolgte konkrete Projektarbeit ohne damit einen Anspruch erheben
zu wollen, dass es sich hierbei um eine repräsentative oder gar
wissenschaftlich belegte Gesamtanalyse der Thematik handelt.

In einem in sich geschlossenen Vortrag lässt sich zwar ein Thema
als Ganzes sehr gut von einer theoretischen Warte aus beleuchten.
Als Zuhörer bleibt man am Schluss jedoch oft alleine mit der
Frage:"...und wie kann nun das theoretische Modell umgesetzt
werden?"

Mit diesem Vortrag versuchen wir auf eine dieser praktischen
Fragen eine mögliche Antwort zu geben, nämlich:

> "Wie lässt sich ein DBM(IR)S in eine
> gewachsene, heterogene Systemumgebung
> eines Grossunternehmens integrieren und
> welche Probleme treten dabei zu Tage?"

1.1   Kurzvorstellung SBV

Der SBV zählt zu den drei führenden schweizerischen Grossbanken.
In der Schweiz besitzt das Institut über 280 Geschäftsstellen und
mehrere Tochtergesellschaften. Daneben verfügt der SBV mit einem
weitverzweigten internationalen Netz von Vertretungen über eine
gut ausgebaute Organisation im Ausland.

Die Geschäftstätigkeit des SBVs umfasst sämtliche Dienstlei-
stungen einer Universalbank, die überwiegend computerunterstützt
abgewickelt werden.

1.2   Bürokommunikation beim SBV

Beim SBV wird dem Bereich Bürokommunikation ein grosser Stellen-
wert beigemessen. In diesem Zusammenhang treten "intelligente"

Arbeitsstationen zunehmend an die Stelle der herkömmlichen Bild-
schirmarbeitsplätze. Zum heutigen Zeitpunkt sind rund 8000
Workstations in der Schweiz im Einsatz.
Wie bei den meisten Grossfirmen werden auch beim SBV Systeme von
mehreren Herstellern eingesetzt.

Auf Grossrechner-Ebene sind Systeme von IBM vertreten. Auf diesen
Grossrechnern befinden sich die sog. "Produktionsdaten" der Bank,
sprich sämtliche Kundendaten mit Konto-, Kredit-, Depotinforma-
tionen, etc. Ebenfalls auf dem IBM-Grosssystem angesiedelt ist
die Bürokommunikationsplattform OFFICE VISION (von IBM), welche
zum heutigen Zeitpunkt dem elektronischen Austausch von Informationen dient.

Neben den Grosssystemen sind in dem über die ganze Schweiz verteilten Niederlassungsnetz des SBVs auf dezentraler Seite
grösstenteils UNISYS-Systeme (CTOS Betriebssystem) im Einsatz.
Neben der Möglichkeit, innerhalb des lokalen Bereichs gemeinsam
Daten und Infrastruktur zu nutzen, ist der Zugriff auf den HOST
gewährleistet.

Zusätzlich zu den UNISYS-Systemen werden in diversen Ressorts und
Abteilungen auf lokaler Ebene auch Arbeitsplatzrechner von IBM
eingesetzt (Verhältnis 1:3, d.h. rund 2000 IBM (DOS, OS/2) und
6000 UNISYS (CTOS)).

Für beide Plattformen wurden Standards bezüglich einzusetzender
Tools (Textverarbeitung, Tabellenkalkulation, Graphik, etc.)
definiert. So wird eine einheitliche / gemeinsame Basis für die
Bürokommunikation geschaffen und damit v.a. die Möglichkeit des
elektronischen Datenaustausches gewährleistet.

Durch die zunehmende Bedeutung der elektronischen Erstellung und
der elektronischen Verteilung von Informationen wurde und wird
ein Bedarf mehr und mehr geweckt: Die bereits in elektronischer
Form verfügbaren Daten sollen auch elektronisch abgelegt werden
können. Je intensiver von den Möglichkeiten der Bürokommunikation
Gebrauch gemacht wird, umso mehr steigt der Bedarf für eine
elektronische Unterstützung im Ablagebereich.
Dabei sollen die dezentral (auf der Workstation) erstellten
und/oder benötigten Daten und Dokumente dezentral abgespeichert
werden, während die sog. "Produktionsdaten" (wie vorne erwähnt)
auch weiterhin auf der Mainframe verbleiben.

1.3   Das Arbeitsgebiet ELA

Zur Sicherung der Leistungsfähigkeit und zur rechtzeitigen
Reaktion auf sich ändernde Anforderungen wurde das Projekt
"Elektronische Ablage und Archivierung (ELA)" im Departement
Informatik/Organisation des SBV initialisiert.

Schon erste Ueberlegungen zeigten, dass in diesem Bereich speziell die "interdisziplinäre" Zusammenarbeit von grosser Bedeutung ist, da wie o.e. die unterschiedlichsten Anforderungen und eine grosse Anzahl von Schnittstellen zu berücksichtigen sind. Aus diesem Grund wurde das Projekt weitergefasst und das **Arbeitsgebiet ELA** definiert, in dem mehrere Teilprojekte zusammengefasst und koordiniert werden. In den einzelnen Projekten werden parallel verschiedene Teilbereiche bearbeitet; in unseren weiteren Ausführungen werden wir uns auf das Teilprojekt "Basisentwicklung und Kreditablage" konzentrieren.

ELA hat zum Ziel, sämtliche unternehmensrelevanten Informationen/Dokumente zu verwalten, dem Retrieval zugänglich zu machen, zu speichern und zu sichern, sofern diese nicht schon mit bestehenden Systemen verwaltet werden. Schwerpunkte des Projektes sind:

- Definition von Strukturen und Standards einer Elektronischen Ablage und Archivierung

- Konzeption betrieblicher Ablagevorgänge unter Berücksichtigung der abteilungsspezifischen Aufbau- und Ablauforganisation

- Konzeption von Schnittstellen zu Bürokommunikations-Tools und Definition von Schnittstellen zu operationellen Applikationen

Die elektronische Ablage und Archivierung soll als ein Modul in die heutige Infrastruktur des SBVs eingebunden werden. ELA soll folgende Aufgaben bewältigen:

- Abbildung des Ordnungssystems jeglichen Ablagegutes durch eine elektronische Verwaltung von Ablageregeln, Dokumentarten und Dossierstrukturen

- Aufnahme von physisch (extern) abgelegten Dokumenten (in Papierform) mittels beschreibender Informationen (Deskriptoren, Metadaten über Dokumente)

- Aufnahme von elektronischen Dokumenten (nicht nur beschreibend, sondern als elektronische Vollinformation) aus dezentralen Bürokommunikations- Tools. Das bedeutet, dass verschiedene **physische Dateiformate** verwaltet werden müssen: Im Falle einer Textverarbeitung ist es ein Textfile in einem bestimmten Format, im Falle einer Scan-Software ist es ein Image-File, im Falle eines Business-Graphic-Programms ist es eine Graphik usf.

- Automatischer Zugriff auf Online- und automatisierter Zugriff auf Offline-Ablagemedien (z.B. elektronisches Bestellwesen für Papierdokumente aus zentralem Archiv).

Die Ablagemedien können z.B. Magnetplatten oder Optische Platten, Magnetbänder oder auch Papier sein.

Eine Priorisierung erfahren diese Aufgaben durch die im folgenden aufgeführten Leistungsansprüche.

2. Anforderungen an die Ablösung konventioneller Ablagen durch EDV

Neben den globalen Zielen des Ablagesystems, nämlich der Reduktion des Verwaltungsaufwandes bei den mittelfristig aufbewahrten Akten mit hoher Zugriffshäufigkeit und der Reduktion des Suchaufwandes bei den langfristig aufbewahrten Akten, müssen diverse Anforderungen aus den unterschiedlichsten Bereichen erfüllt werden.

2.1 Benutzeranforderungen

Die Ansprüche seitens der Benutzer sind v.a. dadurch sehr hoch, weil ihre Erwartungen aufgrund von "Hochglanz-Versprechungen" diverser Anbieter sehr forciert werden. Selbstverständlich geht der Benutzer auch davon aus, dass die "elektronische Ablage Version 1" vergleichsweise die Funktionalität eines "Porsche Carrera 911 TURBO" aufweist und nicht etwa nur einem "VW Passat" ähnelt....

Gleichwohl stellen die folgenden Benutzeranforderungen ernstzunehmende Funktionsansprüche dar:

- der Zugriff in einem Arbeitsschritt auf die Gesamtheit der Unternehmensdaten

- kurze Zugriffszeiten

  sowie

- wenig oder gar kein Zusatzaufwand.

Im projektbegleitenden Dialog soll mit dem zukünftigen Anwender eine Konkretisierung der Benutzerbedürfnisse vom Wünschbaren zum Machbaren erfolgen.

Dabei muss klar festgehalten werden, dass auch eine elektronische Ablage mit Aufwand verbunden sein wird; dieser Aufwand wird nur dann akzeptiert werden, wenn er durch einen evident grösseren Nutzen aufgewogen wird.

2.2 Betriebswirtschaftliche Anforderungen

Zu den betriebswirtschaftlichen Anforderungen gehören v.a.

- die Forderungen nach der Rationalisierung der Arbeitsabläufe

- dem Abbau der Raumkosten für
  konventionelle (Papier-)Archive

sowie

- der besseren Nutzbarmachung der Ressource
  Information mittels der Datenbanktech-
  nologie.

Bei der Forderung nach Rationalisierung der Arbeitsabläufe sowie
der Nutzbarmachung der Ressource Information ergibt sich stets
das Problem der quantitativen Messbarkeit des Erfolgs.

Anhand eines Beispiels möchten wir aufzeigen, wie bei der Forderung nach "Abbau der Raumkosten für konventionelle Papierarchive"
der Erfolg hingegen messbar und kontrollierbar wird:
Die zunehmende Papierflut erfordert einen immer grösser werdenden
Platzbedarf für die physische Ablage von Dokumenten/Akten. So
wurde 1990 ein durchschnittliches Ablagevolumen von ca. 2-3
Laufmetern pro Mitarbeiter und Jahr erhoben. Umgerechnet auf das
gesamte Institut (innerhalb der Schweiz) ergibt dies ein Ablagevolumen von ca. 40 000 Laufmetern, was etwa der Luftlinie Frankfurt - Wiesbaden entspricht.
Um der bestehenden Forderung nach <u>kurzer</u> <u>Zugriffszeit</u> Rechnung zu
tragen, wird die Ablage heute vielfach in zentral gelegenen
Büroräumlichkeiten mitten in der City angelegt. Unter Berücksichtigung der fixen Liegenschaftskosten, die sich beispielsweise
in Basel auf rund Fr. 350.--/m2 belaufen, resultiert daraus ein
jährlicher Gesamtaufwand von gut 10 Mio Franken.
Durch eine, auch nur teilweise Entlastung der bisherigen Ablage-
flächen mittels elektronischer Ablage- und Archivierungsmittel
wird eine spürbare Reduktion der Fixkosten resp. eine wirt-
schaftlichere Nutzung des Raumangebotes möglich.

2.3   Rechtliche Anforderungen

Die <u>rechtlichen Anforderungen</u> erschweren eine Realisierung im
Bereich der elektronischen Ablage v.a. deshalb, weil sich die
heutige Rechtsprechung noch primär auf die konventionelle Art der
Speicherung in Papierform stützt. Die noch fehlenden, gesetzlich
verbindlichen Aussagen führen unweigerlich zu Problemen. Aufgrund
der hohen Sensitivität von Bankdaten und der wie erwähnt fehlenden juristischen Regelung stehen die bankinternen Rechtsstellen
dieser "neuen Art" der Ablage eher konservativ und zurückhaltend
gegenüber.

Im speziellen besteht eine gewisse Rechtsunsicherheit deshalb,
weil der Gesetzgeber (nach schweizerischem Recht) zwar die
Aufzeichnung und Aufbewahrung auf Bild- und Datenträgern erlaubt,
andererseits jedoch nicht garantiert, dass die Wiedergabe auf
elektronischen Datenträgern in einem konkreten Prozess vom Richter als übereinstimmend mit dem Original angesehen wird.

In diesem Zusammenhang sei erwähnt, dass selbst eine Mikro-
verfilmung vom schweizerischen Bundesgericht als ungenügend
erachtet wird.

Sämtliche weiteren Ueberlegungen bezüglich elektronischer Ablage
und Archivierung müssen daher unter den oben dargelegten Aspekten
angestellt werden. Das Risiko, dass ein Dokument nicht als
Beweismittel anerkannt wird, darf <u>nicht</u> eingegangen werden.

Kurz- und mittelfristig muss aufgrund der obigen Ausführungen
damit gerechnet werden, dass - abhängig von der Dokumentart - aus
rechtlichen Gründen eine <u>nur auf elektronischen Medien</u> basierende
Ablage <u>nicht</u> realistisch ist. Eine Koexistenz unterschiedlicher
Medien (insbesondere Papier und elektronische Speicherung) ist
daher bei der Konzeption mit zu berücksichtigen.

Eine weitere Problematik besteht im Bereich des Zugriffsschutzes:
Kundenbezogene Daten durften bis anhin aus Sicherheitsgründen nur
auf der Mainframe gespeichert werden. Zur Bearbeitung von Daten
auf der dezentralen Workstation (z.B.für Auswertungen) mussten
sie kryptographiert werden. Ob für ELA "normale" Zugriffssiche-
rungen (Passwort, Zugriffsberechtigungen) ausreichen, oder ob die
Dokumente zusätzlich in kryptographierter Form abgespeichert
werden müssen, ist noch zu prüfen.

2.4 Systemtechnische Anforderungen

Die Planung / Konzeption kann nicht auf der grünen Wiese erfolgen; daraus ergibt sich die <u>Mussanforderung</u>, dass ELA in das
bestehende Systemumfeld zu integrieren ist.

Da nicht nur Dokumente und (Meta-)Daten zu Dokumenten, sondern
generell Daten aus und für beliebige(n) Applikationen abgespeichert werden sollen, stellt sich die Frage, ob als Basis für
ELA ein dediziertes System zur Dokumenten-Ablage und -
Archivierung genommen werden kann.

Auf der Suche nach einem geeigneten System bieten sich zwei
Lösungen an: Information-Retrieval-Systeme (IRS) und Daten-
bank-Management-Systeme (DBMS). Beide Bezeichnungen werden oft
synonym benutzt und eine scharfe Abgrenzung fällt schwer. Ein
mögliches Unterscheidungsmerkmal ist für uns, dass bei IRS die
Textbearbeitung im Vordergrund steht. Aus beliebigen Texten
werden automatisch Wörter (i.d.R. strings) selektiert und inklu-
sive Fundstellenangabe in einem speziellen Index-File abgelegt.
Ueber dieses 'Register' können Texte aufgrund der in ihnen
vorkommenden Begriffe schnell gefunden werden. Derartige Anforderungen an eine elektronische Ablage sind benutzerseitig heute
jedoch kaum vorhanden. Systemseitig bedeutet dies, dass
Information-Retrieval-Funktionen zwar vorzusehen sind, ihre
Realisierung aber nicht Priorität eins hat. Im Bankbereich werden
Dokumente vornehmlich nach stark strukturierten Kriterien abgelegt (Kundennummer, Kontonummer). In Folge dessen besteht
(heute!) auch noch wenig Bedarf, Dokumente nach inhaltlichen

Kriterien in einer Elektronischen Ablage zu suchen. Da strukturierte Daten aber typischerweise in Datenbank-Management-Systemen verwaltet werden, liegt es nahe ELA auf der Basis eines DBMS zu entwickeln.

Ein weiterer Faktor ist, dass Daten aus allen im dezentralen Bereich zu entwickelnden Anwendungen im selben System abgelegt werden sollen. Das erhöht die Verfügbarkeit von Informationen und reduziert den allfälligen Datenaustausch (Import/Export).

Eine weitere systemtechnische Anforderung ist der gleichzeitige Zugriff auf Daten auf der Workstation und auf Produktionsdaten (auf der Mainframe).

Neben der Forderung nach einer hundertprozentigen Verfügbarkeit des Systems muss ein differenziertes und automatisches Backup- und Recovery-Verfahren gewährleistet werden. Rechtlichen Anforderungen muss beispielsweise durch den Einsatz entsprechender Medien (z.B. WORM als Speichermedium von abgelegten, nicht mehr änderbaren Dokumenten) entgegen gekommen werden.

Von grosser Bedeutung ist die Definition von Integritätsbedingungen, Constraints/Business-Rules im Data Dictionary und nicht in den Applikationen.
Dadurch sollen u.a. Ablage- und Archivregeln abgebildet und deren Einhaltung erzwungen werden. Das können teilweise sehr einfache Regeln sein, wie etwa die Zuordnung einer definierten Dokumentart zu einem Dokument; über die Dokumentart wird wiederum die Ablageerlaubnis definiert, so dass z.B. die Dokumente einer bestimmten Dokumentart nur dann archiviert werden dürfen, wenn bestimmte Attributwerte vorliegen.

Damit sollen die Grundlagen für ein allgemeingültiges und verbindliches Ablagewesen - und in einem späteren Schritt: Archivwesen - geschaffen werden.

3. Gegenüberstellung von konzipierten, verfügbaren und integrierbaren Systemen

3.1 Die Visionen der Anbieter

In gewissen Hochglanzbroschüren verschiedener Anbieter wird darauf hingewiesen, dass ihr "Informationssystem über den Leistungsumfang bisheriger Archivierungs-Systeme weit hinaus geht" oder dass das Produkt "xy mehr ist als ein Ablagesystem". Noch erfolgversprechender tönt es, wenn einem versichert wird, dass das "Sicherheits- und Datenschutzkonzept von xy sämtliche gesetzlichen Bestimmungen im Bereich der elektronischen Archivierung erfüllt".

Beim näheren Betrachten dieser "Lösungen" stellt sich jedoch bald heraus, dass damit zwar recht gute Ablagelösungen angeboten werden, die Leistungsfähigkeit im allgemeinen jedoch nur zur Abdeckung ablagespezifischer Anforderungen reicht.

Typische Schwachstellen sind: Abdeckung von lediglich Teilbe-
reichen (z.B. Ablage nur von Images; Verwaltung nur eines
Ablagemediums i.d.R. WORM), isolierte/inkompatible Lösungen
(dedizierte Systeme auf spezieller Hardware; Schnittstellen zu
anderen Applikationen z.B. Textverarbeitung werden nicht unterstützt), fehlende Standards (z.B. bezüglich Text- und Graphik-
formaten), mangelnde Integration mit Funktionen der Bürokommunikation wie Electronic Mail, unklare strategische Sicherheit (d.h.
es ist unsicher, ob und wie lange Anbieter und/oder Produkt am
Markt sind), mangelnde Offenheit für Weiterentwicklungen, etc.

3.2   Die verfügbaren Systeme

Zur Beurteilung der tatsächlichen Leistungsfähigkeit der auf dem
Markt befindlichen DBM(IR)-Systeme wurden elf namhafte Anbieter
zur Offertstellung eingeladen.
Die Auswahl der Anbieter erfolgte aufgrund der zwei folgenden,
generellen Lösungsansätze:

<u>Lösungsansatz 1:</u>

Dediziertes Ablage-, Archivsystem auf der Basis einer standardi-
sierten oder spezifischen Datenbank mit verfügbaren Spezialfunktionen (z.B. Thesaurus)

<u>Lösungsansatz 2:</u>

Allgemeines standardisiertes RDBMS (entwicklungsintensiver
Ansatz)

Um Informationen <u>über die Marketingargumente hinaus</u> zu erhalten,
sowie um bei jedem Anbieter die Messlatte gleich hoch zu setzen,
wurde ein detailliertes Pflichtenheft mit Fragenkatalog erstellt.

Schwerpunktmässig wurden die Bereiche

- Datenbankfunktionalität
- Retrievalfunktionen
- Client-Server-Architektur
  und
- die Integrationsmöglichkeiten in die
  bestehende SBV-EDV

untersucht.
Dabei wurden folgende Muss-Anforderungen festgelegt:

<u>DBMS-Funktionen</u>   -Deadlock-Detection
                          -Row-Level-Locking
                          -Definition von
                           Integritätsbedingungen im
                           Data Dictionary
                          -SQL als Data Definition und
                           Data Manipulation Language
                          -Feld zum Speichern binärer Daten

```
                          -Online Backup
                          -Rollback und Rollforward
                          -Import- und Exportfunktionen

IR-Funktionen            -Aufbau des Inverted Files
                         -Negativ- und Positivliste
                          definierbar
                         -Adjacency-Funktionen
                         -Trunkierungs-Funktionen
                         -Thesaurus-Funktionen

Client-Server-Architektur

                         -Two-Phase-Commit
                         -Zugriff auf DB2-Datenbank
                         -Netzprotokoll auf Token-Ring
                          parallel zu LU 6.2
                         -Frontend-Software auf MS-DOS
                          und OS/2
```

Während im Bereich der DB-Funktionalität nur marginale Unterschiede zu verzeichnen waren, wichen die einzelnen Offerten hinsichtlich der Integrationsmöglichkeiten in das bestehende SBV-Systemumfeld weit voneinander ab. Hier zeigen sich die Unterschiede zwischen 'Planung und Realität' am deutlichsten: Ist z.B. die Unterstützung eines Netzwerkprotokolls erst geplant, kann über die Einbindung des Produkts in das bestehende LAN eben nur spekuliert, aber nicht diskutiert werden.
Neben diesen Produkte-Fragen wurde im weiteren auch nach dem Vorhandensein von User-Groups oder nach Referenzinstallationen gefragt. Bei der Beurteilung von angegeben Referenzinstallationen muss jedoch berücksichtigt werden, dass die jeweiligen konzeptionellen Lösungsansätze sehr spezifisch sind (Einflussfaktoren: Aufbau-, Ablauforganisation, technische Infrastruktur). Ein einfaches Portieren von (Referenz-)Konzepten ist daher kaum möglich.
Da man mit dem Entscheid FÜR ein Datenbankprodukt eine enge Kooperation mit dem Anbieter eingeht, bilden Kriterien wie das Einhalten von Terminen, Verbindlichkeit der Offerte (primär Antworten bezüglich <u>verfügbarer</u> Produkte anstatt Hinweise auf Version nn), firmeninternes Know-how, "Nähe" zum Entwicklungszentrum, etc. ebenfalls Mosaiksteine, die das Gesamtbild einer Offerte abrunden.

3.3 Die integrierbaren Systeme

Aufgrund der Erkenntnisse aus den vorliegenden Offerten hat sich
gezeigt, dass es keine Fixfertig-Lösung gibt, welche gekauft und
installiert werden kann.
Bei den offerierten dedizierten Ablage- und Archivsystemen
(Lösungsansatz 1) steht primär das Problem im Vordergrund, dass
es sich hierbei um HOST-basierende Produkte handelt. Eine Integration der dezentralen CTOS-, DOS- und OS/2-Workstations wäre
lediglich über den Umweg einer Emulation möglich. Diese Art der
Integration entspricht jedoch nicht den Zielvorstellungen.
Vielmehr soll die wegweisende Client-Server-Architektur die Basis
für ein Projekt wie ELA bilden. Damit soll einerseits die Intelligenz der Workstation genutzt und andererseits eine
anforderungsgerechte Verteilung der Datenhaltung gewährleistet
werden.

Die Basisentwicklung wird daher mit einem allgemeinen RDBMS
geschehen (Lösungsansatz 2). Aufgrund der nur teilweise oder
nicht vorhandenen Spezialfunktionen (wie z.B. IR-Funktionen oder
die Einbindung optischer Datenträger) handelt es sich hierbei um
einen entwicklungsintensiven Ansatz. Im Mittelpunkt bei dieser
Eigenentwicklung steht das permanente Ueberprüfen der Annahmen
zur Abschätzung des Entwicklungsaufwandes sowie das Austesten
mittels Prototyping.

Der vermehrte Aufwand dieses Lösungsansatzes wird dadurch aufgewogen, dass das System durch seine Offenheit die schrittweise
Integration einzelner, weiterer Bürokommunikations-Anwendungen in
ELA ermöglicht und somit die Datenbasis für sämtliche
operationellen Applikationen bilden kann.

4 Ein Lösungsansatz

4.1 Der gewählte technische Approach

Zur Entwicklung des ELA-Systems wird die folgende Strategie nun
weiterververfolgt werden:

> Phase 1: - Entwicklung des Verwaltungs-
> systems mit Hilfe eines RDBMS mit
> spezieller Berücksichtigung der
> technischen Integrations-
> möglichkeiten in das bestehende
> Systemumfeld

> Phase 2: - Erweiterung des DBMS um Informa-
> tion Retrieval-Komponenten

Für die Stufe 1 wird/wurde vor dem Hintergrund des Globalen
Datenmodells (GDM) des SBVs für ELA ein Datenmodell entwickelt,
das die verteilte Datenhaltung vorsieht und den Konventionen des
GDM entspricht. Das Modell ist als ein erster Entwurf zu

betrachten, der im Laufe des Projektes erweitert oder verändert
werden kann. Inwieweit normalisierte Tabellen z.B. aus Gründen
der Perfomance wieder denormalisiert werden müssen, kann erst mit
der Realisierung des Prototyps ermittelt werden.
Die Integration in die bestehende EDV-Landschaft sieht modellhaft
folgendermassen aus:

Im LAN, beim SBV der Token-Ring, werden ein oder mehrere
dezentrale SQL-Server auf UNIX-, CTOS- oder OS/2-Maschinen
installiert. Clients können in diesem Verbund OS/2- oder MS-
DOS-Maschinen oder CTOS-Workstations sein.
Ueber Frontend-Software soll dadurch von den Workstations trans-
parent auf Datenbanken zugegriffen werden können, die auf einem
oder mehreren Servern liegen. Auf diese Weise sollen Informati-
onen/Dokumente dort gespeichert werden, wo sie benötigt werden
und somit die Belastung des Netzes so gering als möglich gehalten
werden.

4.2 Erweiterung des Database-Management-Systems um Information-Retrieval-Funktionen

Die Verknüpfung von Data-Base-Management- und Information-
Retrieval-Systemen zu einem DBMIRS wird bereits seit einigen
Jahren in der Forschung diskutiert[1], stark vertreten sind
derartige Hybridsysteme auf dem Markt jedoch bis anhin nicht.

Durch die Verknüpfung zweier 'verwandter' Typen von Informationssystemen, nämlich DBMS und IRS, sollen die Vorteile des
einen mit den Vorteilen des anderen verbunden werden.

Drei der elf Offertsteller bieten ein, in das DBMS integriertes
Volltext-Retrieval an. D.b., ein Text (i.d.R. im ASCII-Format)
kann in das DBMIRS geladen und für das Retrieval aufbereitet
werden. Alle Produkte beinhalten dafür den Aufbau eines Inverted
Files unter Verwendung von Stoppwort- oder Präferenz-Listen,
jedoch auf der Basis der Stringinvertierung.

Die Funktionalität der gebotenen Volltext-Indexierung ist speziell unter zwei Aspekten zu betrachten:

- Aufgrund der speziellen sprachlichen
  Konstellation der Schweiz (Deutsch,
  Französisch und Italienisch sind
  Landessprachen) wird die Suche in Texten
  multilingual möglich sein müssen.

---

1) U.a. beschäftigt sich Horst Biller bereits 1982 mit
seinem Beitrag 'On the Architecture of a System integration
Data Base Management and Information Retrieval' mit einer
Synthese von DBM und IRS.

- Beim SBV bereits vorhandene Thesauri
  sollen auch bei der Recherche in ELA
  genutzt werden können.

Beide Forderungen sind jedoch nur auf der Basis eines
wortorientierten Verfahrens sinnvoll realisierbar:

Für ein (zunächst einmal) in der gesamten Schweiz einsetzbares
Ablage- und Archivsystem muss der Zugriff auf Dokumente in jeder
Landessprache gewährleistet werden. D.h. aber auch, dass auf
französische und/oder deutsche Texte mittels italienischer
Stichwörter zugegriffen werden soll. Es müssen also
Uebersetzungen der Stichwörter entweder zusätzlich abgespeichert,
oder ad hoc bei der Abfrage über Relationierungen gebildet
werden. Gerade bei stark flektierenden Sprachen wie Deutsch,
Französisch und Italienisch ist dies nur mit vertretbarem Aufwand
möglich, wenn die Uebersetzung auf der Grundform (bei Substan-
tiven z.B. der Nominativ Singular) beruhen.
Der Einsatz von Thesauri beim SBV dient vor allem der Verein-
heitlichung und exakten Definition von Bezeichnungen und Vorgän-
gen. Erhöht man auf der einen Seite durch die Verwendung einer
Volltext-Indexierung den Recall (Dokumente können nicht nur über
stark selektive Schlagwörter sondern auch über Stichwörter[2)]
gefunden werden), so müssen auf der anderen Seite Verfahren zur
Verfügung gestellt werden, auch die Precision zu erhöhen. Eine
Möglichkeit sehen wir hier in der Ablösung von Adjacency- und
Trunkierungs-Funktionen durch den Einsatz von Thesauri. Eine
Recherche muss also nicht mehr durch die Angabe eines 'Abstands
zwischen zwei Begriffen', sondern durch Angabe der gewünschten
Relation präzisiert werden.

Da keiner der drei Anbieter Verfahren zur Grundformenermittlung
in den benötigten Sprachen anbietet, gehen wir von der
Ueberlegung aus, dass an Stelle einer integrierten
Textinvertierung ein externes Programm diese Funktionalität
übernehmen kann.

Das Konzept einer Elektronischen Ablage und Archivierung (die
sowohl über Funktionen eines DBMS als auch eines IRS verfügt),
beruht deshalb auf folgenden Annahmen:

> 1. Das Ergebnis einer automatischen
>   Indexierung von Texten (Invertierte Liste)
>   kann in eine Form gebracht werden, die das
>   Laden in ein beliebiges DBMS erlaubt.

---

2) Unter Stichwörtern werden Deskriptoren verstanden, die
aus dem Text selbst stammen; unter Schlagwörtern werden
Deskriptoren verstanden, die zusätzlich zu einem Text
vergeben werden.

2. Je nach Genauigkeit des Indexierungsver-
   fahrens[3] können Adjacency-Funktionen mit
   jedem DBMS realisiert werden.
   Wird z.B. zu jedem Stichwort die laufende
   Wortnummer vergeben, kann die Folge zweier
   Suchbegriffe einfach durch ein entspre-
   chendes Select-Statement abgefragt werden.

3. Durch den Einsatz von wortorientierten
   Verfahren kann die Funktion der
   Trunkierung durch die der Relationierung
   abgelöst werden.
   Während bei stringorientierten Verfahren
   die verwendeten Suchbegriffe häufig
   trunkiert werden (z.B. Suchbegriff=BEIN%,
   d.h. der gesuchte Begriff muss lediglich
   mit dem angegebenen String beginnen) damit
   alle zu dem Stichwort gehörenden Formen
   gefunden werden (hier z.B. BEINE, BEINES,
   BEINBRUCH, BEINBRUECHE, aber auch BEINA-
   ME), kann bei wortorientierten Verfahren
   allein mit der Grundform (hier BEIN)
   gesucht werden. Sollen Komposita in die
   Recherche mit einbezogen werden, kann eine
   entsprechende Relationierung erfolgen.
   Dadurch wird die Recherche um die
   gewünschten Begriffe erweitert, ohne dass
   es zu fehlerhaften Ergebnissen kommt
   (Erhöhung des Recall und der Pecision).

Voraussetzung für den Einsatz einer externen Textinvertierung
ist, dass ein derartiges Programm so in die Applikation integriert wird, dass es für Benutzer nicht bemerkbar ist. Das
erfordert eine sehr gute Performance des Programms sowie der
entsprechenden Load-Funktionen zum Datenimport in die Datenbank.

4.3 Aus einem DBMIRS wird eine elektronische Ablage und Archivierung

Die bis jetzt aufgezeigte Funktionalität ist der erste Schritt in
Richtung einer umfassenden elektronischen Ablage und
Archivierung. Zunächst können elektronisch erstellte Dokumente
lediglich elektronisch abgelegt werden. Zum Zweck der
Archivierung müssen sie nach wie vor in Papierform vorliegen.
Dieser Medienbruch soll durch den Einsatz geeigneter elek-

---

3) Genaue Fundstellenangabe: Text#, Kapitel#, Absatz#,
Satz#, Wort#

tronischer Speichermedien vermieden werden, die in einem separaten Projekt untersucht werden.
Letztendlich sollen mit ELA alle, beim SBV vorhandenen Speichermedien verwaltet werden.
Neben systemtechnischen Lösungen ist hier aber vor allem die Neugestaltung organisatorischer Abläufe erforderlich.
Die Arbeitsweise der Benutzer ist geprägt von einem stark ·strukturierten Arbeitsumfeld. Der Aufbau der heutigen Ablagen entspricht dieser Struktur, da jede abgelegte Akte eingebunden ist in einen Ablauf bzw. Geschäftsvorgang. Das macht u.a. die Mehrfachablage notwendig, da ein und das selbe Dokument verschiedenen Geschäftsvorfällen zuzuordnen ist und dementsprechend in verschiedenen Akten oder Dossiers abgelegt wird. Während eine derartige Unterteilung bei elektronisch abgelegten Dokumenten über entsprechende Mehrfach-Klassifizierungen erreicht werden kann, müssen für Papierdokumente neue Abläufe festgelegt werden.
Ein Beispiel: Ein Vertrag von einem Kunden erreicht den Kundenbetreuer. Er erstellt allfällige Kopien und legt den Vertrag in seinem Dossier ab. Zukünftig wird er dieses Kundendokument scannen, das Image-File mit Deskriptoren versehen in die Ablage einspeisen und das Original mit einer eineindeutigen Nummer versehen an eine zentrale Papierablage weiterleiten. Dort wird das Dokument nach der angegebenen Nummer abgelegt. Benötigt ein Mitarbeiter zu einem späteren Zeitpunkt diesen Vertrag (Original) wieder, so wird eine entsprechende Nachricht auf elektronischem Weg an die zentrale Papierablage abgesetzt und die Bereitstellung des Dokuments ausgelöst.

Die Erweiterung von ELA um sogenannte 'Value Added Services' wird bereits in der ersten Stufe beginnen. Auf der Basis von einfachen Auswertungen soll der Mehraufwand (z.B. die Deskriptierung der Dokumente), den der Benutzer durch ELA hat, kompensiert werden.
In diesem Zusammenhang ist die Kumulation von Informationen auf verschiedenen Ebenen vorgesehen.

Während es heute nicht möglich ist zu überprüfen, ob z.B. sämtliche für einen Geschäftsfall relevanten Dokumente dem SBV bereits vorliegen, wird dies durch entsprechende Verwaltungs-Einträge mit ELA leicht möglich: Zu einem Geschäftsfall A gehören Dokumente der Dokumentarten 1, 2 und 5. Ueber eine einfache Abfrage ist es möglich zu überprüfen, ob alle für einen Geschäftsfall relevanten Dokumente vorliegen. In einer späteren Phase können dann aufgrund solcher Stati entsprechende Meldungen wie 'Geschäftsfall A des Kunden Felix Muster kann jetzt bearbeitet werden' ausgegeben werden.
Darüberhinaus können statistische Auswertungen gemacht werden, die je nach Zugriffsberechtigung mehr oder weniger umfangreich sein können. Während sich der Sachbearbeiter einen Ueberblick z.B. über abgeschlossene Kredit-Verträge in einem bestimmten Zeitrahmen in einem bestimmten ihm zugeordneten Bereich verschaffen kann, steht dem Management die entsprechende Funktion auf Unternehmensbasis zur Verfügung.

Neben diesen rein ablageorientierten Funktionen wird das ursprünglich passiv angelegte ELA nach und nach um 'aktive' Funktionen erweitert werden. Dazu gehört z.B. eine Pendenzenkontrolle. Eine derartige Funktion bezieht sich auf noch nicht abgeschlossene Vorgänge und dient dem Benutzer als "Reminder". Sie zeigt z.B. dem Benutzer die in Bearbeitung befindlichen Dokumente an oder macht ihn auf ausstehende Aktionen aufmerksam.

5.   ... auch der SBV hat Visionen

Das, was in anderen Bereichen 'Ganzheits-Methode' genannt wird, heisst im Bankbereich Cross-Selling oder Allfinanz. Gemeint ist damit eine veränderte Sicht auf die Kundenbeziehungen: Während bisher die einzelnen Geschäftsbeziehungen separat abgewickelt und der Kunde von verschiedenen Kundenberatern betreut wurde, soll in Zukunft der Kunde mit allen Geschäftsbeziehungen betrachtet werden. Informationen über die verschiedenen Geschäfte wurden bislang separat in verschiedenen Bereichen gesammelt und gespeichert. Wenn dies auch zunehmend elektronisch geschah, so waren es doch 'Dateninseln', die nur spezielle Bedürfnisse abdeckten. Die Beschaffung bereichsübergreifender Informationen war sehr zeitintensiv und die Vollständigkeit nicht unbedingt gewährleistet. Zur Unterstützung des Cross-Selling muss deshalb die Ressource Information anders genutzt werden. Dazu wird ein (logischer) unternehmensweiter Informationspool benötigt, in welchem sämtliche, für eine Kundenbeziehung notwendigen Informationen gespeichert sind.

Dadurch, dass sich die Funktion des Sachbearbeiters von einem Spezialisten hin zu einem Generalisten ändert, müssen ihm Entscheidungshilfen zur Verfügung gestellt werden. Der Sachbearbeiter muss also systemseitig z.B. Vorschläge für eine Anlage aufgrund bestimmter Kundendaten erhalten und anschliessend muss die getroffene Entscheidungen automatisch überprüft werden.

Das hier vorgestellte Konzept einer elektronischen Ablage und Archivierung ist dabei der erste Schritt in Richtung eines derartigen, umfassenden Bankinformationssystems.

Literaturangaben:

Paul Bantzer, Claudia Toussaint: Information Retrieval - relational? Nachrichten für Dokumentation 38, 1987, S.351-360

Robert G. Crawford, Michael Kim-to Yeung: Specifying information retrieval models in a relational system. The Canadian Journal of Information Science Vo. 13, No. 1/2, September 1988

David J. Harper, John D. Shortridge: What can a Database Management System do for an Information Retrieval System? Proceedings, Australian Computer Conference 9th, August 1982

Ian A. Macleod: A Model for Integrated Information Systems. 9th Int. Conference on Very Large Data Bases, 1983

Jean Rohmer: An approach to Office Information Storage and Retrieval: Hardware and Software Issues for Electronic Filing. INRIA/North-Holland Publishing Company, 1982

Horst Biller: On the Architecture of a System Integration Data Base Management and Information Retreival'. Proceedings, Research and Development in Information Retrieval, 1989

WIDAB - Konzeption und Pilotrealisierung eines experimentellen Information Retrieval-Systems

Kurt Englmeier
Ifo-Institut für Wirtschaftsforschung
Poschinger Straße 5
8000 München 86

Kurzfassung

Die Konzeption des Informationssystems WIDAB (Wirtschaftsinformationen- und Datenbank) orientiert sich an dem Ziel, aus einer wahrhaftig unübersehbaren Menge an Wirtschaftsdaten, die bei den statistischen Ämtern und Wirtschaftsforschungsinstituten gehalten werden, Informationen werden zu lassen, die so einfach zugänglich sind wie der Inhalt einer Zeitung. Dies ist vor dem Hintergrund zu sehen, daß einerseits für viele Unternehmen die Bedeutung von Wirtschaftsinformationen aus Datenbanken stetig wächst, die derzeitigen Informationsdienste die Ansprüche der Nutzer nach Aktualität, Vollständigkeit, vor allem aber nach Problemorientiertheit, Integrationsfähigkeit sowie leichtem und kostengünstigen Zugang nur sehr unzureichend erfüllen können. Anstelle einer Retrieval-Sprache soll ein Menüsystem die Nutzer in die Lage versetzen, ihre Suchanfrage präzise zu formulieren. Es ermöglicht die Navigation in Begriffshierarchien, die nach den Sachgebieten Regionen, Branchen und Variablen getrennt sind. Ziel ist es, die Mensch-Computer-Schnittstelle so zu gestalten, daß den Nutzern thematische Zusammenhänge näher gebracht und mit dem Navigieren die Formulierung der Suchanfrage nahtlos verbunden werden kann, die ihren Ausdruck im ''Ankreuzen'' für das Informationsproblem relevanter Begriffe findet. Diesem Ansatz liegt die These zugrunde, daß Benutzer die ihr Informationsproblem charakterisierenden Begriffe mit denen in den Hierarchien assoziieren können.

Zu diesem Zweck wird Sachwissen in Form dieser Begriffsrelationen in den Retrievalprozeß integriert. Diese zusätzlichen Daten werden zentral von Informationsmittlern für alle Benutzer verwaltet und diesen zur Formulierung ihrer Suchanfragen zur Verfügung gestellt. Die Nutzer recherchieren nicht direkt in der Datenbank, von der sie vermuten, ihr Inhalt könnte zur Reduzierung ihres Informationsproblems beitragen, sondern sie bedienen sich eines automatisierten Informationsmittlers, der die Recherche für sie durchführt.

Doch die Begriffshierarchien sind nicht nur für die Steuerung des Menüsystems verantwortlich, sondern auch für die genaue Umsetzung der Suchanfrage in eine automatische Datenbank-Recherche. Deshalb ist es notwendig, den Inhalt der Datenbanken mit den Begriffshierarchien zu verbinden. Erst wenn die Verweise auf die Dokumente in die Begriffsrelationen integriert sind, kann aus der Suchanfrage eine automatische Recherche abgeleitet werden, die als Suchergebnis eine am Informationsproblem orientierte Dokumentensammlung liefert. WIDAB will diesen Zuordnungsprozeß weitgehend automatisieren.

Inhalt

Seit der jüngsten Vergangenheit kann beobachtet werden, daß der Markt für Informationsdienste auf dem Sachgebiet Wirtschaftsinformationen zunehmend an Attraktivität gewinnt. Das Angebot erstreckt sich von Detailinformationen für die Konkurrenzbeobachtung bis zu den Daten für Branchen- oder gesamtwirtschaftliche Betrachtungen. Dabei werden neben Text- immer mehr numerische Dokumente in das Angebot integriert. Im Zuge dieser Entwicklung drängen die elektronischen Medien die traditionell auf diesem Gebiet vorherrschenden Printmedien weiter in den Hintergrund, wobei neben den Online-Diensten vermehrt auch die Informationsträger CD-ROM oder Diskette in Erscheinung treten.
Die Nachfrage nach derartigen Informationen wird von den sich stärker verändernden Marktsituationen belebt. Informationen über neue und veränderte Märkte spielen in den Planungsprozessen der Unternehmen eine bedeutende Rolle: Die Konkurrenzfähigkeit hängt mehr und mehr von den Informationen ab, die in den Entscheidungsprozeß eingehen. Kürzere Reaktionszeiten auf Marktveränderungen und eine größere Komplexität des Marktgeschehens erfordern ein Mehr an Information (Häußler 1990,S.4-19).

Im Zuge der zunehmenden Nachfrage nach Informationen und dem gleichzeitig ungebremsten Anwachsen des Informationsangebots tritt derzeit das Problem der Informationsüberlastung verstärkt in Erscheinung. D.h. der Aufwand, den Benutzer betreiben müssen, um sich Informationen zugänglich zu machen, steht oftmals in keinem Verhältnis zum erreichten Nutzen (Mang/Schweiger 1991,S.47-68). Die heute angebotenen Retrieval-Systeme stützen sich größtenteils auf Retrieval-Verfahren aus den sechziger Jahren. Boolsche Frageformulierungen auf der Basis einer ungewichteten Indexierung mit einem vorgegebenen Deskriptorensystem und/oder als Freitextsuche in Textdokumenten, dazu wenig Unterstützung des Rechercheprozesses durch das System machen den Informationssuchenden das Leben alles andere als leicht (Krause 1990,S.19). Obendrein sind viele Informationsdienste in ihrer Preisgestaltung nicht gerade zimperlich.

Mit WIDAB (**W**irtschaftsinformationen- und **Datenbank**) soll die Schaffung eines Systems zur Informationsorganisation erreicht werden, das eine effiziente Nutzung der wahrhaftig unübersehbaren Mengen an Wirtschaftsinformationen erlaubt, die bei den statistischen Ämtern und Wirtschaftsforschungsinstituten gehalten werden. Die Informationen sollen dabei so aktuell sein wie eine Tageszeitung, gezielt und problemorientiert der augenblicklichen Entscheidungssituation der Nutzer entsprechen und dabei noch so einfach zugänglich sein wie der Inhalt einer Zeitung. Da WIDAB aufgrund dieses Anspruchs grundsätzliche Bedeutung für die Wirtschaft gewinnt, wird das Projekt vom Bundesministerium für Wirtschaft gefördert.

Aus dem genannten Anspruch können die Ziele abgeleitet werden, auf deren Grundlage das Information Retrieval (IR)-System WIDAB entworfen wird:
Der Wunsch nach **Aktualität** verlangt, daß neue Informationen unmittelbar nach ihrer Entstehung in die Informationssammlung aufgenommen werden. Um ein Höchstmaß an **Vollständigkeit** zu erreichen, muß das IR-System den Zugang zu einem großen Anteil potentiell relevanter Informationen gewährleisten (Salton 1987,S.1-17).
Weiter ist es Aufgabe des Systems, durch ein hohes Maß an **Problemorientiertheit** eine Reduktion der Informationsflut zu erreichen. D.h. es soll einerseits den Nutzern die Möglichkeit eröffnen, in der Suchanfrage ihr Informationsproblem möglichst präzise zu umreißen, und andererseits in der Lage sein, aufgrund der Suchanfrage aus dem Gesamtangebot der Informationsautoren die Nachrichten zu selektieren, die sich genau auf den Informationsbedarf beziehen. Der von den Nutzern artikulierte Informationsbedarf resultiert dabei aus dem Wissensdefizit in der jeweiligen Entscheidungssituation. Durch den Informationsgehalt der übermittelten Dokumente wird ihr Wissensdefizit reduziert (Bössmann 1978, S.185/186).
Den Nutzern muß die Möglichkeit geboten werden, die erhaltenen Informationen weiterzuverarbei-

ten, um sie möglichst optimal in die jeweilige Entscheidungssituation integrieren zu können (**Integrationsfähigkeit**). Weitere Informationen können aus den übermittelten Dokumenten gewonnen werden, sobald sie mit den entsprechenden Werkzeugen bearbeitet werden.

Damit das System bei einem großen Kreis von Nutzern Anklang findet, soll die Zugangsschwelle so niedrig wie möglich gehalten, d.h. ein **leichter und kostengünstiger Zugang** gewährt werden. Diese Bedingung beeinflußt in erster Linie die Gestaltung der Benutzeroberfläche und der Preise.

1. Das Informationsmittlerkonzept im Überblick

Um ein Höchstmaß an *Aktualität* und *Vollständigkeit* zu erreichen, sieht das Konzept von WIDAB vor, alle Funktionen, die mit der Sammlung und Pflege aber auch der Indexierung der Dokumente (numerische Daten und Texte) in Zusammenhang stehen, am Ort der Informationsentstehung - bei den Informationsautoren - zu belassen. Dies ist vor dem Hintergrund zu sehen, daß das Zusammenführen der wichtigen Informationen auf eine zentrale Datenbank (das sogenannte "Downloading", das von nahezu allen Informationsdiensten praktiziert wird) zeitintensiv ist und damit die Aktualität beeinträchtigt. Während bei den Informationsdiensten die technische, in erster Linie am Nachrichtenverkehr orientierte Kompetenz überwiegt, steht bei den Informationsautoren eher die inhaltliche im Vordergrund. D.h. Änderungen am Datenbestand, die von den Autoren nach dem "Downloading" vorgenommen werden, sind für die Benutzer nicht mehr wirksam. Die Aktualität bezieht sich aber nicht nur auf die reine Erweiterung des Datenbestandes sondern auch auf die Veränderung bereits existierender Daten.

Die derzeit praktizierte zentrale Haltung der Informationen kann auch die Forderung nach Vollständigkeit insoweit nicht befriedigend erfüllen, als in nahezu allen Fällen die Datenbestände der Informationsautoren nicht vollständig übernommen werden. Die Selektion erfolgt nach Maßgabe der Rentabilität. Speicherplatz ist ein knappes Gut und folglich werden Informationen, die nur selten abgerufen werden, nicht in die zentrale Datenbasis integriert. Arm dran sind jedenfalls die Benutzer, wenn eine umfassende Lösung ihres Informationsproblems auf diese "unrentablen" Informationen angewiesen ist. Derzeit wird zwar verstärkt das sogenannte "Durchschalten" angeboten, d.h. die Möglichkeit des Verbindungsaufbaus zu weiteren zentralen Datenbanken, die vielleicht die noch fehlenden Informationen vorhalten. Es darf aber bezweifelt werden, daß die Nutzer in eine glücklichere Lage versetzt werden, wenn sie ihr Informationsproblem durch mehrere Recherche-Prozesse in unterschiedlichen Datenbanken lösen können, die darüberhinaus oftmals noch unterschiedliche Interaktionsmodi erfordern.

Um den Nutzern einen umfassenden, aber einheitlichen Zugang zu den dezentralen und heterogenen Datenbanken der Informationsautoren bieten zu können, sieht WIDAB eine Vermittlerstelle vor, die eine für die Nutzer virtuell zentrale Datenbasis realisieren soll. Diese recherchieren folglich nicht direkt in der jeweiligen Datenbank, von der sie vermuten, ihre Informationssammlung könne ihren Bedarf decken. Sie bedienen sich eines Informationsmittlers, dem sie ihr Informationsproblem anvertrauen und der aufgrund seines Fachwissens in der Lage ist, daraus eine geeignete Recherche in den relevanten Datenbanken abzuleiten. Der Informationsmittler weiß, in welchem Themengebiet das Informationsproblem anzusiedeln ist und er weiß auch, welche Informationsautoren welche Informationen zu diesen Themen auf ihren Datenbanken vorhalten. Darüberhinaus kennt er auch die Arbeitsweise für den Abruf der nötigen Informationen. Der Dienstleistungsbereich der Informationsvermittler, die auch diesen Aufgabenbereich in etwa abdecken, d.h. für die Nutzer die Datenbank-Recherche durchführen, hat bereits eine beachtliche Verbreitung gefunden. In der Beratung können sich die Nutzer ganz auf das eigentliche Sachproblem, die Artikulierung des Informationsproblems, konzentrieren. Dessen Umsetzung in eine Suchanfrage leistet der Informationsvermittler. Die gesamte Problematik der Interaktion mit einem Retrieval-System bleibt den Nutzern auf diese Weise ebenfalls erspart. Nachdem aber diese Dienstleistung für die große Mehrheit der Benutzer nicht

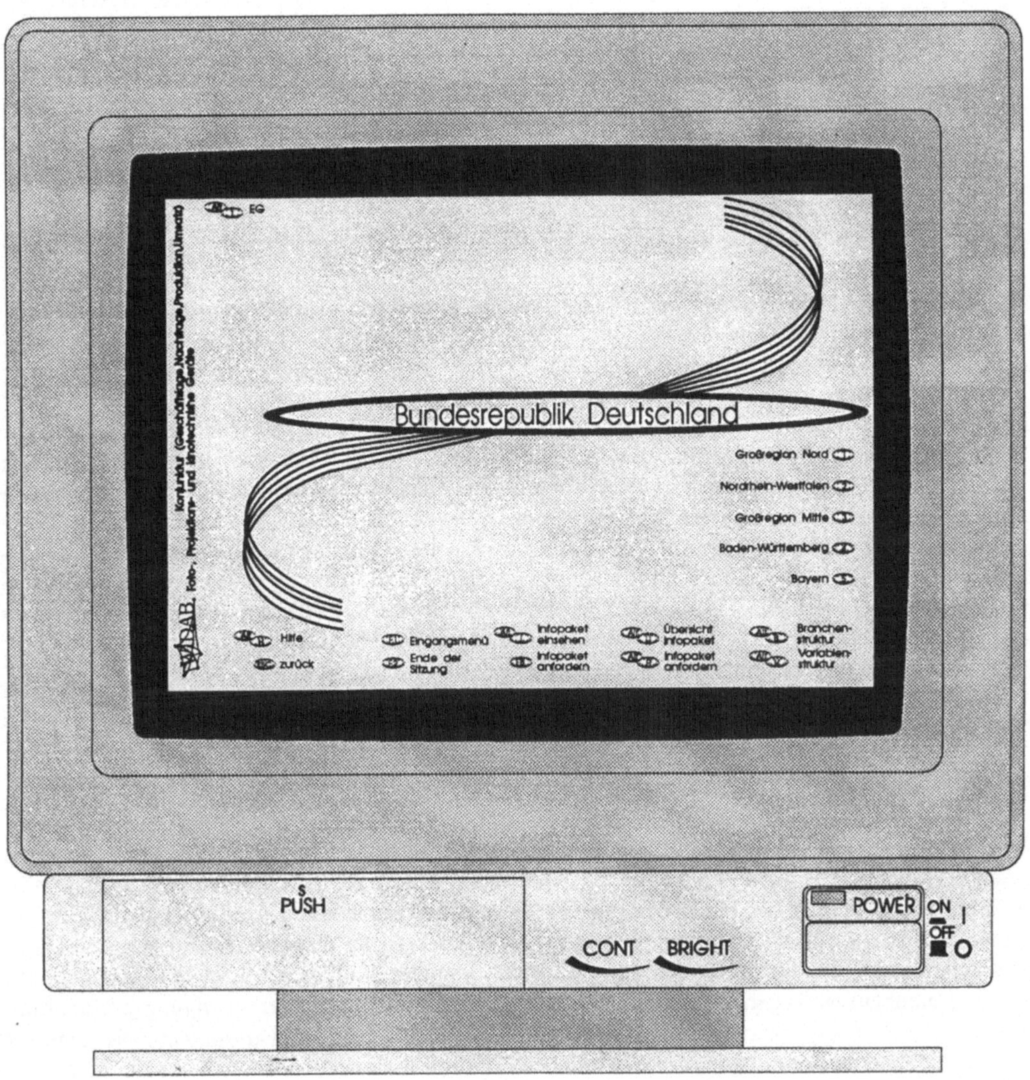

Abb. 1 Die grafische Darstellung der Begriffshierarchien am Bildschirm unterstützt die Verdeutlichung der Kontextabhängigkeit. So kann der Benutzer leicht erkennen, welchem übergeordneten Begriff (am Monitor links oben) der augenblicklich betrachtete (Bildmitte) zugeordnet wurde und welche Begriffe darunter subsumiert wurden (rechts unten). Die geschwungenen Linien, die den augenblicklichen Begriff kreuzen, unterstreichen grafisch den Zusammenhang.

immer verfügbar und vor allem bezahlbar ist, dürfte der Anspruch nach Aktualität etwas darunter leiden und der nach kostengünstigem Zugang gänzlich unter den Tisch fallen.

WIDAB will vor diesem Hintergrund versuchen, den Teil der Informationsmittlerfunktionen in das IR-Systems zu intergieren, der vollständig automatisierbar ist. Beim Design des Systems wird deshalb besonderes Augenmerk auf drei Bereiche gerichtet:

- Die Umsetzung des Informationsproblems in eine genaue Suchanfrage

- die Organisation eines geeigneten Rechnerverbundes zur Generierung der virtuellen Gesamtdatenbank und

- die präzise Verknüpfung der Suchanfrage mit den relevanten Informationen.

WIDAB bietet den Nutzern eine Übersicht der Themen, die auf der Fachkompetenz des Informationsvermittlers gründen und einen Ausschnitt seines Sachwissens abbilden. Diese Übersicht enthält allerdings nicht eine schlichte Auflistung aller Themen sondern vielmehr eine Begriffshierarchie, die auch den nötigen Kontext verdeutlichen soll. D.h. die Nutzer können so erkennen, aus welchen übergeordneten Punkten ein betrachteter Begriff abgeleitet wurde und welche Punkte darunter zu subsumieren sind. Die Umsetzung des Informationsproblems der Benutzer in eine Suchanfrage ergibt sich aus dem "Ankreuzen" der Begriffe, die mit denen korrespondieren, die ihr Informationsproblem charakterisieren. Aus der Suchanfrage generiert das IR-System unter Zuhilfenahme seines Sachwissens (Begriffshierarchie mit Verweisen auf relevante Dokumente) eine Menge an Antwortobjekten (Dokumenten) als Ausschnitt aus der virtuellen Gesamtdatenbank. Die realisierte Datenbank-Recherche liefert dann Informationen, die stark auf die Begriffe des Informationsproblems unter Berücksichtigung ihres jeweiligen Kontexts zugeschnitten sind, wodurch der notwendigen *Problemorientiertheit* Rechnung getragen wird.

2. Mensch-Computer-Interaktion

2.1. Die Gestaltung der Benutzeroberfläche

Krause (1990,S.8) verweist darauf, daß Benutzer einen nicht unerheblichen Teil ihrer Energien darauf verwenden, zu lernen und darüber nachzudenken, wie sie ihr Sachproblem, die Suchanfrage, so formulieren, daß sie die Funktionalität des Systems nutzen können. Deshalb ist die Mensch-Computer-Schnittstelle so zu gestalten, daß sie zur Verbesserung dieses Verständigungsproblems zwischen Mensch und Computer beiträgt. Damit die Benutzer die für sie relevanten Informationen aus der Datenbank abfragen können, müssen sie sich zusätzlich zum Verständigungsproblem mit dem zu lösenden Sachproblem auseinandersetzen. Das eigentliche Retrievalproblem zielt damit bei WIDAB nicht nur auf den Zugang zur eigentlichen Zielinformation, sondern auch auf die Integration von zusätzlichem Sachwissen, die diesen Zugang unterstützen sollen. Zentrales Moment bei der Gestaltung der Benutzeroberfläche, der Interaktionskomponente, ist die Integration des Sachwissens des Informationsmittlers, das auf Begriffshierarchien reduziert wird. Diese Relationen vermitteln Zusammenhänge der in der virtuellen Gesamtdatenbank gespeicherten Sachgebiete.

Hierarchische Begriffsrelationen setzen semantisches Wissen über die Strukturierung des Gegenstandsbereichs ein. "Durch die schrittweise Weitergabe dieses Wissens an die Benutzer reduziert sich die Komplexität der Suchanfrage" (Krause 1990,S.46). Sie erleichtern den Nutzern den Einblick in die thematischen Zusammenhänge der Sachgebiete, die ihr Informationsproblem tangieren. Die Benutzeroberfläche präsentiert die Begriffshierarchie in grafischer Darstellung. Die Navigation in den Begriffsrelationen kann damit nahtlos mit der Formulierung der Suchanfrage verbunden werden. Die grafische Darstellung der Begriffshierarchie und die Gestaltung der Navigationsmöglichkeiten wird deshalb zum zentralen Baustein für ein effizientes und benutzerfreundliches IR-System. Ziel ist es, daß die Benutzer die Schlüsselbegriffe, die sie intuitiv ihrem Informationsproblem zuordnen, mit den Begriffen der entsprechenden Kontextpositionen in der Begriffshierarchie assoziieren können.

Diese Vorgehensweise wird wesentlich von der Grundannahme beeinflußt, daß Benutzer bei der Problembearbeitung (Formulierung der Suchanfrage) auf eine **interne (mentale) Repräsentation thematischer Zusammenhänge** zurückgreifen (Krause 1986,S.10-12; ausführlich: Gentner u.a. 1983).

2.2. Die Repräsentation der Suchanfrage

Die grafische Darstellung der Begriffshierarchie erleichtert den Benutzern das Verständnis des jeweiligen Kontexts. Benutzer fassen die Schlüsselbegriffe zu einem Cluster zusammen, der ihr Informationsproblem umreißt und die kognitive Zusammengehörigkeit der Begriffe repräsentiert (Krause 1990,S.46). Während der Navigation durch die Begriffshierarchie kann der urspüngliche Cluster in der Auseinandersetzung mit den Begriffsrelationen durchaus modifiziert werden. In jedem Fall aber entsteht in der Markierung relevanter Begriffe ein neuer Cluster, der Ergebniscluster, der dem internen gegenübergestellt wird. Die Suchanfrage gilt dann als formuliert, wenn die Benutzer eine ausreichende Übereinstimmung der gegenübergestellten Cluster feststellen. Der Ergebniscluster repräsentiert dann die Suchanfrage.

Den Benutzern stellt WIDAB insgesamt drei Begriffshierarchien entsprechend den drei Hauptbezugsebenen der Wirtschaftsinformationen zur Verfügung. Jedes Dokument weist im Zusammenhang mit Wirtschaftsdaten einen regionalen, Branchen- und Variablenbezug auf. Nachdem dies auch im mentalen Modell der Benutzer eine Entsprechung findet, wurden die Navigationsmöglichkeiten dahingehend erweitert. Durch die Markierung werden Begriffstripel dem Ergebniscluster zugeordnet. Zusätzlich können die Benutzer noch entscheiden, ob die Begriffe des Tripels isoliert, d.h. ausschließlich, oder unter Hinzunahme ihrer nachgeordneten Begriffshierarchie übernommen werden sollen.

Dadurch kann die Suchanfrage auch den spezifischen Recall- und Precisionanforderungen (Salton 1987,S.167-210) angepaßt werden. Um einen hohen Recall zu erzielen, werden die Nutzer ihr die gesamte Teilhierarchie, also den Begriff und seine nachgeordneten Relationen zuschlagen. Soll hingegen hohe Precision sichergestellt werden, findet ausschließlich der relevante Begriff Berücksichtigung.

Nachdem die Begriffstripel auf die Menge bzw. die Kosten der ihnen zugeordneten Dokumente verweisen, liefert das System den Nutzern auf Wunsch eine Abschätzung der Informationskosten, die mit der getroffenen Markierung verbunden sind. Dadurch wird es den Nutzern ermöglicht, ihre Auswahl auch unter dem Gesichtspunkt der zu erwartenden Kosten zu treffen.

Das Design der Benutzeroberfläche zielt aber nicht nur auf eine klare Darstellung der thematischen Zusammenhänge, sondern auch auf eine möglichst einfache Gestaltung der Interaktionen. Das Drücken einer Taste bzw. Tastenkombination reicht aus, um von einem Thema ins nächste zu navigieren oder das Suchergebnis zu manipulieren. Sämtliche für die aktuelle Situation anwendbaren Interaktionsmöglichkeiten sind vollständig am Monitor dargestellt. Im Zuge der Weiterentwicklung des Prototypen sind der Einsatz der Maus sowie Ikonen und Fenster vorgesehen.

Selbstverständlich sind die Ansprüche an die Benutzeroberfläche auch bei der Form der Ergebnisrepräsentation zu berücksichtigen, der Repräsentation der Dokumente, wie sie das System als Antwort

auf die Suchanfrage der Nutzer ausgibt. Der Aufwand für das Sichten der Ergebnisse aus der Informationssuche wird zunächst reduziert, indem die auf die Anfrage zugeschnittene Dokumentensammlung in die Begriffshierarchie eingeordnet und damit gegliedert wird. Die Bezeichnungen in den Begriffshierarchien werden dann zu Gliederungspunkten der Dokumentensammlung.
Für die numerischen Daten werden unterschiedliche Repräsentationen angeboten, da bspw. die gemeinsame Darstellung von Zeitreihen in einem Diagramm die Information über deren Entwicklung eher verständlicht als die parallele Darstellung in Tabellen.

Die Form der Ergebnisrepräsentation beeinflußt darüberhinaus auch die weitere Verwendung der Suchergebnisse und damit den Grad der *Integrationsfähigkeit* des IR-Systems. WIDAB überträgt die Dokumente in einer transparenten Form in den Arbeitsplatzrechner der Nutzer und schafft damit die Möglichkeit, die Daten mit anderer Anwendungssoftware weiterzubearbeiten.

3. Das distribuierte System

3.1. Die logisch-technische Struktur

Ebenso wie die Benutzerschnittstelle beeinflußt die logisch-technische Struktur den intellektuellen oder physischen Aufwand, den die Nutzer treiben müssen, um eine Suchanfrage zu formulieren, die Informationsermittlung durchführen zu lassen und das Suchergebnis einzusehen. Dieser Aufwand dient den Nutzern als Parameter, inwieweit ihrem Wunsch nach *leichtem und kostengünstigen Zugang* entsprochen wird.

Nachdem die Kosten einen nicht zu unterschätzenden Faktor bei der Akzeptanz des Systems darstellen, ist es wirtschaftlich sinnvoll, den gesamten Teil der Datenhaltung am Entstehungsort der Informationen zu belassen und über einen Verbund dieser Datenbanken, der Informationsmittler-Stationen und der Benutzerrechner nur diejenigen Daten zwischen ihnen auszutauschen, die zum jeweiligen Zeitpunkt für die Nutzer von Bedeutung sind.

Um den gesamten Prozeß der Informationserstellung durchführen zu können, wird ein temporäres Rechnernetz realisiert. D.h. die Kommunikationsverbindungen zwischen den jeweiligen Datenstationen werden nur für den Zeitraum der Nachrichtenübermittlung aufrecht erhalten.
Unter Nachrichten sind in diesem Zusammenhang
a)   die Suchanfragen der Benutzer,
b)   die Begriffshierarchien der Informationsmittler (Sachwissen),
c)   die aus diesen beiden Teilen abgeleitete Liste der Schlüssel, die die für die Suchanfrage relevanten Dokumente repräsentieren,
d)   die mit Hilfe der Liste an den Datenbanken der Informationsautoren produzierte Dokumentensammlung selbst und
e)   das Informationspaket (als Suchergebnis) mit der Dokumentensammlung und modifizierten Begriffshierarchien.

Die Datenstationen der Informationsautoren stellen dabei im Gesamtsystem diejenigen Systemelemente dar, an denen die Informationen (d) entstehen, die dem Netz zur Übermittlung an die Datenstationen der Informationsmittler übergeben werden. Von dort erhalten sie über das Netz deren Anforderungen (c). Die Datenstation des Informationsmittlers, die aufgrund ihrer Funktionszuordnung auch mit dem Fachbegriff ''Terminal Interface Processor'' (TIP) bezeichnet werden kann, wickelt im Gegenzug den Nachrichtenverkehr (bzgl. a,b und e) mit den Nutzern ab. (Schnupp 1982,S.19-27) Sie empfängt die Suchanfrage der Nutzer, übersetzt sie in Algorithmen der jeweiligen Datenbank-Recherche und führt diese an den Datenbanken durch. Nachdem sie alle notwendigen

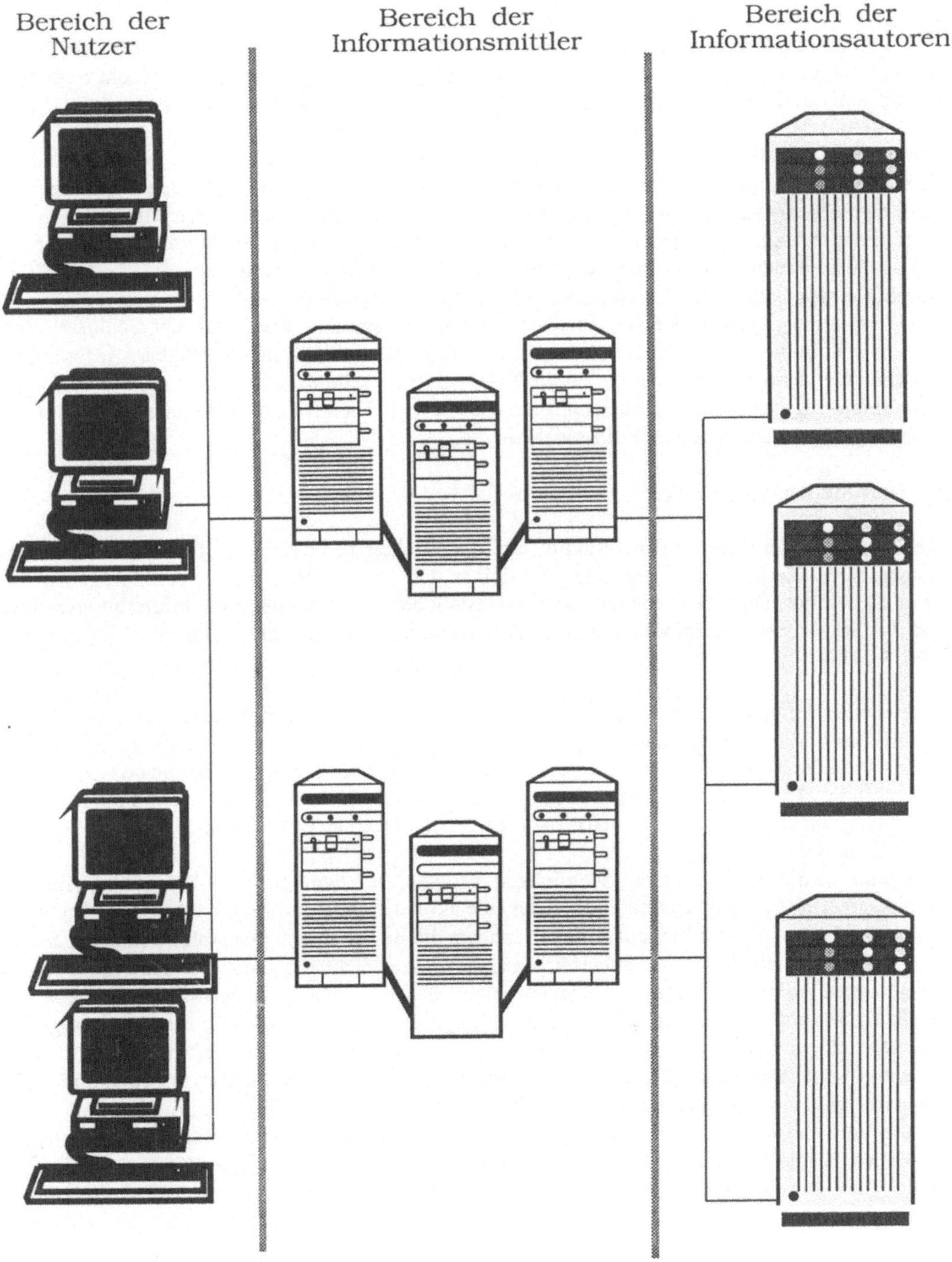

Abb. 2 Schema des distribuierten Systems in WIDAB.

Dokumente gesammelt und aufbereitet hat, übermittelt sie das fertige Informationspaket an die Nutzer. Die Datenkommunikation basiert ausschließlich auf Filetransfer und ist automatisiert, so daß für die Nutzer hier kein Aufwand entsteht.

Das System WIDAB realisiert aufgrund dieser Darstellung ein temporäres Rechnernetz, das aus einer Menge von Funktionskomponenten besteht, die einerseits in räumlicher Distanz zueinander stehen und andererseits Benutzeraufträge in kooperativer Autonomie bearbeiten. Der einzelne Nutzer braucht die Arbeitsgliederung und den Ort der jeweiligen Funktionskomponenten nicht zu kennen. Ein System mit derartigen Eigenschaften nennt Jessen (1988) **"Distribuiertes System"**.

Die zentrale TIP-Datenstation ist nicht nur für die Verbindung zu den zahlreichen Benutzern einerseits und den unterschiedlichen Datenbanken andererseits von Bedeutung, sondern auch für die Integration des Sachwissens der Informationsmittler. Die Verwaltung der Begriffsrelationen liegt ausschließlich in ihren Händen. Sie sichten darüberhinaus das Angebot der Informationsautoren und stellen die Verbindung der Dokumentschlüssel mit den Begriffshierarchien her.

Durch die Möglichkeit der individuellen Strukturgestaltung unterscheiden sich letztendlich auch die Informationsangebote der verschiedenen Informationsmittler. Erst wenn der Schlüssel eines Dokumentes in die Struktur integriert ist, ist es für das Retrieval-System verfügbar. Aufgrund der Individualität der Strukturen kann es für die Nutzer sinnvoll sein, zu mehr als einem Mittler Kontakt zu knüpfen. Diese aber werden Beziehungen zu möglichst vielen Datenbanken unterhalten, um eine größtmögliche Informationsvielfalt zu wahren.

3.2. Die funktionale Struktur

Die Gestaltung der funktionalen Struktur, d.h. der Struktur der Daten und Prozesse sowie deren systeminterne Wechselwirkungen, orientiert sich an dem Ziel, im Rahmen des definierten distribuierten Systems die Datenbestände mehrerer Datenstationen (die Dokumente der Informationsautoren und das Sachwissen der Informationsmittler) logisch zusammenzufassen. (Jessen 1988; Schnupp 1982,S.24)

Die Benutzer definieren mit Hilfe der Menünavigation, die auf den Begriffshierarchien der Informationsmittler basieren, ihre Suchanfrage. Dies geschieht lokal ohne Verbindung zu irgendeiner Datenstation des Netzes. Erst wenn die Benutzer diesen Prozesses abgeschlossen und den Auftrag zur Übermittlung der Suchanfrage an den Informationsmittler erteilt haben, wird die Kommunikationsverbindung zur TIP-Datenstation aufgebaut, die entsprechende Datei dorthin geschickt und die Verbindung wieder abgebaut.

Einleitend wird den Nutzern die Möglichkeit geboten, auf dem gleichen Weg (automatischer Verbindungsauf- bzw. Abbau und Filetransfer) die aktuellen Begriffsstrukturen für ihre Menünavigation vom Informationsmittler abzurufen. Nachdem die Begriffshierarchien relativ statische Strukturen darstellen, sich also im Zeitablauf kaum ändern, ist es nicht angebracht, diesen Prozeß fest in den gesamten Ablauf zu integrieren. Dynamischen Charakter besitzen sicherlich die Verweise aus den Strukturen auf die Schlüssel der Dokumente. Doch diese Verweise sind für die Menünavigation irrelevant und werden daher ausschließlich zentral bei den Informationsmittlern verwaltet. Eigentlich würde es ausreichen, den Nutzern einen Update der Strukturen automatisch mit einem Informationspaket zu übermitteln, sobald sie verändert wurden. Der Grund für diese Option aber liegt darin, daß die Verweise auf die Menge bzw. Kosten der Dokumente ähnlich angelegt sind, aber in die Relationen für die Menünavigation integriert werden, um den Nutzern einen Kostenüberblick zu ermöglichen. Die diesbezüglichen Werte sind deshalb Schwankungen unterworfen. Für eine genaue Kostenberechnung mögen diese von Bedeutung sein, für eine grobe Abschätzung sicher nicht.

Nach dem Eingang der Suchanfrage (d.h. der sie charakterisierenden Liste mit Begrifsstripeln) bei der TIP-Datenstation führt das System einen Abgleich mit den Begriffsstrukturen durch. Dabei werden die Teile extrahiert und neu zusammengefügt, die notwendig sind, um die markierten Begriffe der Suchanfrage anzusteuern. Diese neu enstandenen Strukturen sollen später die Nutzer bei der Einsicht der Dokumentensammlung führen. Irrelevante Verzweigungsmöglichkeiten wären dabei nur hinderlich. Die Dokumentensammlung bildet zusammen mit den an ihrem Inhalt orientierten Begriffsstrukturen das Informationspaket (Suchergebnis).

Die Verwaltung der Verweise aus den Begriffsstrukturen auf die Schlüssel der Dokumente fällt ausschließlich in den Tätigkeitsbereich der Informationsmittler. Jeder Kombination aus jeweils einem Knoten der drei Begriffshierarchien (entsprechend den Bezugsebenen Branchen, Regionen und Variablen) ist eine (durchaus auch leere) Liste der Schlüssel für die entsprechenden Dokumente zugeordnet. Auf diese Weise erzeugt das System eine für die Suchanfrage spezifische Referenzliste. D.h. es erarbeitet eine Anforderungsliste für die Datenbanken, in der alle Schlüssel für die Dokumente enthalten sind, die in Zusammenhang mit der Suchanfrage stehen. Diese neu entstandenen Dateien werden den zuständigen Informationsquellen zugeordnet und anschließend per Filetransfer an die jeweiligen Datenbanken transferiert.

Dort werden vorgefertigte Queries angestoßen, die die genannte Anforderungslisten abarbeiten und das Query-Ergebnis, die Dokumentensammlung in weiteren Dateien in einem zwischen Informationsmittler und -autor vereinbartem Format abgelegt. Nach dem die automatische Recherche durchgeführt wurde, senden die Datenstationen der Informationsautoren die Dateien zurück an die TIP-Stationen.

Nach Erstellung dieser Dokumentensammlung bei den Datenanbietern und ihrer Übermittlung an den Informationsmittler wird die Generierung des Informationspaketes (d.h. die Verknüpfung der neu erstellten Begriffshierarchien mit der Dokumentensammlung und ihre Abspeicherung in einer Datei) an den TIP-Datenstationen vorgenommen. Das letzte Glied der Transaktionskette aktiviert den relevanten Transportweg zu den Nutzern und realisiert den Filetransfer des gewünschten Informationspaketes. Mit Hilfe der Menünavigation kann nun die Dokumentensammlung eingesehen werden.

4. Wissensrepräsentation des automatisierten Informationsmittlers

WIDAB stellt keine direkte Verbindung zu den unterschiedlichen, für die Fragestellungen der Nutzer relevanten Datenbanken her, sondern bedient sich eines automatisierten Informationsmittlers. Diese zentrale Vermittlungsstelle produziert aus der Suchanfrage der Nutzer ein aktuelles und problemorientiertes Informationspaket unter Zuhilfenahme der Datenbestände, die bei den Informationsautoren verwaltet werden.

4.1. Das Sachwissen abgebildet in Begriffshierarchien

Während die Benutzeroberfläche von WIDAB dafür verantwortlich ist, daß die Benutzer des IR-Systems ihr Informationsproblem in der Suchanfrage soweit präzisieren bzw. modifizieren können, um es möglichst scharf abzugrenzen, muß der automatisierte Informationsmittler für eine genaue Übersetzung der Suchanfrage in geeignete Datenbank-Recherchen sorgen. Beide Prozesse aber stützen sich auf weitere Daten, die - in das System integriert - das Sachwissen des Analytikers, d.h. des Informationsmittlers, in strukturierter Form abbilden.

Durch den rekursiven Prozeß der thematischen Untergliederung entsteht für jedes Sachgebiet (z.B. eine Branche) eine hierarchische Begriffsstruktur. Diese bildet dann nicht nur Begriffe ab, sondern auch die Beziehungen zwischen ihnen und erzeugt so die Repräsentation der Zusammenhänge. Jeder der darin enthaltenen Begriffe wird deshalb nicht mehr isoliert betrachtet, sondern in Wechselbeziehung mit den ihn umgebenden Begriffen. Dadurch wird deutlich, in welchem Kontext er zu sehen ist. Mittels dieser Abstraktion wird dem Nutzer eine schnelle Information über das gesamte Wissensterrain geliefert, mit dem sein Wissensdefizit, d.h. sein Informationsproblem, abgedeckt werden kann (Winston 1987,S.265/266). Die Nutzer ordnen intuitiv ihrem Informationsproblem bestimmte Schlüsselbegriffe zu und grenzen es dabei anhand charakterisierender Begriffe ab (siehe Abschnitt 2). Diese oder deren Synonyma finden sie im durch die Begriffsstruktur dargestellten Kontext wieder. Diese Identifikation der Begriffe ihres Interesses, dieses "Anklicken" ihrer relevanten Knoten, verkörpert die Artikulation ihres Informationsproblems.

Die Begriffshierarchien unterstützen im gesamten Prozeß der Informationserstellung folgende Funktionen:
Sie steuern das Menüsystem, mit dessen Hilfe die Nutzer in ihrem Arbeitsbereich ihre Suchanfrage einfach, aber präzise definieren können. Durch die gleiche Herangehensweise können sie Dokumentensammlung einsehen. Das System bietet dann an den Begriffsknoten Funktionen zur Darstellung der Dokumente (Texte und Zeitreihen).
Sie dient der automatischen Generierung der Informationspakete beim Informationsmittler (siehe Abschnitt 3.2).
Sie unterstützt die automatische Zuordnung der Dokumente - genauer gesagt ihrer Schlüssel anhand ihrer charakterisierenden Begriffe.

4.2. Die Repräsentation des Sachwissens in einem semantischen Netz

Für WIDAB wird derzeit ein Modul geschaffen, das die komplexen Begriffshierarchien, sowie ihre vielfältigen Beziehungsarten verwaltet. Diese Entwicklung orientiert sich an der strukturierten Wissensrepräsentationsmethode, d.h. an der Darstellung von Objekten und Beziehungen in einem **semantischen Netz** (Winston 1987,S.267).
Die Syntax eines semantischen Netzes, d.h. die Symbole und ihre Verwendungsmöglichkeiten, sind einfach: Es gibt Objekte, und es gibt Beziehungen zwischen Objektpaaren. In grafischer Form sind Objekte durch benannte Kreise und die Beziehungen zwischen ihnen durch benannte Pfeile gekennzeichnet. In der Standardterminologie werden die benannten Kreise Knoten und die benannten Pfeile Kanten genannt. Die Beschreibungen der Objekte (Begriffshierarchien) liegen in natürlicher Sprache vor, wodurch das semantische Netz, das in Zusammenhang mit WIDAB Anwendung findet, auf der deskriptiven Semantik basiert (Winston 1987,S.266/267). Weiter wird vereinbart, "daß die Slots eines Knoten den unterschiedlich benannten Kanten entsprechen" (Winston 1987,S.269).

In Anlehnung an die Graphentheorie (vgl. Schmidt 1988,S.81-143; Domschke 1989,S.10/11) kann eine Begriffshierarchie als ein Wurzelbaum mit seiner begrifflichen Hauptbezugsebene als Wurzel ("Einstiegspunkt") betrachtet werden. In dieser Betrachtung werden die Begriffe durch Knoten und die Beziehungen zwischen ihnen durch Pfeile repräsentiert. Die Slots eines Knotens entsprechen den unterschiedlich benannten Pfeilen. Die unterschiedlichen Funktionen, die das Netz unterstützen soll, spiegeln sich auch in den unterschiedlichen Slot-Klassen wieder.

Die KONTEXT-Slots verkörpern die Kontextabhängigkeit der Knoten und erzeugen damit die thematische Gliederung eines Sachgebiets. Im IR-System WIDAB unterstützen sie den Aufbau der Substrukturen für die Sachgebiete Branchen, Variablen und Regionen.
Die Kanten der KONTEXT-Slots legen die Pfade der Menünavigation fest. Im Nutzerbereich wird so die Möglichkeit geschaffen, die Suchanfrage zu definieren bzw. die Dokumentensammlung einzusehen. Im Informationsmittler-Bereich kommt ihnen eine wichtige Funktion im Rahmen der Verwaltung der Strukturdaten zu: Sie ermöglichen die automatische Zuordnung neuer Dokumente (genauer, ihrer Schlüssel) durch Abgleich ihrer charakteristischen Begriffe mit den Knotenbegriffen.

Die SUBSUMTION-Slots stellen Beziehungen zu Begriffen her, die unter dem Begriff des Knotens zu subsumieren sind, von dem sie ausgehen. Sie unterstützen die Funktion der KONTEXT-Slots, indem sie diese weiter spezifizieren. Deren Aussagekraft wird erhöht, da sie um weitere charakterisierende Elemente ergänzt werden. Sie steigern damit die Fähigkeit des Systems, die korrekte Zuordnung der Dokumente automatisch vorzunehmen. Für den Benutzerbereich sind sie unbedeutend, da sie in der Menüauswahl nicht dargestellt werden.

Die DETAIL-Slots hingegen realisieren die Verbindung zwischen Knoten in den Begriffshierarchien der drei thematischen Hauptbezugsebenen (Begriffstripel) und den Schlüsseln der Dokumente. Sie stellen das zentrale Bindeglied zwischen den Begriffshierarchien und den Datenbankinhalten der Informationsautoren dar.

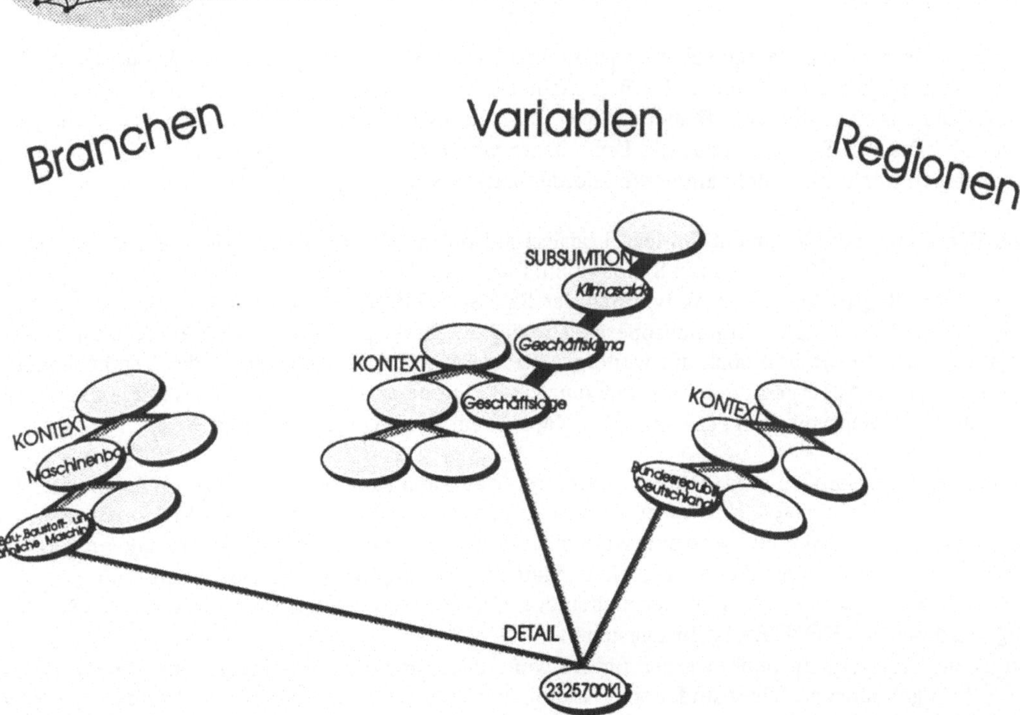

Abb. 3 Während die KONTEXT-Slots die Kontextabhängigkeit verdeutlichen, stellen die SUBSUMTION-Slots Beziehungen zu Begriffen her, die unter dem Begriff zu subsumieren sind, von dem sie ausgehen. Die DETAIL-Slots realisieren die Integration der Dokumente in die Begriffshierarchien.

Im Mittelpunkt des besagten Moduls für das Retrieval-System WIDAB steht nicht die automatische Generierung der Begriffshierarchien. Sie werden ebenso wie die Zuordnung der Dokumente im derzeitigen Prototyp auf manuellem bzw. halbautomatischem Wege erzeugt. Es wird aber das Ziel verfolgt, diesen Zuordnungsprozeß so weit als möglich zu automatisieren.

Ausgangspunkt ist dabei die Katalogisierung der Datenbankinhalte durch die Informationsautoren. D.h. diese erstellen eine Liste, in der die Deskriptoren ihrer Dokumente zusammen mit den notwendigen Schlüsseln für die Datenbankabfrage (Query) enthalten sind. Die Deskriptoren sind entweder Schlagworte, die als charakterisierende Begriffe aus den Textdokumenten gewonnen wurden, oder können aus sogenannten ''sprechenden Schlüsseln'' abgeleitet werden. Diese Art von Schlüssel ist bei der Verwaltung von numerischen Daten (Zeitreihen) oft anzutreffen. ''Sprechend'' bedeutet, daß diese Schlüssel als zusammengesetzte Teilschlüssel betrachetet werden. Ein Teilschlüssel aber besitzt keine Schlüsselfunktion im Rahmen des Datenbanksystems; d.h. er verweist auf kein Element in der Datenbasis. Er ist lediglich Repräsentant eines bestimmten Begriffs. Die aus den Teilschlüsseln ableitbaren Begriffe stellen die eigentlichen Deskriptoren der numerischen Daten dar.

Aus dem Schlüssel 2325700KLS, der den Zugriff auf eine Zeitreihe aus der Ifo-Datenbank ermöglicht, lassen sich folgende Deskriptoren ableiten:

2   : Verarbeitendes Gewerbe
32   : Maschinenbau
5700 : Herstellung von Bau-, Baustoff- und ähnlichen Maschinen
KLS : Klimasaldo

Mit Hilfe derartiger Kataloge soll eine weitgehend automatische Manipulation der Zuordnung von Dokument-Schlüssel und Knoten der Begriffshierarchie erreicht werden. Durch das ''Schütten des Kataloginhalts über die Begriffshierarchien'' soll die meiste Arbeit, die mit der Verwaltung der Verweise aus den Strukturen auf die Dokumente verbunden ist, erledigt werden - bis auf wenige Ausnahmen (nicht bzw. nicht eindeutig zuordenbare Dokumente).

Die Zuordnung der Dokument-Schlüssel basiert auf einem Vergleich der Dokument-Deskriptoren mit den Knotenbegriffen und ihren Synonymen. Für jeden Knoten in der Hierarchie kann ausgehend von seinem Begriff und unter Aktivierung der SUBSUMTION-Slots eine Folge von Deskriptoren gebildet werden. Diesem Vergleichsoperanden wird die Deskriptorenfolge aus dem Katalog gegenübergestellt, die eventuell noch um weitere Attribute aus der ''Übersetzung'' der ''sprechenden'' Schlüssel und aus übergeordneten Gesichtspunkten (regionaler, Branchen- oder Variablenbezug der betrachteten Datensammlung, des aktuellen Kapitels im Katalog o.ä.) erweitert wird.

Beim Zuordnungsprozeß wird die Deskriptorenfolge aus dem Katalog ausgehend von der Wurzel der jeweiligen Hierarchie von Knoten zu Knoten gereicht, um sie mit deren Deskriptorenfolgen zu vergleichen. Für jeden Punkt wird eine Knotenbewertung vorgenommen, d.h. jedem Knoten wird die Anzahl der durch Zeichenkettenvergleich (Matching) nachgewiesenen Übereinstimmungen von Deskriptoren zugeordnet. Das Weiterreichen des Vergleichsoperanden aus dem Katalog, das Routing, wird von den KONTEXT-Slots gesteuert.

An jedem Verzweigungspunkt werden für das weitere Routing die Pfeile nicht mehr weiterverfolgt, die auf Folgeknoten gerichtet sind, deren Knotenbewertung sich signifikant von denen der benachbarten unterscheidet und gleichzeitig auf keinerlei Übereinstimmung hindeutet. Durch die rekursive Anwendung dieses Prozesses werden die Hierarchien abgearbeitet und eine Menge markierter Punkte mit positiven Knotenwerten erzeugt. Bei mindestens einer festgestellten Übereinstimmung läßt sich in der jeweiligen Hierarchie mindestens ein einfacher Weg erkennen. Sein initialer Punkt ist die Wurzel, sein terminaler Punkt der Knoten mit positivem Wert, in dessen Folgestruktur kein positiver Knotenwert festgestellt werden kann. Jedem Weg wird nun seinerseits eine Maßzahl zugeordnet. Diese Pfeilbewertung wird von Prozeduren vorgenommen, die mit den KONTEXT-Slots in Verbindung stehen. In Abhängigkeit vom Pfeilwert wird über die Zuordnung des Dokument-Schlüssels entschieden, die sich in der Generierung eines entsprechenden DETAIL-Slots ausdrückt.

Im Gegenzug führt ein Abgleich der einerseits in den Knotenverweisen und andererseits in den Katalogen enthaltenen Schlüssel zu einer Entfernung der Verweise auf die Dokumente, die nicht mehr im Angebot der Informationsautoren enthalten sind.

5. Die Realisierung eines Software-Prototypen

Von Projektbeginn an war vorgesehen, parallel zur Konzeptionsphase auch die Entwicklung eines Software-Prototypen voranzutreiben. Die Konzeption stellt allerdings die Grundlage für die Realisierung eines IR-Systems für Wirtschaftsinformationen dar, das die Gesamtheit der eingangs erwähnten Ansprüche abdecken soll. Aufgrund der beschränkten Ressourcen, die vom Zuwendungsgeber zur Verfügung gestellt werden, kann sie nur teilweise in die Entwicklung des Prototypen eingehen. Ziel ist es deshalb, aus der Konzeption eine Pilotrealisierung abzuleiten, die zwar naturgemäß hinter deren Ansprüchen zurückbleibt, aber dennoch deren Umsetzbarkeit beweist. Die Software stellt in einem etwas kleineren Rahmen das System vor, das die Konzeption vorsieht. D.h. sie enthält alle vorgesehenen Funktionen, wenn auch nicht in der Qualität und dem Ausbauumfang, wie man es von einem marktreifen Software-Produkt erwarten würde. Es reicht aber aus, um das System potentiellen Anwendern zu präsentieren. In dieser Auseinandersetzung können wertvolle Anregungen für die weitere Konzept-Entwicklung gewonnen werden.

Wenn auch der Prototyp derzeit als Inhouse-System am Ifo-Institut in München zu Test- und Präsentationszwecken eingesetzt wird, so wird er nie den Stand eines breit einsetzbaren Software-Produkts erreichen, sondern allenfalls die Grundlage für einen Auftrag an ein Softwarehaus bilden. Dennoch wird durch den Einsatz der objektorientierten Programmierung die Voraussetzung geschaffen, bei der Software-Weiterentwicklung auf den bestehenden Prototyp zurückzugreifen. Dadurch wird die Wiederverwertbarkeit der bereits produzierten Software erreicht und eine vollständige Neuprogrammierung vermieden. So wird eine leichte Adaptierbarkeit des Systems an neue Anforderungen erreicht.

Literaturhinweise

Bössmann,E.: **Information**. In: Albers,W. u.a.: Handwörterbuch der Wirtschaftswissenschaften. Stuttgart 1978. S.185/186.

Domschke,W.: **Logistik: Transport**. 3.Auflage. München 1989. S.3-15.

Gentner,D. u.a.: **Mental Models**. Hillsdale 1983.

Häußer,E.: **Perspektiven und Strukturen elektronischer Informationssysteme**. In: Häußer,E.: Auf dem Weg zum europäischen Informationsverbund: Von CD-ROM bis Informationsdatenbanken. Velbert 1990.

Jessen,E.: **Rechnernetze**. Vorlesungsskript, Wintersemester 1988/89.

Krause,J.: **Direkte Manipulation elektronischer Objekte und Metaphernverwendung**. LIR-Arbeitsbericht. LIR Regensburg 1986. S.10-12.

Krause,J.: **Zur Architektur von Wing: Modellaufbau, Grundtypen der Informationssuche und Integration der Komponenten eines intelligenten Information Retrieval**. WING-IIR-Arbeitsbericht 7. LIR Regensburg 1990. S.8-48.

Mang,E.; Schweiger,J.: **Der Akzeptanztest bei den Unternehmen**. In: Englmeier,K. u.a.: WIDAB-Projekt. Ergebnisse der Praxisphase. Deutsches Institut für Wirtschaftsforschung, Berlin, und Ifo-Institut für Wirtschaftsforschung, München 1991. S.47-68.

Salton,G.: **Information Retrieval - Grundlegendes für Informationswissenschaftler**. Hamburg u.a. 1987. S.1-17,167-210.

Schmidt,G.; Ströhlein,T.: **Relationen und Graphen**. Berlin u.a. 1989. S.81-143.

Schnupp,P.: **Rechnernetze**. 2.Auflage. Berlin 1982. S.19-27.

Winston,P.H.: **Künstliche Intelligenz**. Bonn u.a. 1987. S.265-278.

Wissensbasiertes, inhaltsorientiertes Retrieval statistischer Daten mit EISREVU

W. Augsburger, H. K. Rieder, J. Schwab
Universität Bamberg, Wirtschaftsinformatik

Zusammenfassung

Derzeit verfügbare statistische Retrievalsysteme haben eine Architektur nach dem Paradigma der traditionellen Programmierung: der Trennung von Programmen und Daten. Diese Systemarchitektur stößt bei den Anforderungen an ein intelligentes Informationssystem an ihre systemimmanenten Grenzen. Um diese zu überwinden, wird eine neue Systemarchitektur, basierend auf einem objektorientierten Datenmodell, vorgeschlagen. Diese hebt die klassische Trennung zwischen numerischen Daten und Programmen auf. Die Darstellung des Modellansatzes erfolgt dabei am Beispiel der Zeitreihenanalyse.

1 Motivation

Ausgangspunkt der nachfolgenden Überlegungen war die Konzeption eines Informationssystems für Führungskräfte in Wirtschaft und Verwaltung auf der Grundlage numerischer Daten[1]. Dabei zeigte sich, daß die nach dem Paradigma traditioneller Programmierung aufgebauten numerischen Informations- und Retrievalsysteme bei Bildung komplexer Modelle, bei der Klassifikation numerischer Daten nach inhaltlichen Gesichtspunkten und bei kontinuierlicher Überwachung komplexer Datenbestände ihre Grenzen finden. Diese Grenzen lassen sich nicht durch Kosmetik an bestehenden Systemen überwinden, sondern fordern einen neuen Modellansatz. Nach einer kurzen Betrachtung der systemimmanenten Schwächen traditioneller Systemarchitekturen wird als Lösungsmöglichkeit ein objektorientierter Ansatz vorgeschlagen. Durch Ausnutzung der Möglichkeiten eines objektorientierten Konzepts können neue Objekte ohne eine Änderung von Programmen generiert werden. Die Vererbung von Attributen und Werten auf Klassen- wie auf Objektebene eignet sich besonders zur Darstellung einer Halbordnung über einer Objektmenge. Diese Struktur findet sich oft in einem betriebswirtschaftlichen Kennzahlensystem über Einzelkennzahlen.

2 Statistische Analyse- und Retrievalsysteme

... sind in ihrer Grundkonzeption noch dem Batch-Zeitalter verhaftet. Wie in Abb. 1 dargestellt, unterstützen Statistikprogramme eine einmalige Analyse des zuvor eingegebenen Datenbestands. Sie unterstützen verschiedene statistische Verfahren und eine graphische Aufbereitung. Die Ausgabe von Texten

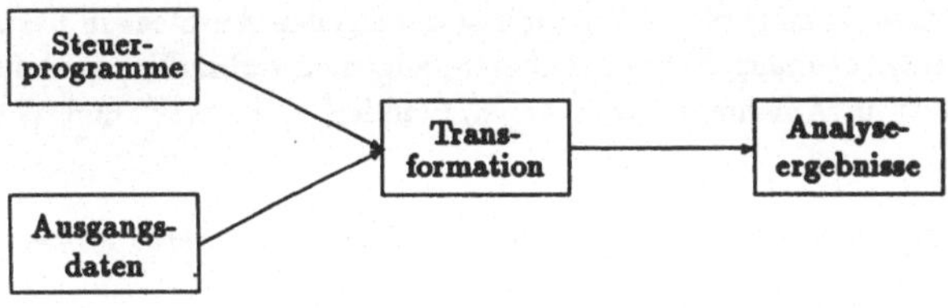

Abb. 1: Arbeitsweise eines Statistikpaketes

ist (wie beispielsweise bei SPSS) möglich, doch muß der Text auf Programmiersprachenlevel codiert werden. Der interaktive Modus beschränkt sich auf das schrittweise Absetzen von Kommandos[2]. Statistische

---

[1] Das Projekt EISREVU (Entscheidungsunterstützendes Informationssystem für Energieversorgungsunternehmen) wird finanziell und durch fachliche Zusammenarbeit von den Unternehmen Mainkraftwerke AG Frankfurt Höchst (MKW) und Energieversorgung Oberfranken AG (EVO) gefördert. Es wurde eine in [Augs 90] beschriebene Pilotversion implementiert.

[2] vgl. [SPSS 88, S. 155ff.]

Retrievalsysteme[3] ergänzen das Statistikpaket durch eine integrierte Datenbank. Diese enthält jedoch nur die nackten numerischen Daten und ist somit lediglich ein Ersatz für den Batch-File.

Statistikpakete und Auswertungen auf statistischen Datenbanken sind darauf angewiesen, die benötigten Daten beim Programmaufruf in einem Batch-File[4] oder in der systemeigenen Datenbank[5] vorzufinden. Kopplungen zwischen Statistiksystemen und Wissensbasierten Systemen haben i. d. R. die Zielsetzung, Statistiksysteme für den Anwender besser zugänglich und begreifbar zu machen[6]. Die Aufgabenstellung eines intelligenten Zeitreihenverwaltungssystems erfordert jedoch genau das Gegenteil; nämlich die Nutzbarmachung statistischer Teilkomponenten in einem Wissensbasierten System.

Zeitreihenverarbeitende Statistikpakete und Zeitreihendatenbanken unterstützen eine strikte Trennung von Daten und Programmen. Auch Systeme mit einer integrierten Datenbank sind aufgrund ihrer prinzipiellen Systemarchitektur nur für Schnappschußanalysen einsetzbar. Für die Überwachung sich laufend ändernder Datenbestände und für ein Retrieval nach inhaltlichen Gesichtspunkten sind sie eher ungeeignet. Eine derartige Aufgabenstellung erfordert vielmehr einen Ansatz, der die numerischen Daten zusammen mit ihren Attributen und Methoden in einer Objektstruktur integriert.

3 Die Idee der Zeitreihenobjekte

Kern des vorgestellten Modellansatzes zur Lösung der o.g. Problemstellung sind sogenannte Zeitreihenobjekte. Diese stellen einen neuen abstrakten Modellansatz zur Darstellung von zeitabhängigen numerischen Daten dar. Seine Grundbausteine sind sogenannte Zeitreihenobjekte. Die Idee der Zeitreihenobjekte besteht darin, als Zeitreihen dargestellte Kennzahlen zusammen mit allen zu einer Zeitreihe gehörenden Informationen, d.h. auch Methoden, die auf die Zeitreihe anwendbar sind, in einem Zeitreihenobjekt zu kapseln und als strukturiertes Zeitreihenobjekt abzulegen. Damit ist die Trennung von Daten und Programmen aufgehoben.

Die Verwendung eines objektorientierten Ansatzes als Grundlage eines Systems zur Zeitreihenanalyse war bzgl. der EISREVU-Projekthistorie nicht etwa der Ausgangspunkt des wissenschaftlichen Ansatzes, sondern wurde im Laufe des Projekts als geeignetes Instrument zur Modellierung der vorliegenden Aufgabenstellung "entdeckt". Die Definition der Objekte wurde (auch) deshalb in keiner eingeführten Objektbeschreibungssprache durchgeführt. Sie leitet sich vielmehr aus den Anforderungen an die Ausdrucksfähigkeit einer derartigen Beschreibung ab und ist bewußt idealtypisch, d.h. es wird keine Rücksicht auf eine eventuelle Implementierbarkeit genommen.

Es erscheint berechtigt, zu fragen, inwieweit das im folgenden dargestellte Modell wirklich dem Paradigma objektorientierter Systeme genügt, oder ob es nur des besseren Images wegen "objektorientiert" getauft wurde. Hier stellt sich jedoch das Problem, daß in der Literatur der Begriff "objektorientiert" nicht immer ganz einheitlich verwendet wird[7]. Erschwerend kommt hinzu, daß es für den Autor nicht nachzuvollziehen war, von wem und in welchem Zusammenhang der Begriff "objektorientiert" geprägt wurde. Da aufgrund der hier angedeuteten Begriffsverwirrung eine Überprüfung des eigenen Ansatzes in bezug auf die Erfüllung der Kriterien für "objektorientiert" mangels einer sauberen, allgemeinverbindlichen Definition leider unmöglich ist, wird "objektorientiert" in Anlehnung an Kempel/Pfander[8], Kreutzer[9] und Wegner[10] folgendermaßen definiert:

Objektorientierung = gekapselte Objekte + Klassen + Vererbungsmechanismen

Der gewählte Ansatz von Zeitreihenobjekten wird als objektorientiert betrachtet, weil er die folgenden Eigenschaften besitzt:

---

[3] vgl. hiersu [Stau 85]
[4] das war früher der Kartenstapel mit den Kommandos
[5] das war früher der Kartenstapel mit den Daten
[6] vgl. hiersu [Gale 85]
[7] vgl. in diesem Zusammenhang Stoyans Vergleich swischen den Charakteristiken objektorientierter Programmiersprachen nach den Kriterien von Wegner [Wegn 87] und eigenen Kriterien in [Stoy 91, S. 192ff.].
[8] vgl. [Kemp 90, S. 12]
[9] vgl. hiersu [Kreu 90, S. 213]
[10] vgl. [Wegn 87] und [Wegn 89]

- Realisierung eines Klassen[11]/Instanzen-Konzepts.

- Kapselung: Zeitreihen bilden zusammen mit allen zu einer Zeitreihe gehörigen Informationen[12] eine Einheit, die in einem Objekt gekapselt ist[13]. Die einzelnen Objekte können nur mit Operationen bearbeitet werden, die in dem Objekt selbst definiert sind.

- Attribute (bzw. Sloteinträge) sind keine untrennbaren Einheiten. Dadurch ergibt sich definitionsgemäß ein NF^2-Modell[14].

- Vererbung: Es existiert eine Vererbung auf Klassenebene und ein (im Vergleich mit dem originären objektorientierten Ansatz) stark modifiziertes Konzept zur Vererbung von Sloteinträgen auf Instanzebene.

Ein rudimentäres Nachrichtenkonzept[15] ist, z.B. zur Kommunikation mit der Außenwelt, ebenfalls vorhanden, wird im folgenden aber nicht weiter dargestellt.

4 Der Aufbau von Zeitreihenobjekten

Im folgenden wird zwischen Klassen und Instanzen von Zeitreihenobjekten unterschieden. Ist von einem Zeitreihenobjekt die Rede, so ist die Instanz gemeint. Klassen werden als ZRO-Klassen bezeichnet. Eine Instanzierung ist von solchen ZRO-Klassen möglich, die *OPERATION create_instance()* besitzen. Dabei wird eine Instanz mit allen in der Objektdefinition definierten Slots, allen ererbten Slots[16] und allen Subobjekten[17] erzeugt. Andere ZRO-Klassen sind entweder Basistypen, die an andere instanzierbare ZRO-Klassen vererbt werden oder Teilobjekte von instanziierbaren ZRO-Klassen, die bei einer Instanzierung ihre Teilobjekte mitgenerieren. Die folgende Definition von Zeitreihenobjekten ist idealtypisch. Es wird keine Rücksicht auf die Ausdrucksfähigkeit von gängigen Implementierungs- und/oder Spezifikationssprachen[18] genommen.

Die Modellierung erfolgt auf der Grundlage eines hybriden Ansatzes mit Elementen aus frameorientierten—objektorientierten Ansätzen[19] und deklarativ-regelorientierten Ansätzen[20]. Jede Objektbeschreibung besteht aus einem OBJ_Header und der Slotliste. Der OBJ_Header besteht aus dem Schlüsselwort *"OBJECT"* und dem Objektnamen in Form eines Strings. Eine Slotliste ist folgendermaßen aufgebaut:

slot
  : slottyp, slotname, slotbeschreibung
  | slot, slot

slotname ist ein innerhalb des Objekts eindeutiger Bezeichner in String-Konventionen[21]. Slots werden über ihren Slotnamen angesprochen. *slottyp* ist genau ein Bezeichner aus einer definierten Menge möglicher Bezeichner für Slottypen. In jedem Objekt muß genau ein Slot des *slottyps FATHER_OBJ* vorhanden sein. Alle anderen Slottypen können beliebig oft auftreten. Die Syntax der *slotbeschreibung* steht in Abhängigkeit vom jeweiligen Slotnamen. In Abhängigkeit vom *slotnamen* hat die *slotbeschreibung* folgende Funktion:

---

[11]im folgenden wird der Begriff Klasse verwendet, wenn es sich um einen leeren Frame handelt, der Begriff Typ bleibt für Datentypen reserviert

[12]d.h. Attributen und Methoden

[13]vgl. hierzu die Betrachtung von Objekten als Datenkapseln in [Flei 91, S. 26 (1-6)]

[14]zur Definition von NF^2-Modellen s. z.B. [Pare 89, S. 177ff.]

[15]vgl. hierzu als kurze Einführung in ein derartiges Konzept [Rich 89, S. 139ff.]

[16]da es sich hierbei um eine Instanzierung von einer Klassendefinition handelt, sind auch diese slots nach der Erzeugung der Instanz zunächst leer

[17]um ein Sub-Objekt als Instanz erzeugen zu können, ist in der Klassendefinition des Subobjekts keine *OPERATION create_instance()* erforderlich

[18]einen Überblick über derartige Sprachen bieten Stoyan ([Stoy 88], [Stoy 91]) und Hawley ([Hawl 87])

[19]Verwendung eines Klassen-Instanzen-Konzepts, einer Modelldefinition mit Klassen, von Slots und von Demons

[20]zur Definition der Berechnungsvorschrift von berechneten Zeitreihenobjekten und von Demons

[21]vgl. hierzu die Definition von Strings in Programmiersprachen

slottyp	*slotbeschreibung*

ARGUMENT   Argument (String, Integer oder Real) in 1. Normalform oder eine Menge derartiger Argumente

L_ARGUMENT   Wohlgeformter Ausdruck einer formalen Sprache – z.B. der Sprache zur Beschreibung von Zeitreihenobjekten oder der Sprache zur Beschreibung von Demons.

V_ARGUMENT   Definition eines Arguments in 1. Normalform, dessen Inhalt dynamisch durch eine Funktion erzeugt wird. Die Ausprägung folgt dabei dem Schema:
datentyp "←" *funktion*

P_OBJ   Definition eines Teilobjekts, das bei einer Instanzierung miterzeugt wird. Als Ausprägungen sind die Namen von Objektklassen zugelassen.

FATHER_OBJ   Definition Objektklasse, deren Slots geerbt werden sollen. Als Ausprägungen sind die Namen von Objektklassen zugelassen.

CONSTRAINT   Formulierung einer semantischen Integritätsbedingung über die Ausprägungen der *Slotbeschreibungen* des jeweiligen Objekts. Sie enthält eine prädikatenlogische Formel zur Überprüfung der semantischen Integrität von Objekten dieser Objektklasse, die bei allen Kombinationen zulässiger Ausprägungen aller Variablen stets den Wert *true* zu haben hat.

OPERATION   Definition einer zulässigen Operation auf den Ausprägungen der *slotbeschreibung* eines Objekts. Die Ausprägung enthält einen Funktionenamen, ggf. mit Parameter(n). Operationen können auch durch eine Bedingung konditioniert sein. Dabei bedeutet:
$B \Rightarrow op\,(V) \;:\Leftrightarrow\; op$ kann auf V nur ausgeführt werden, wenn die Bedingung B erfüllt ist.

Zur Symbolik in den Slotbeschreibungen:

Im folgenden werden nur solche Sprachkonstrukte erklärt, deren Semantik nicht selbstverständlich ist.

a) Sprachkonstrukte zur Definition von *ARGUMENT-Slotbeschreibungen*:

$< zro - klasse >$ Der Name einer ZRO-Klasse[22]

$\{el_1, \ldots, el_n\}$ Auswahl: ein Element aus der definierten Menge von Elementen gleichen Datentyps

SET OF $<zro\text{-}klasse>$ Eine Instanz oder mehrere Instanzen der *zro-klasse*

SET OF $\{el_1, \ldots, el_n\}$ Ein Element oder mehrere Elemente der definierten Menge von Elementen gleichen Datentyps.

ARRAY OF $<datentyp>$ Eine Reihung aus Elementen von *datentyp*

b) Sprachkonstrukte zur Definition von *V_ARGUMENT-Slotbeschreibungen*:

$< datentyp > \leftarrow func()$ Die Funktion *func()* errechnet einen Sloteintrag vom Typ *datentyp*. Die Ausprägung des Slotinhalts errechnet sich dabei durch die Funktion *func()*

c) Sprachelemente zur Konstruktion von *CONSTRAINT-Slotbeschreibungen*:

<zro> INSTANCE_OF <zro-klasse>	Logischer Ausdruck: liefert den Wahrheitswert true, wenn *<zro>* eine Instanz von $<zro - klasse>$ ist
< date > AFTER < date >	Logischer Ausdruck: liefert den Wahrheitswert true, wenn das erste Zeitreihenobjekt vom Typ $< date >$ das neuere ist
$\Rightarrow$	Bezeichnet eine Implikation
XOR	Logischer Junktor zur Darstellung des exklusiven OR
<slotname> ⋈ *<zro-klasse>*, *<datentyp>*	Dieses Konstrukt ist anwendbar, wenn im Slot *<slotname>* verschiedene *<zro-klasse>*-en und/oder $< datentyp >$-en als Einträge zulässig sind. Der logische Ausdruck nimmt den Wahrheitswert *true* an, wenn die aktuelle Ausprägung von $< slotname >$ vom Typ $< zro - klasse >$ oder $< datentyp >$ ist

5 Elementare Zeitreihenobjekte

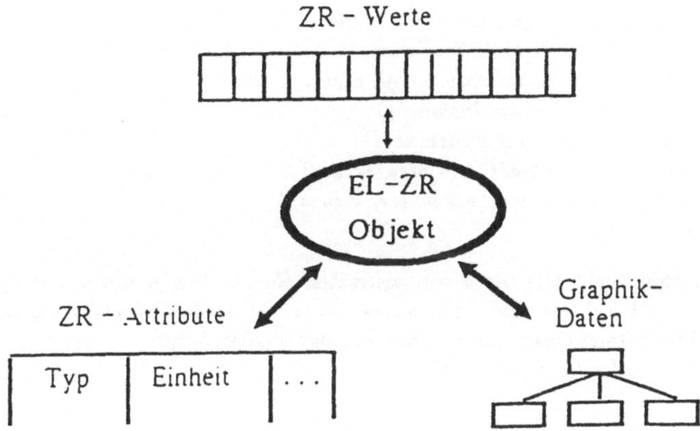

Abb. 2.: Aufbau eines elementaren Zeitreihenobjekts

Zeitreihenobjekte gliedern sich in elementare und höhere Zeitreihenobjekte. Elementare Zeitreihenobjekte wurden zur Repräsentation von Basiswerten, die von außen eingespeist werden, konzipiert. Die Klassenbeschreibung zur Definition von elementaren Zeitreihenobjekten besitzt, wie in Abb. 2. dargestellt, eine innere Struktur mit identifizierenden Namen und einer Zeitreihe mit Zusatzangaben (Einheit, Periodizität etc.). Bei der Konstruktion eines konkreten Modells wird dabei jeder von außen in das System eingeführten Zeitreihe einer betriebswirtschaftlichen Größe ein elementares Zeitreihenobjekt zugeordnet.

Das Objekt *zeitreihen_object* ist die gemeinsame Grundlage für elementare und höhere ZRO-Klassen. Seine Slots werden an beide vererbt. Die Ausprägung im Slot *name* ist der modellweit eindeutige Identifikator für das Zeitreihenobjekt. *level* ist eine natürliche Zahl. Für elementare Zeitreihenobjekte ist *level* stets 0[23]. *graphic_data* beinhaltet ein Teilobjekt. *update* merkt sich das Datum des letzten Updates der *values* bei

---

[23]vgl. hiersu den *CONSTRAINT* in der Definition von *el_zeitreihen_object*

jedem schreibenden Zugriff auf das Objekt mit der Funktion *systemdate*. Die Operationen *op1 und op2* definieren lesbare und beschreibbare Bereiche. *read()/write()*-Operationen auf nachgeordnete Objekte sind so definiert, daß diese Operationen auf allen Slots mit einer *ARGUMENT*-Definition möglich sind, ohne daß bei den nachgeordneten Objekten eine explizite *OPERATION*-Definition erforderlich ist.

```
OBJECT all zr objects:
      FATHER OBJ:       OBJECT all objects


OBJECT zeitreihen object:
      FATHER OBJ:                  OBJECT all zr objects
      ARGUMENT      name           STRING
      ARGUMENT      level          INTEGER
      P OBJ         graphic data   OBJECT graphik-daten
      P OBJ         update         OBJECT date ← systemdate()
      OPERATION:    op1            read({name, level, graphic data})
      OPERATION:    op2            write({name, graphic data})


OBJECT el zeitreihen object:
      FATHER OBJ:                  OBJECT zeitreihen object
      P OBJ         attributes     OBJECT zr attribute
      P OBJ         values         OBJECT zr werte
      CONSTRAINT:   c1             el zeitreihen object.level == 0
      OPERATION:    o1             create instance()
      OPERATION:    o2             remove instance()
      OPERATION:    o3             read({attributes, values})
      OPERATION:    o4             write({attributes, values})
```

Das Objekt *el zeitreihen object* erbt alle Slots von *zeitreihen object*. Des weiteren hat es die im folgenden noch erläuterten Teilattribute *attributes* und *values*. *el zeireihen object* enthält die *OPERATION o1* "create instance()", da eine Instanz dieser ZRO-Klasse erzeugt werden kann[24]. Weitere Operationen erlauben das Lesen und Schreiben auf *attributes* und *values*.

```
OBJECT zr attribute:
      FATHER OBJ:                  OBJECT all zr objects
      ARGUMENT      type:          {value, relation, index}
      ARGUMENT      d unit:        OBJECT date
      P OBJ         index date:    OBJECT date
      CONSTRAINT:   c1             d unit == NULL XOR index date == NULL
      CONSTRAINT:   c2             type == index ⇒ d unit == NULL
      CONSTRAINT:   c3             type <> index ⇒ str unit == NULL
```

Das Objekt *zr_attribute* enthält den Typ der Zeitreihe (d.h Werte, Index oder Verhältnis) und die Einheit der Zeitreihe. Ist die Zeitreihe vom Typ *index*, so hat diese keine Einheit. In diesem – und nur diesem – Fall wird unter *index_date* das Datum, auf das sich der Index bezieht, festgelegt (vgl. hierzu die *CONSTRAINTs* c1, c2, c3).

Das Objekt *zr_werte* beinhaltet die Werte des Zeitreihenobjekts als *ARRAY* von Zahlen. Bei Nichtvorliegen

---

[24]Im Gegensatz dazu besitzt beispielsweise das Objekt *zeitreihen_object* keine Operation *create_instance()*, da es nicht sinnvoll ist, Objekte dieser Klasse zu erzeugen. Es können jedoch Instanzen von Objekten erzeugt werden, deren Vater-Klasse *zeitreihen_object* ist. Ebenso besitzt das Objekt *zr_werte* keine Operation *create_instance()*, da keine eigenständigen Objekte dieser Klasse erzeugt werden können. Ein Objekt *zr_werte* wird z.B. dann erzeugt, wenn ein Objekt *el_zeitreihen_object* erzeugt wird, als dessen Teilobjekt *zr_werte* definiert ist.

des Wertes ist auch der *NULL*-Wert zugelassen. Weiterhin enthält das Objekt *zr_werte* das erste und das letzte Datum, für das ein Wert existiert. Das *COSTRAINT* $c1$ überprüft, ob die notwendige Anzahl von Werten zwischen dem ersten und dem letzten Datum mit der tatsächlich vorhandenen Anzahl an Werten übereinstimmt.

```
OBJECT zr_werte:
    FATHER_OBJ:                 OBJECT all_zr_objects
    ARGUMENT     values_list:   ARRAY OF {INTEGER,REAL,NULL}
    P_OBJ        first_date:    OBJECT per_date
    P_OBJ        last_date:     OBJECT per_date
    CONSTRAINT:  c1             distance(first_date, last_date) == number_of(values)
```

Das Objekt *per_date* dient (einschl. seiner von *date* geerbten Slots) zur Darstellung von Datumsangaben. Eine Datumsangabe besteht aus 1-3 Stellen und kann nur in Abhängigkeit von der Periodizität semantisch interpretiert werden. Hat diese die Ausprägung *year*, so ist sie einstellig. Die andereren Stellen sind in diesem Fall mit NULL-Werten zu belegen[25] . Bei den Periodizitäten *halfyear*, *quarteryear* und *month* sind zwei Stellen mit Werten belegt. Bei der Periodizität *day* sind alle Stellen mit Werten belegt. Je nach Periodizität hat der Wert des Attributs *n_idf* somit verschiedene Grundmengen als Wertebereiche. Diese werden in den *CONSTRAINT*s $c1$, $c2$, $c3$ definiert. Die *CONSTRAINT*s $c4$, $c5$, $c6$, $c7$, $c8$ definieren den Wertebereich von *day* in Abhängigkeit von *n_idf* (als Feld für den Monatswert) und *year*[26]. Die *CONSTRAINT*s von per_date sind somit Integritätsbedingungen für wohlgeformte Datumsangaben.

```
OBJECT date:
    FATHER_OBJ:             OBJECT all_zr_objects
    ARGUMENT    year:       1500 .. 2200
    ARGUMENT    n_idf:      {1 ... 12, NULL}
    ARGUMENT    day:        {1 ... 31, NULL}
```

---

[25] siehe erstes *CONSTRAINT* von *per_date*
[26] Anzahl der Tage einschließlich Berücksichtung der Schaltjahrprobleme

```
OBJECT per_date:
    FATHER_OBJ:              OBJECT date
    ARGUMENT      period:    {year,quarteryear,halfyear,month,day}
    CONSTRAINT:   c1         per_date.period == year ⇒
                                 per_date.n_idf == NULL ∧
                                 per_date.day == NULL
    CONSTRAINT:   c2         per_date.period == quarteryear ⇒
                                 per_date.n_idf == {1,2,3,4} ∧
                                 per_date.day == NULL
    CONSTRAINT:   c3         per_date.period == halfyear ⇒
                                 per_date.n_idf == {1,2} ∧
                                 per_date.day == NULL
    CONSTRAINT:   c4         per_date.period == month ⇒
                                 per_date.n_idf == {1,2, ..,12} ∧
                                 per_date.day == NULL
    CONSTRAINT:   c5         per_date.period == day ⇒
                                 per_date.n_idf == {1,2, ..,12} ∧
                                 per_date.day == {1,2, .. ,31}
    CONSTRAINT:   c6         per_date.period == day ∧
                             per_date.n_idf == {4,6,9,11} ⇒
                                 per_date.day == {1,2, .. ,30}
    CONSTRAINT:   c7         per_date.period == day ∧
                             per_date.n_idf == {2} ⇒
                                 per_date.day == {1,2, .. ,29}
    CONSTRAINT:   c8         per_date.period == day ∧
                             per_date.n_idf == {2} ∧
                             ( per_date.year mod 1000 <> 0 ∧
                               ( per_date.year mod 4 <> 0 ∨
                                   per_date.year mod 100 == 0
                             ) )⇒ per_date.day == {1,2, .. ,28}
```

Im OBJECT *graphik_daten* können die Koordinatenwerte zur graphischen Visualisierung von Systemen aus Zeitreihenobjekten abgelegt werden. Es wäre auch denkbar, das Objekt durch zusätzliche Slots (wie z.B. "Hintergrundfarbe") über die Koordinatenangaben hinaus zu erweitern.

```
OBJECT graphik_daten
    FATHER_OBJ:              OBJECT all_zr_objects
    ARGUMENT      x         INTEGER
    ARGUMENT      y         INTEGER
```

6 Höhere Zeitreihenobjekte

Inhaltliche Aufgabe des Konzepts höherer Zeitreihenobjekte ist die Verdichtung der Vielzahl von in elementaren Zeitreihenobjekten repräsentierten Basisdaten auf Maßzahlen.

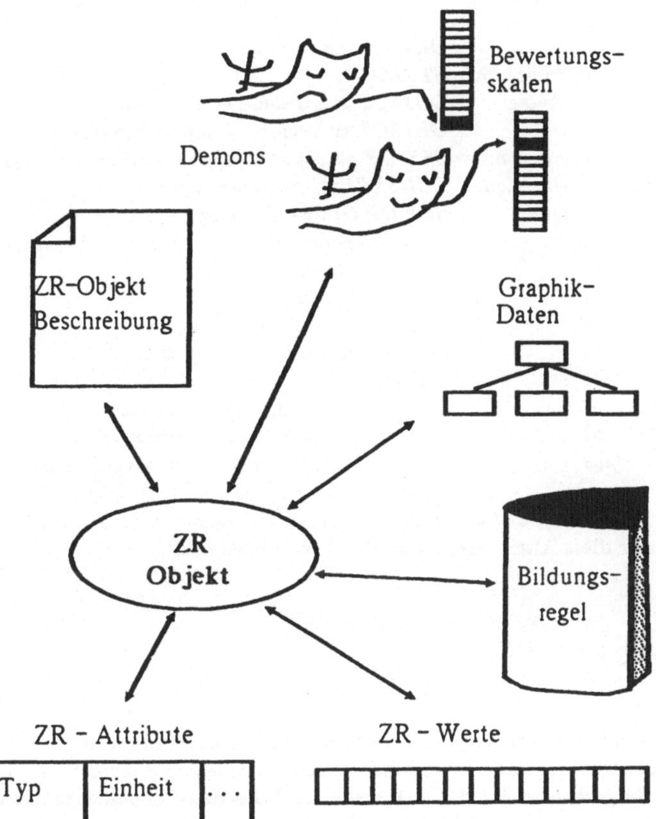

Abb. 3.: Aufbau eines höheren Zeitreihenobjekts

Der in Abb. 3 veranschaulichte Aufbau eines höheren Zeitreihenobjekts ist wie folgt definiert: *hzr* ist der Name der ZRO-Klasse "höheres Zeitreihenobject". *zr_obj_beschr* bietet die Möglichkeit der Generierung einer natürlichsprachlichen Beschreibung der dem Zeitreihenobjekt zugrunde liegenden Konstruktionsvorschrift. *attributes* und *values* werden nicht – wie bei elementaren Zeitreihenobjekten – mit einer write-Operation gefüllt, sondern mit einer Funktion dynamisch errechnet.

Der Slot *construction* beinhaltet ein Objekt mit einer Vorschrift zur Berechnung der Werte und der Attribute eines Zeitreihenobjekts. Wird diese Regel mit den Funktionen *com_attr()* bzw. *comp_val()* aktiviert, so kann der Inhalt der Subobjekte *zr_attributes* bzw. *zr_values* und damit der Sloteintrag in die Slots *hzr.attributes* bzw. hzr.values berechnet werden. Analog dazu kann mit der Funktion *obj_constr()* die Menge der Zeitreihenobjekte, von denen die Werte und Attribute des (aktuellen) Zeitreihenobjekts funktionell abhängen, bestimmt werden.

Das *CONSTRAINT c1* prüft, ob der Level des *hzr*'s höher ist als der Level aller Zeitreihenobjekte, aus denen es errechnet wird. Operationen ermöglichen die Erzeugung einer Instanz der *hzr*-Klasse und können diese wieder löschen. Die Konstruktionsvorschrift *construction* und ihre natürlichsprachliche Beschreibung *zr_obj_beschr* kann gelesen und neu beschrieben werden. Demons können neu angelegt werden (*o5*) und vorhandene Demons gelesen, aktualisiert und gelöscht werden (*o6* bis *o8*).

```
OBJECT hzr:
     FATHER_OBJ:                    OBJECT zeitreihen_object
     ARGUMENT        zr_obj_beschr: STRING
     P_OBJ           attributes:    OBJECT zr_attribute ← comp_attr(hzr.construction)
     P_OBJ           values:        OBJECT zr_werte ← comp_val(hzr.construction)
     V_ARGUMENT      depends_on:    SET OF all_object ← obj_constr(hzr.bildungsobject)
     L_ARGUMENT      construction:  CONSTRUCT_OF descr_lan
     P_OBJ           demons:        SET OF OBJECT demon
     CONSTRAINT:     c1             ∀x (x ∈ hzr.depends_on ⇒ x.level < hzr.level)
     OPERATION:      o1             create_instance()
     OPERATION:      o2             remove_instance()
     OPERATION:      o3             read(zr_obj_beschr, construction )
     OPERATION:      o4             write(zr_obj_beschr, construction )
     OPERATION       o5             write(demon)
     OPERATION       o6             (demon ∈ hzr.demons) ⇒ read(demon)
     OPERATION       o7             (demon ∈ hzr.demons) ⇒ update(demon)
     OPERATION       o8             (demon ∈ hzr.demons) ⇒ remove(demon)
```

Das Object *all_object* dient dazu, daß an Stellen, an denen ein elementares Zeitreihenobjekt oder ein *hzr* stehen kann, nicht immer diese Alternative ausgeschrieben werden muß:

```
OBJECT all_object:
     FATHER_OBJ:     f1     OBJECT el_zeitreihen_object
     FATHER OBJ:     f2     OBJECT hzr
     CONSTRAINT:     c1     f1 == NULL   XOR   f2 == NULL
```

Aufgabe des Slots *hzr.construction.bildungsregel* eines höheren Zeitreihenojekts ist die Definition des Berechnungsalgorithmus für den Sloteintrag *hzr.values* und den Slot-Eintrag *zr_attributes*[27]. Bei der Definition bzw. der Auswahl eines hierfür geeigneten Formalismus war es zunächst naheliegend, auch hier einen objektorientierten Ansatz in Erwägung zu ziehen. Allerdings sollte das berühmt-berüchtigte Beispiel der Realisierung von 1 + 1 in Smalltalk[28] zur Vorsicht mahnen und den Designer veranlassen, objektorientierte Ansätze nur in für diesen Formalismus geeigneten Aufgabenstellungen einzusetzen. Da im vorliegenden Fall arithmetische Verknüpfungen und statistische Umformungen von Zeitreihenobjekten unterstützt werden sollen und dabei ein Mechanismus angeboten werden sollte, mehrere Verfahren hintereinander zu schalten, um auf die Speicherung von Zwischenergebnissen – wie etwa von temporären Hilfs-Zeitreihenobjekten – verzichten zu können, erscheint ein mehr funktionsorientierter Ansatz als Grundlage zur Definition der Beschreibungssprache naheliegender[29].

Aus diesem Grund besitzt der Slot *bildungsregel* den Eintrag *CONSTRUCT OF descr_lan*, der für Instanzen der Klasse *hzr.construction* einen wohlgeformten Ausdruck der Beschreibungssprache *descr_lan* erfordert. Diese ist modellierungstechnisch auf der gleichen Ebene wie die Regelsprachen von Expertensystemen angesiedelt.

---

[27] die selbst widerum eine komplexe Struktur haben
[28] vgl. hierzu [Smal 88,S. 49]
[29] vgl. hierzu auch andere Ansätze mit hybriden Wissensrepräsentationen wie z.B. [Chri 89]

Die Regelsprache für die Bildungsregel[30] eröffnet dem modellierenden Benutzer die Möglichkeit, höhere Zeitreihenobjekte einschl. der Berechnungsvorschrift für Werte und Attribute zu definieren. Unbenommen vom funktionalen Ansatz der Beschreibungssprache ist es vom Modellansatz her prinzipiell möglich, statistische[31] und arithmetische Operationen als Objekte zu definieren, deren Berechnungsverfahren von der Beschreibungssprache aus aufgerufen werden können.

Die Beschreibungssprache ermöglicht somit eine Art *Vererbung* von Werten und Attributen der Quell-Zeitreihenobjekte auf das Zeitreihenobjekt, in dessen Slot sie sich befindet. Im Gegensatz zur normalen Vererbung werden die Ausprägungen in den Slots *values* und *attributes* nicht (nur) kopiert, sondern aufgrund der in der Beschreibungssprache codifizierten Vorschriften modifiziert.

Über sein Vater-Objekt erbt eine höhere ZRO-Klasse (durch Vererbung auf Klassenebene) auch den *values*-slot. Dieser ist in der ZRO-Klasse *hzr* eigentlich redundant, da mit der Bildungsregel ein Algorithmus zur Berechnung existiert. Denkt man an eine Implementierung des dargestellten Modells, so müßten bei häufigen Zugriffen auf die *values*[32] eines höheren Zeitreihenobjekts diese bei jeder Anfrage, ggf. über Kaskaden von höheren Zeitreihenobjekten hinweg, stets neu berechnet werden, was eine permanente Residenz der Werte in höheren Zeitreihenobjekten - auch im Modellentwurf - ratsam erscheinen läßt.

7 Die Datenüberwachung durch Demons

Operationelle Mittel für die Datenbewertung sind die Demons. Diese untersuchen Zeitreihenwerte[33] auf vorgegebene Muster hin und erstellen, falls diese Muster vorliegen, Meldungen. Nach der Klassifikation von [Gene 89] handelt es sich bei den Demons um tropistische Agenten. Muster innerhalb einer Zeitreihe können beispielsweise periodische Schwankungen, Trends oder das Über- oder Unterschreiten vorgegebener Werte sein.

Bedingt durch den Sloteintrag *SET of demon* des slot *demon* der ZRO-Klasse *hzr* kann jedes höhere Zeitreihenobjekt keinen, einen odere mehrere Demons besitzen.

```
OBJECT demon:
    FATHER_OBJ:                     OBJECT all_zr_objects
    L_CONSTRAINT    trigger:        CONSTRUCT OF demon_lan
    L_CONSTRAINT    action:         CONSTRUCT OF demon_lan
    OPERATION:      op              trigger()  ⇒  action()
```

Jeder Demon besteht aus einem System von Produktionsregeln[34]. *trigger* und *action* sind Konstrukte in der Demon-Beschreibungssprache, die durch eine *OPERATION* aktiviert werden können. *trigger* liefert einen Wahrheitswert zurück. Im Gegensatz zu manchen Produktionsregeldefinitionen ist es mit derartigen Aktionen nicht möglich, die Regeln des Regelsystems selbst zu verändern. Ebenfalls ist es nicht möglich, damit die Definition höherer Zeitreihenobjekte zu verändern. Gilt

$$trigger() \ == \ true,$$

so wird *action* ausgeführt und liefert selbst bei erfolgreicher Ausführung den Wahrheitswert true. *trigger* selbst ist im Prinzip eine prädikatenlogische Formel und wird in der Syntax der Beschreibungssprache für Demons formuliert. Aus dieser heraus können statistische Verfahren aufgerufen werden. Diese können eine Zeitreihe auf einen Wert oder einen Wahrheitswert abbilden. Im ersten Fall ist dann (innerhalb des Demons) noch eine Abbildung des Wertes auf einen Wahrheitswert notwendig. Bei den implementierten Verfahren wurde eine Auswahl von gut interpretierbaren, wenig Voraussetzungen benötigenden statistischen Verfahren getroffen, deren Anwendungsmöglichkeit gegeben schien. Dabei handelt es sich unter anderem um:

---

[30] eine detaillierte Bechreibung dieser findet sich in [Augs 90]

[31] wie in [Oldf 86] vorgeschlagen

[32] z.B. von Demons im Bewertungsprozeß

[33] d.h. dessen numerische Werte

[34] zur Begriffsdefinition s. z.B. [Wins 82,S. 201ff.]

- statistische Tests wie Run-Test und Tests auf Basis des einfachen linearen Modells,

- Verfahren, die Istwerte der Zeitreihen oder Maßzahlen, deren Wachstum etc., mit Sollwerten vergleichen.

Bei den Aktionen handelt es sich um Verfahren zur:

- Ausgabe von Zeitreihenwerten,

- Berechnung von Maßzahlen etc.,

- Ausgabe von Meldungen.

Letzteres entspricht damit dem "Versenden einer Meldung" in der objektorientierten Terminologie. Die Resultate von Aktionen können sich auch an das Betriebssystem des Rechners wenden. Sei *VORSTAND* eine Adresse des E-Mail-Systems, welches von der Objektwelt der Zeitreihenobjekte aus erreichbar ist, so kann an diese eine Meldung gesendet werden:

$$
\begin{array}{lll}
IF & \textit{"Vgl.\_Lagerkosten\_Vorjahr"} & > +20\% \\
AND & \textit{"Vgl.\_Lagerbewegungen\_Vorjahr"} & < +10\% \\
\hline
THEN & SEND\ MAIL\ TO\ VORSTAND &
\end{array}
$$

Die Meldungen können neben Texten auch statistische Informationen usw. umfassen, die vom einem Demon berechnet werden. Zur Beschreibung der Demons wurde eine formale Sprache entwickelt, die aber zu umfangreich ist, um sie im Rahmen dieses Artikels vorzustellen.

Ein Beispiel für einen einfachen Demon ist die Überwachung einer Kostenstelle in Relation zum Vorjahreswert. Wird überdurchschnittliches Wachstum oder überdurchschnittliche Abnahme der Kostengrößen festgestellt, so löst dies eine Demonmeldung aus. Im allgemeinsten Fall besagt die Demonmeldung, daß hier eine auffällige Entwicklung eingetreten ist, die von zuständiger Stelle näher betrachtet werden sollte.

8 Implementierung

Auf Grundlage des vorgestellten Modellansatzes wurde ein Prototyp in C und Prolog implementiert[35]. Durch die Beschränkung der Ausdrucksfähigkeit der verwendeten Implementierungssprachen kann diese Implementierung jedoch nur eine Annäherung an den vorgestellten Modellansatz darstellen.

Literaturverzeichnis

[Augs 90]   Augsburger W., Rieder H., Schwab J., 1990
Endbenutzerorientierte Informationsgewinnung aus numerischen Daten am Beispiel von Unternehmenskennzahlen; in: Herget J., Kuhlen R.; Pragmatische Aspekte beim Entwurf und Betrieb von Informationssystemen; Proc. 1. Int. Symp. für Informationswissenschaft; Konstanz

[Chri 89]   Christaller T., di Primo F., Voss A., 1989
Die KI-Werkbank Babylon; Bonn

[Flei 91]   Fleischer P., Behdjati A., Bagdon S., Schlüter P., 1991
Der objektorientierte Software-Entwicklungsprozeß und seine Unterstützung durch Werkzeuge; in: Softwaretechnik-Trends, 11 (1991) 1, S. 24-53

---

[35] für Details siehe [Augs 90]

[Gale 85]   Gale W., 1985
               Artificial Intelligence Research in Statistis; in: The AI Magazine 4 (1985), S. 72-75

[Gene 89]   Genesereth M. R., Nilson N. J., 1989
               Logische Grundlagen der Künstlichen Intelligenz; Braunschweig / Wiesbaden

[Hawl 87]   Hawley R., 1987
               Artificial Intelligence Programming Environments; Chichester

[Henn 90]   Hennerkes, W. A., 1990
               MAXDATA; Berlin u.a.

[Kemp 89]   Kempel H.-J., Pfander G., 1990
               Praxis der objektorientierten Programmierung; München, Wien

[Kreu 90]   Kreutzer W., 1990
               Grundkonzepte und Werkzeuge objektorientierter Systementwicklung - Stand der Forschung
               und Anwendung; in: Wirtschaftsinformatik 32 (1990) 3, S. 211-227

[Oldf 86]   Oldford R., Waterloo, Peters S, 1986
               Object-Oriented Data Representations for Statistical Data Analysis; in: Compstat 1986, S.
               301-306, Heidelberg

[Pare 89]   Paredaens J., De Bra P., Gyssens M., Van Gucht D.; 1989
               The Structure of the Relational Database Model; Berlin et. al.

[Rich 89]   Richter M. M., 1989
               Prinzipien der Künstlichen Intelligenz; Stuttgart

[Smal 88]   Smalltalk; 1988
               Smalltalk/V286, Object-Oriented Programming System (OOPS); Los Angeles

[SPSS 88]   SPSS, 1988
               SPSS-X User's Guide, 3rd edition; Chicago

[Stau 85]   Staud Josef, 1985
               Online Retrieval in Numeric Data Bases; in: IATUL Proceedings 17; pp. 164-228

[Stoy 88]   Stoyan H., 1988
               Programmiermethoden der Künstlichen Intelligenz; Band 1; Berlin u.a.

[Stoy 91]   Stoyan H., 1991
               Programmiermethoden der Künstlichen Intelligenz; Band 2; Berlin u.a.

[Wegn 87]   Wegner P., 1987
               Dimensions of Object-Based Language Design; in: OOPSL 1987 Proceedings, New York ACM
               Sigplan Notices 22 (Octr. 1987), pp. 168-182

[Wegn 89]   Wegner P., 1989
               Learning the Language; in: BYTE March 1989, pp. 245-253

[Wins 82]   Winston, P. H., 1984
               Artificial Intelligence; Addison-Wesley Deutschland, Reading Mass.

Forensisches Informationssystem Handschriften

- Ein Beispiel für ein klassifizierendes Rechercheverfahren -

M. Münzenberger
Kriminalistisches Institut
Bundeskriminalamt, Wiesbaden

Abriß

Das forensische Informationssystem Handschriften, Kurzbezeichnung FISH, wurde für den Handschriften-Erkennungsdienst des Bundeskriminalamtes entwickelt. Ziel des Projektes war es, die Arbeitsabläufe im Handschriften-Erkennungsdienst zu vereinheitlichen und zu rationalisieren. Insbesondere sollte die Klassifizierung von Handschriften objektiviert und eine effektive Recherche ermöglicht werden. Hierzu wurden Verfahren der Mustererkennung und des Information Retrieval eingesetzt.

1. Einleitung

Neben der traditionellen Verarbeitung von strukturierten, alphanumerischer Daten in Datenbanksystemen gewinnt die Einbeziehung von anderen Medien, wie zum Beispiel von Bildern, immer mehr Eingang in die Informationsverarbeitung. Die Speicherung und die Verarbeitung, hier insbesondere das Wiederauffinden bestimmter Informationen bedarf anderer Verarbeitungstechniken, und zwar dann, wenn zusätzlich vage und unvollständige Daten zu verwalten sind.

Im Bereich der Polizei existieren eine Reihe von Sammlungen, deren Führung unter Ausnutzung dieser Techniken rationalisiert und objektiviert werden kann. Stellvertretend für solche Anwendungen, wurde bereits 1977 im Bundeskriminalamt mit einem vom Bundesminister für Forschung und Technologie geförderten Grundlagenprojekt zur Objektivierung und Automatisierung des Handschriftenvergleichs begonnen. Ziel dieses Projektes war es, die prinzipiellen Möglichkeiten zur Gewinnung von Merkmalen aus Handschriftenbildern aufzuzeigen. Im Anschluß an diese Studie, wurde 1982 mit der Entwicklung des forensischen Informationssystem Handschriften, Kurzbezeichnung FISH, für den Handschriften-Erkennungsdienst des Bundeskriminalamts begonnen. Mit FISH soll dem Erkennungsdienst ein System zur Verfügung stehen, welches ihn bei allen Routinearbeiten unterstützt. Insbesondere ist hier aber die klassifizierende Recherche zu nennen, mit der eine Handschriftenprobe eines unbekannten Urhebers, die auch als fragliche Schreibleistung bezeichnet wird, anhand seiner Merkmale mit einer Handschriften-Sammlung automatisch verglichen werden kann.

Seit 1990 wird FISH zur Bearbeitung eines Teilbereich der Handschriften-Sammlung für den Wirkbetrieb eingesetzt; auch andere Länder sind an dem Einsatz von FISH interessiert.

2. Entwicklung von FISH

2.1 Vorgehen

Die Entwicklung des Systems erfolgte schrittweise. Funktionen, die den Anwender wesentlich unterstützen und die mit Standardtechniken realisiert werden konnten, wurden zuerst implementiert, um so die Investitionen für das System abzusichern. Aber auch die nicht zu unterschätzende Rückkopplung durch den Anwender und die oftmals notwendige Korrektur von einigen Verfahrensschritten konnte so möglichst frühzeitig erreicht werden.

Zuerst wurde dem Erkennungsdienst ein Verwaltungssystem zur Verfügung gestellt, in dem die für ihn typischen Objekte: Vorgang, Person, Zuordnung und Schriftmaterial in einem relationalen Datenbanksystem abgebildet wurden.

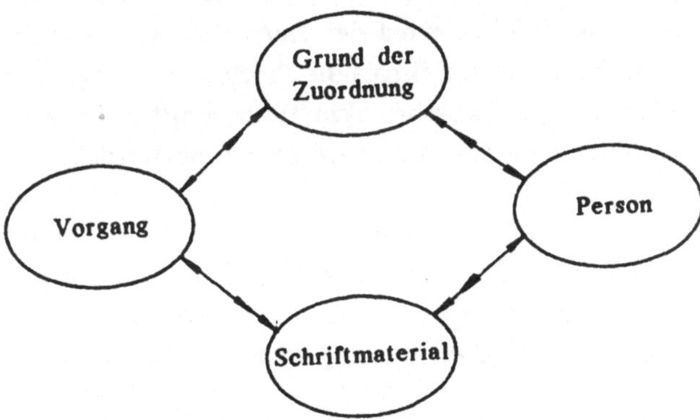

Bild 1: Objektstruktur
◄──────► 1: m – Beziehung

Die Objekte konnten damit erfaßt, geändert und gelöscht werden auch eine boolische Suche der Objekte war möglich. Welche Arbeitserleichterung bereits mit einem solchen System zu erreichen ist, läßt sich an den jährlich anfallenden ca. 50.000 Tatschriften abschätzen.

Erst in den folgenden Projektphasen wurden die innovativen Komponenten der Merkmalextraktion und der klassifizierenden Recherche entwickelt und in das System integriert.

2.2 Merkmalextraktion

Die Schreibleistung, die für diese Anwendung von besonderem Interesse ist, wird durch folgende vier Merkmalskategorien beschrieben:

- deskriptive,
- graphische,
- textbezogene,
- textinsensitive.

Der Typ der Merkmale ist bei den deskriptiven Merkmalen nicht numerisch, und bei den anderen Merkmalen numerisch. Die Erfassung dieser Merkmale erfolgt je nach Kategorie unterschiedlich. Es wurde jeweils das Verfahren gewählt, mit dem die Merkmale mit vertretbarem Aufwand am besten gewonnen werden können.

So werden die deskriptiven Merkmale, wie die Sprache, das Schriftsystem, die Schriftart und die Bindungsform der Schreibleistung, durch den Schriftprüfer ermittelt und eingegeben.

Die anderen Merkmalskategorien werden vom Schriftprüfer mit Rechnerunterstützung an einem Arbeitsplatzrechner gewonnen. Hierzu wird das Handschriftenbild eines Dokuments mit Hilfe eines Scanners digitalisiert und als Binärbild abgelegt. In diesem Bild markiert der Schriftprüfer einen homogenen, quadratischen Schriftausschnitt mit etwa 6,5 cm Seitenlänge, die Schreibleistung, aus dem dann die Merkmale gewonnen werden.

Zuvor ist oft ein Hintergrund, z.B. ein Formularvordruck, der nicht zu der Handschrift gehört, zu eliminieren. Auch hierbei erfolgt eine interaktive Rechnerunterstützung. Es können mit Verfahren der Bildverarbeitung horizontale bzw. vertikale Linien automatisch ausgeblendet oder es kann ein "elektronischer Radiergummi" benutzt werden.

Aus dem so aufbereiteten Bild der Schreibleistung können die textinsensitiven Merkmale mit statistischen Auswertungen gewonnen werden. Der statistische Ansatz zur Gewinnung von repräsentativen Merkmalen bedingt, daß die Schreibleistung eine genügend große Textmenge enthält. Man kann davon ausgehen, daß etwa drei Schriftzeilen (gemäß Bild 2) ausreichend sind. Zur Merkmalsgewinnung wurden zwei unterschiedliche Methoden implementiert.

Bei der einen Methode, die auf Steinke (1981) zurückgeht, wird die Schreibleistung als Textur angesehen, die sich aus zufällig wiederholenden primitiven Formelementen zusammensetzt. Für die Formelemente werden acht richtungsorientierte Linienketten gewählt. Dies sind in einem Binärbild ununterbrochene Ketten von schwarzen oder weißen Bildpunkten in einer bestimmten Richtung. Die Kettenlänge, das heißt die Anzahl der Bildpunkte gleicher Farbe, wird auch als Lauflänge bezeichnet. Bei dem betrachteten Verfahren werden die Lauflängen der Ketten in acht Richtungen, die gleichmäßig über 360 Grad verteilt sind, berechnet. Je nach der Farbe der berücksichtigten Bildpunkte, sprechen wir von der Weißkettenstatistik oder von der Schwarzkettenstatistik.

Um Schreibleistungen mit unterschiedlicher Textmenge vergleichen zu können, werden die Kettenstatistiken auf die Textmenge normiert. Zur Dimensionsreduktion werden die Kettenstatistiken durch ein orthogonales Polynomsystem dritten Grades angenähert und die Koeffizienten des Polynomsystems als Merkmale verwendet.

Bei dem zweiten Verfahren wird das Bild der Schreibleistung als Realisierung eines stationären Zufallsprozesses aufgefaßt. Die Autokorrelationsfunktion R ist dann nur durch die relativen Verschiebungen u bzw. v bestimmt.

$$R(u,v) = \sum_m \sum_n s(m,n)\, s(m+u,n+v)$$

Für die Anwendung ist die Autokorrelationsfunktion nur für Verschiebungen von Interesse, die die statistischen Bindungen benachbarter Bildpunkte innerhalb eines Buchstabens bestimmen. In diesem Bereich wird die Autokorrelationsfunktion an 32 Punkten bestimmt.

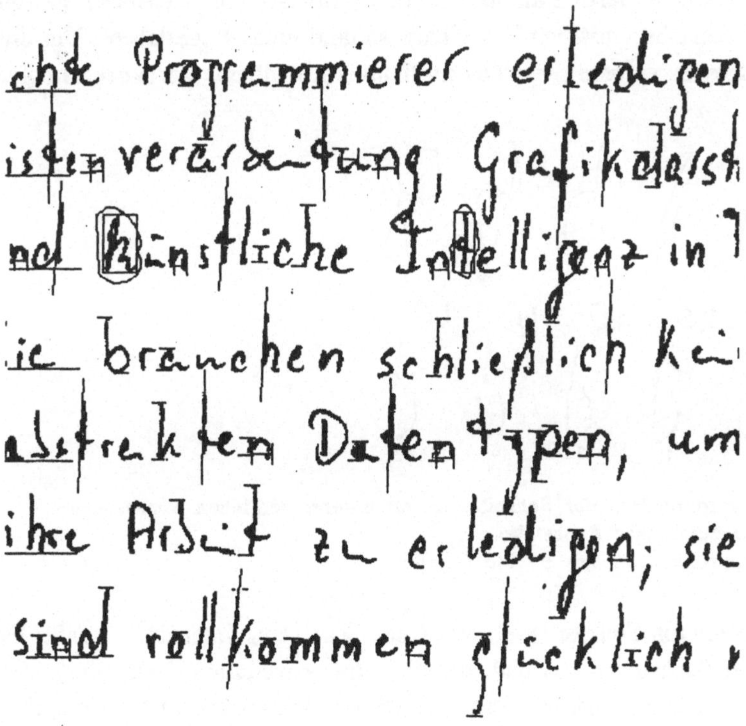

Bild 2: Beispiel einer Schreibleistung
- mit vermessenen graphischen Merkmalen (siehe Begrenzungslinien)
- mit isolierten Buchstaben
- mit linienverfolgten Buchstaben

Als nächstes vermißt der Schriftprüfer die graphischen Merkmale. Dies sind anschauliche Merkmale der Schrift, wie Höhe, Weite, Neigung, Schleifenform und Zeilenabstand. Sie werden interaktiv an verschiedenen, katalogisierten Buchstaben vermessen. Der Schriftprüfer gibt das zu vermessende Merkmal an (z.B. Höhe oder Neigung der Schrift) und markiert einen Meßpunkt im Schriftbild. Je nach Art des zu vermessenden Merkmals wird entweder die Messung vom System unmittelbar ausgeführt, oder das System fordert auf weitere Meßpunkte vorzugeben. Zum Abschluß ist die korrekte Durchführung der Messung durch den Schriftprüfer zu bestätigen. Um exemplartypische Schwankungen des Meßergebnisses gering zu halten, sind die graphischen Merkmale möglichst an verschiedenen Buchstaben zu erfassen, im weiteren wird dann nur der Mittelwert dieser Messungen verwendet.

Die textinsensitiven und die graphischen Merkmale setzen eine gewisse Textmenge voraus, um hieraus repräsentative Merkmale zu gewinnen. Oft steht jedoch dem Handschriften-Erkennungsdienst nur sehr wenig Text zur Verfügung, zum Beispiel bei dem Delikt "Scheckbetrug". Deshalb ist es notwendig, auch aus Einzelbuchstaben Merkmale zu gewinnen, und zum anderen erhofft man, durch weitere Merkmale insgesamt ein besseres Klassifikationsergebnis zu erreichen.

Textbezogene Merkmale werden an speziellen, katalogisierten Buchstaben gewonnen. Sie beschreiben den schreibertypischen Schriftzug anhand eines Buchstabens. Um die Merkmale des Schriftzuges zu erfassen, wurden zwei unterschiedliche Verfahren implementiert.

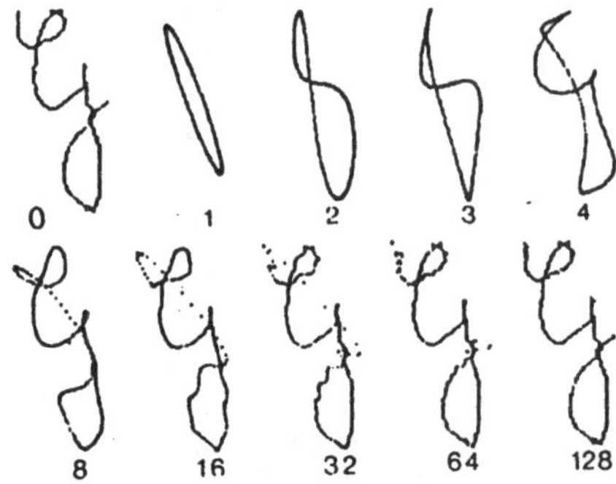

Bild 3: Approximation der Schreiblinie mit unterschiedlichen Anpassungen
0:      geschriebener Buchstabe
1 - 128 : Approximation mit 1 - 128 Glieder

Bei dem Verfahren von Steinke (1981) wird der Schriftzug interaktiv erfaßt. Der Schriftprüfer wählt den Buchstaben aus und markiert die Schreiblinie durch einige Stützpunkte, deren Sequenz die Schreibfolge wiedergibt. Dies ist inbesondere in Kreuzungsbereichen wichtig, in denen die Schreibfolge nicht eindeutig ist. Im Anschluß rekonstruiert ein Linienverfolgungsprogramm die Schreiblinie und beschreibt sie in Form der durchlaufenen Bildpunkte. Dieses Vorgehen setzt einen einzügig geschriebenen Buchstaben voraus. Zur Normierung des Schriftzuges auf eine feste Länge werden die durchlaufenen Bildpunkte durch zwei diskrete Fourierreihen angenähert. Je mehr Glieder dieser Reihen verwendet werden, desto besser ist die Approximation an die Schreiblinie.

Bei Anwendungen der Mustererkennung kommt es jedoch nicht auf eine besonders gute Approximation an, sondern das Klassifikationsergebnis steht im Vordergrund. Im implementierten Verfahren wurden je vier Glieder der Fourierreihe benutzt, damit werden beide Fourierreihen durch 16 Koeffizienten beschrieben, die als Merkmale verwendet werden.

Bei dem zweiten Verfahren zur Gewinnung von textbezogenen Merkmalen, das Naske (1983) angegeben hat, ist es nur notwendig, den Buchstaben aus seinem Kontext zu isolieren. Das Verfahren basiert auf der Modellvorstellung, daß jeder Mensch eine prototypische Vorstellung von den Zeichen seines Schriftsystems hat. Während des Schreibens wird dieser Prototyp durch Störungen deformiert. Beim Lesen tritt ein umgekehrter Vorgang auf: Aus einem vorliegenden Buchstaben wird ein Prototyp rekonstruiert. Das Verfahren versucht diesen Schreib- bzw. Lesevorgang nachzuempfinden. Die berechneten Merkmale beschreiben die Verzerrung zwischen Prototyp und Buchstaben.

Bild 4: Rekonstruktion des Prototypen
- links: Prototyp
- mitte geschriebener Buchstabe
- rechts: rekonstruierter Prototyp

Im Gegensatz zu dem ersten Verfahren können hier auch aus mehrzügig geschriebenen Buchstaben (z.B. das kleine i) Merkmale gewonnen werden. Dagegen ist die Anwendung dieses Verfahrens problematisch, wenn die Schreibweise des Buchstabens vollkommen von der des Prototypen abweicht.

Bei allen Verfahren erfolgt die Berechnung der Merkmale nicht unmittelbar bei der Erfassung, sondern es werden nur die benötigten Daten auf eine Datei ausgegeben und ein Auftrag zur Merkmalsberechnung generiert. Dieser Auftrag wird in der Regel in der folgenden Nacht bearbeitet. Dadurch werden die rechenzeitintensiven Berechnungen abgekoppelt von dem interaktiven Prozeß, um zum einen für den Anwender eine kurze Antwortzeit zu erreichen und zum anderen die Rechnerausnutzung zu optimieren. Weiterhin ist so die Möglichkeit gegegen, modifizierte Merkmale zu berechnen ohne die Schreibleistungen neu zu erfassen.

2.3 Merkmaltransformation und Ähnlichkeitsfunktion

Zur Beurteilung der Ähnlichkeit der Schreibleistungen anhand der numerischen Merkmale einer Kategorie wählen wir folgendes Modell. Wir nehmen an, daß die Handschrift eines Schreibers weitgehend homogene Eigenschaften aufweist und nur einer geringen Variation unterliegt. Diese Variation sei für alle Schreiber gleich. Somit sind die extrahierten Merkmalvektoren $\underline{v}$ Realisationen eines normalverteilten Zufallsprozesses, der durch einen schreiberspezifischen Mittelwertsvektor $\underline{m}_{\underline{v}}$ und eine schreiberunabhängige Kovarianzmatrix $\underline{C}_{\underline{v}}$ beschrieben werden kann. Die Kovarianzmatrix $\underline{C}_{\underline{v}}$ kann aus der vorliegenden Sammlung nach der Beziehung

$$\underline{C}_{\underline{v}} = \sum_{k=1}^{K} \sum_{n=1}^{N_k} (\underline{v}_{(k,n)} - \underline{m}_{\underline{v}(k)})(\underline{v}_{(k,n)} - \underline{m}_{\underline{v}(k)})^t$$

geschätzt werden. Dabei ist K die Anzahl der Schreiber, $\underline{m}_{\underline{v}}(k)$ der Mittelwertsvektor und N_k die Anzahl der Merkmalvektoren $\underline{v}_{(k,n)}$ des k-ten Schreibers.

Diese Situation ist in Bild 5 für vier Schreiber und einem Merkmalsvektor mit zwei Komponenten dargestellt.

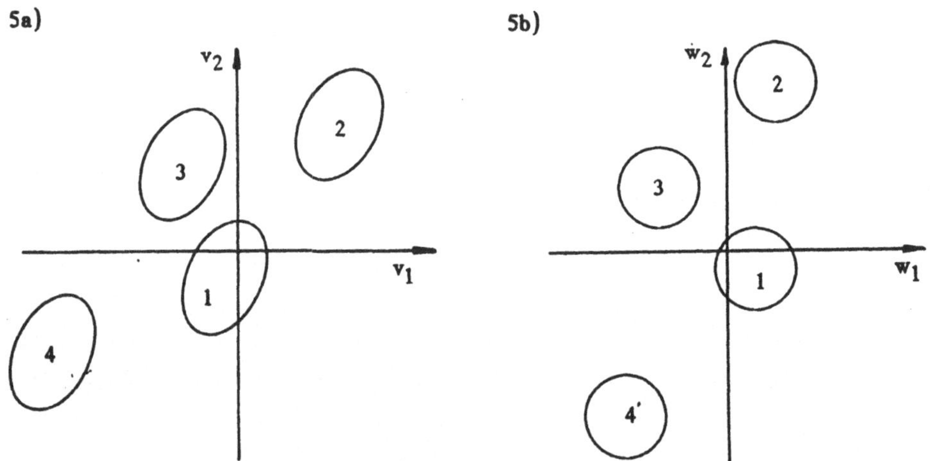

Bild 5: Beispiel für schreiberspezifische Verteilungen im zweidimensionalen Merkmalraum
a) mit Rohmerkmalen
b) mit transformierten Merkmalen

In diesem Modell kann als Maß für die Wahrscheinlichkeit, daß die Schreibleistung von dem k-ten Schreiber der Sammlung geschrieben wurde nach Fukunaga (1972) der Mahalanobis-Abstand

$$d(k) = (\underline{v} - \underline{m}_{V(k)})^t \; \underline{C}^{-1} \; (\underline{v} - \underline{m}_{V(k)}) \quad \text{mit } k=1,...,K$$

verwendet werden. Der Schreiber mit dem geringsten Abstand ist dann der wahrscheinlichste Schrifturheber der fraglichen Schreibleistung.

Anstatt bei jeder Recherche den rechenintensiven Mahalanobis-Abstand zu berechnen, ist es günstiger, durch eine lineare Transformation den Merkmalraum auf den Euklidischen Raum abzubilden. Diese Abbildung wird durch eine Hauptachsentransformation erreicht:

$$\underline{w} = A \, \underline{v}$$

In die Transformationsmatrix A gehen die Eigenwerte und die Eigenvektoren der Kovarianzmatrix $\underline{C}_V$ ein. Die Komponenten des so transformierten Zufallsvektors $\underline{w}$ sind untereinander unkorreliert, und die Varianz der Merkmale ist eins. Das heißt, die Kovarianzmatrix $\underline{C}_W$ entspricht der Einheitsmatrix, somit entspricht der Mahalanobis-Abstand dem Euklidischen-Abstand

$$d(k) = (\underline{w} - \underline{m}_{W(k)})^t \, (\underline{w} - \underline{m}_{W(k)}) \, .$$

Diese lineare Transformation erfolgt im FISH-System im Anschluß an die oben beschriebenen Merkmalsberechnungen.

3. Die klassifizierende Recherche

Bei einer großen Handschriften-Sammlung mit vielen möglichen Schrifturhebern ist eine eindeutige automatische Identifikation einer fraglichen Schreibleistung anhand der beschriebenen Merkmale bei geringer Fehlerrate kaum zu erwarten. Deshalb wird mit der klassifizierenden Recherche ein anderer Weg beschritten.

Ausgehend von einer booleschen Vorauswahl der Sammlung, zum Beispiel anhand der Deliktart, nach dem Geschlecht des Schreibers oder den deskriptiven Merkmalen, werden von dem System für jede zu untersuchende Merkmalskategorie nach Ähnlichkeit geordnete Ranglisten erzeugt. Diese werden von dem Schriftprüfer sequentiell, rechnergestützt bearbeitet. Entsprechend der Reihenfolge der Rangliste werden die digitalisierten Bilder der Handschrift dem Schriftprüfer zusammen mit den wichtigsten administrativen Daten angezeigt. Durch schriftvergleichende Analyse der angebotenen Handschriften kann der

Schriftprüfer entweder die fragliche Schreibleistung identifizieren oder stellt fest, daß die Sammlung keine Schreibleistung des gesuchten Schreibers enthält. Die durchschnittliche Bearbeitungszeit des Schriftprüfers soll mit diesem Vorgehen minimiert werden.

Wurden bei einer Recherche mehrere Ranglisten erzeugt, kann der Schriftprüfer beliebig zwischen diesen Listen wechseln, um so die Suche zu beschleunigen. Dabei ist sichergestellt, daß Schreibleistungen, die der Schriftprüfer in einer Rangliste verwirft, auch in allen anderen Listen automatisch gestrichen werden. Eine umfangreiche Listeninspektion kann zu jedem Zeitpunkt unterbrochen werden, zum Beispiel um bei Zweifelsfällen das Orginal aus der Sammlung zu besorgen und einen genaueren Vergleich daran vorzunehmen. Im Anschluß kann mit dem gleichen Bearbeitungsstatus die Listeninspektion wieder aufgenommen werden.

Die Ordnung der Rangliste ergibt sich aus dem oben definierten Abstandsmaß; jedoch wird noch eine geringe Modifikation vorgenommen. Zur Berechnung des Abstands $d(k)$ ist der Klassenmittelwertsvektor für jeden Schreiber notwendig, dieser kann nur zuverlässig aus einer größeren Anzahl von Schreibleistungen eines Schreibers geschätzt werden. Diese Bedingung ist bei der Anwendung nicht erfüllt, es liegen oft nur einige oder gar nur eine einzige Schreibleistung eines Schreibers vor. Deshalb wird hier nicht der Abstand zu den Klassenmittelwerten aller Schreiber berechnet, sondern der Abstand zu allen vorausgewählten Schreibleistungen. Man bezeichnet dieses Vorgehen, als Nächste-Nachbar-Technik (z.B. Niemann (1984)).

Auch die Berechnung einer umfangreichen Rangliste setzt sehr viel Rechenleistung voraus. Deshalb erteilt der Schriftprüfer im Normalfall für die durchzuführende Recherche einen Auftrag an das System, der im Hintergrund bearbeitet wird. Wurde der Auftrag bearbeitet, kann der Schriftprüfer die berechnete Reihenfolge abrufen und die Listeninspektion durchführen.

Dieses entkoppelte Vorgehen ist bei dieser Anwendung möglich, da hier immer die gleiche Fragestellung vorliegt - zu einer fraglichen Schreibleistung werden ähnliche Schreibleistungen gesucht - und die Auswahlfunktion durch die Merkmale der fraglichen Schreibleistung bestimmt ist. Hierin unterscheidet sich das System FISH von anderen Retrievalsystemen, bei denen unterschiedliche Fragestellungen zu behandeln sind und der Informationsbedarf oft erst im Verlauf einer interaktiven Recherche präziser entwickelt werden kann.

4. Aufbau des Systems FISH

Das System besteht aus einem zentralen Rechner mit über ein lokales Netzwerk ange-
schlossenen Arbeitsplatzrechner. Die Rechner sind vom Typ VAX der Firma Digital.
Vereinfacht dargestellt sind auf dem zentralen Rechner drei Programmsysteme installiert,
das Datenbanksystem ADABAS und zwei rechenzeitintensive Programme. Das eine dient
zur Merkmalbildung aus den Schreibleistungen, und das andere stellt einen Server dar.
Die wichtigsten Funktionen dieses Servers sind die Kommunikation mit der Datenbank
und die Durchführung der klassifizierenden Recherche.

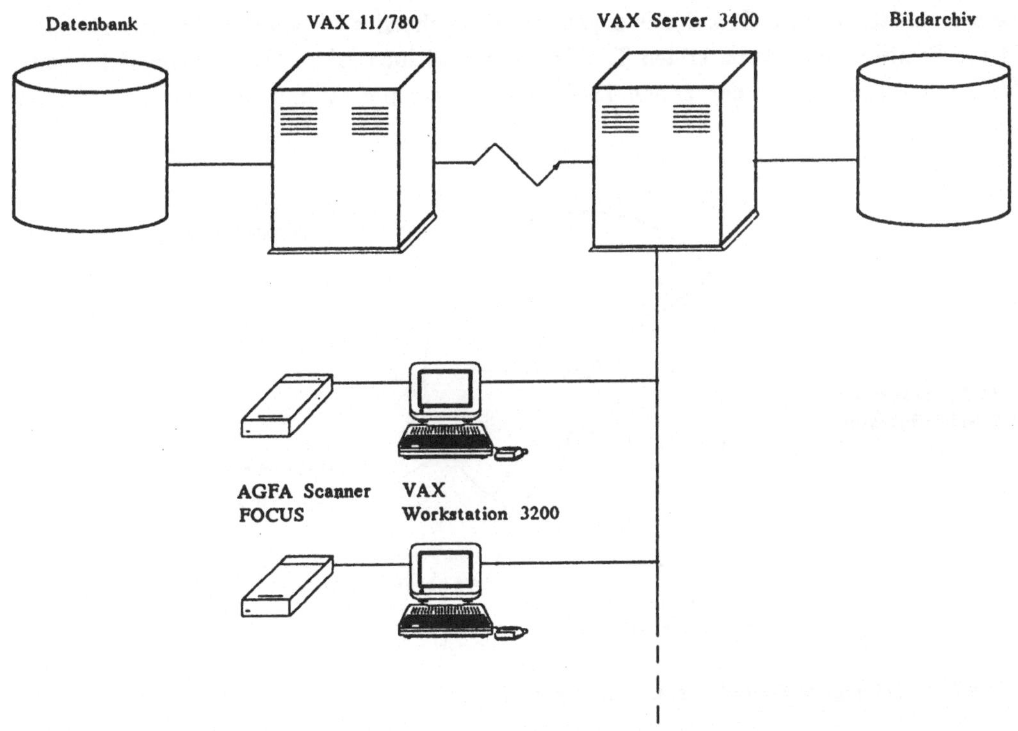

Bild 6: Systemarchitektur von FISH

Wie bereits beschrieben arbeitet der Schriftprüfer an einem Arbeitsplatzrechner. An diesem Arbeitsplatz können Handschriftendokumente durch einen Scanner eingelesen werden.
Aus dem gesamten Dokument kann der Schriftprüfer dann eine Schreibleistung interaktiv
isolieren, aufbereiten, deskribieren und vermessen. Er erstellt dort die Rechercheaufträge
und prüft die Ergebnisse anhand von digitalen Bildern der Handschrift, die ihm in der
Reihenfolge der Ähnlichkeitsrangliste angeboten werden.

5. Ergebnisse und Weiterentwicklung

Bei der klassifizierenden Recherche wird die Handschriftensammlung in bezug auf eine Schreibleistung eines unbekannten Schrifturhebers nach Ähnlichkeit sortiert. Der erste Treffer, das heißt die Antwort auf die Frage, an welcher Position der Rangliste die erste Schreibleistung des gleichen Schreibers liegt, entscheidet über die Selektionskraft des Verfahrens. Für die Anwendung sind die weiteren Treffer von untergeordneter Bedeutung, da man davon ausgehen kann, daß mit dem ersten Treffer der Schreiber bereits identifiziert ist.

Die Selektionskraft kann durch Auswertung der vorliegenden Sammlung beurteilt werden, indem automatisch nach Schreibleistungen mit feststehender Urheberschaft recherchiert und die Position des jeweils ersten Treffers aufgezeichnet wird. Die so empirisch ermittelte Verteilungsfunktion der ersten Treffer entspricht der zu erwartenden Erkennungsrate.

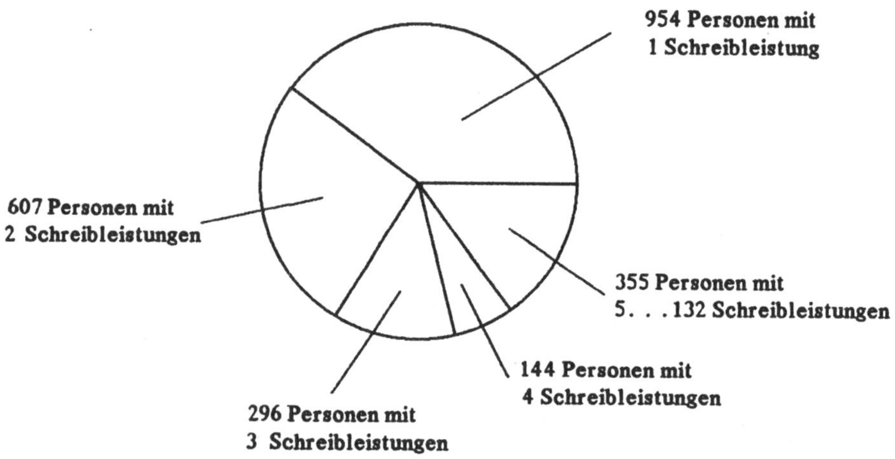

Bild 7: Verteilung der Schreibleistungen pro Person

Die Ergebnisse wurden an einem Bestand mit 7957 Schreibleistungen von 2356 Personen gewonnen. Bild 7 zeigt die Verteilung der vorliegenden Schreibleistungen pro Person. Danach sind die meisten Personen nur mit einer Schreibleistung vertreten, nach diesen Schreibleistungen kann bei der Ermittlung der Erkennungsrate nicht recherchiert werden. Recherchiert werden kann nur, wenn mehrere Schreibleistungen pro Person vorliegen. Danach können am häufigsten Personen mit zwei Schreibleistungen verwendet werden. Im Durchschnitt liegen 3,4 Schreibleistungen pro Person vor.

In Bild 8 ist die Erkennungsrate E für die Kategorie der graphischen Merkmale als Funktion des zu prüfenden Bestands N dargestellt. Zur Normierung auf unterschiedliche Bestände ist der zu prüfende Bestand prozentual zur Größe des Gesamtbestands angegeben. Wie beschrieben werden für das Anwendungssystem transformierte Merkmale benutzt,

die aus dem vorgestellten theoretischen Modell abgeleitet wurden. Die Voraussetzungen
für die Anwendbarkeit dieses Modells sind nur schwer überprüfbar. Dagegen ist die
Wirksamkeit der Transformation einfach zu zeigen, indem die gleichen Recherchen mit
den Rohmerkmalen durchgeführt werden. Dieser Vergleich ist ebenfalls in Bild 8 dargestellt und bestätigt die Richtigkeit der Vorgehensweise. Wird zum Beispiel eine Erkennungsrate von 0,7 als ausreichend festgelegt, so ist bei der Verwendung von Rohmerkmalen 3,8% und bei der Verwendung von transformierten Merkmalen nur 2% des Bestan-
des zu inspizieren. Somit kann der zu prüfende Bestand durch die Transformation nahezu auf die Hälfte reduziert werden.

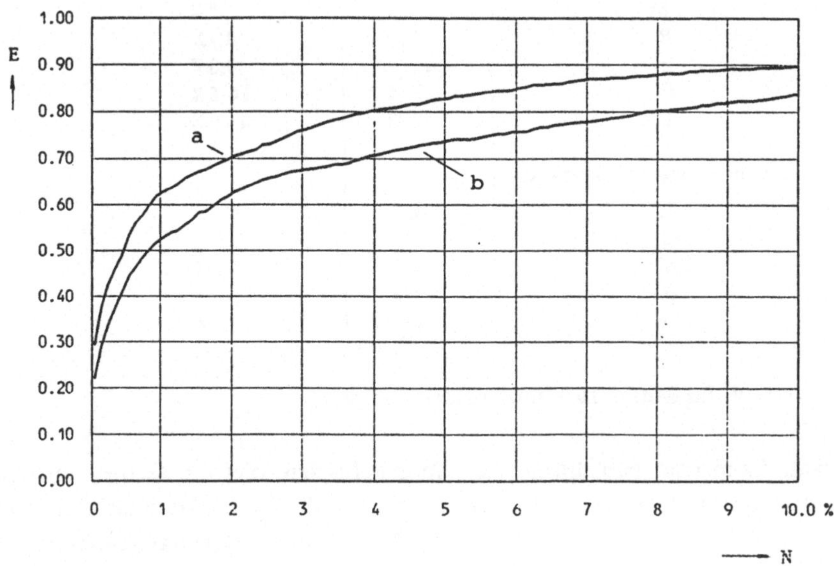

Bild 8: Erkennungsrate der Kategorie graphischer Merkmale
a) transformierte Merkmale
b) Rohmerkmale

Für die anderen Merkmalskategorien ergeben sich ähnliche Erkennungsfunktionen.

Die Erkennungsrate gibt an mit welcher Sicherheit ausgeschlossen werden kann, daß ein
gesuchter Schreiber bereits mit mindestens einer Schreibleistung in der Sammlung einliegt.
Eine weitere Kenngröße ist die mittlere Anzahl der zu inspizierenden Schreibleistungen
bis der erste Treffer erreicht ist. In Bild 9 sind einige typische Werte zusammengestellt.

Der Tabelle kann man entnehmen, daß die graphischen und die textinsensitiven Merkmale
in etwa die gleiche Aussagekraft besitzen, nur die Weißkettenstatistik besitzt einen
schlechteren Kennwert. Dagegen ist bei den Methoden der textbezogenen Merkmale eine
stärkere Streuung ersichtlich. Es ist zu vermuten, daß dies auf die größere Variation der
Schreibweise von Einzelbuchstaben zurückzuführen ist.

Methode	Anzahl der Schreiblei- stungen	im Mittel zu inspizierender Bestand
graphische Merkmale	7952	7,4%
Autokorrelationsfunktion	6975	7,0%
Schwarzkettenstatistik	6975	7,1%
Weißkettenstatistik	6975	9,3%
Isolierte Buchstaben		
G	1111	7,5%
M	1023	7,2%
R	851	8,1%
g	1264	9,3%
k	1574	14,6%
t	1233	11,9%
Linienverfolgte Buchstaben		
A	435	8,8%
G	1392	11,2%
M	697	9,3%
g	1938	11,6%
ch	477	7,1%

Bild 9: Im Mittel zu inspizierender Bestand

Der Tabelle kann man entnehmen, daß die graphischen und die textinsensitiven Merkmale in etwa die gleiche Aussagekraft besitzen, nur die Weißkettenstatistik besitzt einen schlechteren Kennwert. Dagegen ist bei den Methoden der textbezogenen Merkmale eine stärkere Streuung ersichtlich. Es ist zu vermuten, daß dies auf die größere Variation der Schreibweise von Einzelbuchstaben zurückzuführen ist.

Ein Vergleich dieser Ergebnisse mit dem derzeitigen manuellen System, das von Mally (1956) in seinem Grundkonzept entwickelt wurde, ist nur schwer möglich. Denn mit einem manuellen Sytem sind solche Auswertungen mit vertretbarem Aufwand nicht durchführbar.

Um das Sytem zu verbessern, sind zwei Möglichkeiten denkbar. Zum einen können die Einzelverfahren weiter optimiert werden, insbesondere ist hier an eine bessere Bildvorverarbeitung zu denken. Zum anderen bietet es sich an, ein Verfahren zur Kombination der verschiedenen Ranglisten zu entwickeln, so daß eine verbesserte Ähnlichkeitssortierung erreicht werden kann.

Literatur

Fukunaga, K. (1972): Introduction to statistical pattern recognition.
Academic Press New York and London.

Mally, R. (1956): Der Handschriften-Erkennungsdienst.
Internationale Revue, 11, S. 17-21.

Naske, R.D. (1983): Verfahren zur textbezogenen Schreibererkennung aus dem
Handschriftenbild. Dissertation TU Karlsruhe.

Niemann, H. (1983): Klassifikation von Mustern.
Springer-Verlag Berlin Heidelberg New York Tokyo.

Steinke, K. (1981): Entwicklung von Mustererkennungsverfahren zur textunabhängigen
Analyse von Handschriftenbildern. Dissertation TH Aachen.

Suche in Volltextdatenbanken mit Unterstützung von Hypertext

Jörg Herrmann, Dieter Meiser
Universität des Saarlandes
FB 14 Informatik
Lehrstuhl Prof. Dr. Scheidig
D-6600 Saarbrücken
Im Stadtwald 15, Bau 36 - E 16
E-mail: dmeiser@cs.uni-sb.de

1. Einleitung

Die Suche nach einschlägigen Artikeln in einer Volltext- bzw. Abstract-Datenbank kann über Anfragen gesteuert werden, die eine Auswahl von Deskriptoren für das gewünschte Themengebiet enthalten. Um bezüglich der in der Datenbank verwendeten Deskriptoren und ihrer Schreibweise sicher zu gehen, werden die Deskriptoren in einem Thesaurus zusammengefaßt.

Die Antwort auf eine Anfrage besteht aus einer Reihe von Artikeln, die in der Regel sequentiell nach Gewichtungen angeordnet sind. Erfüllt die Antwort nicht die Anforderungen, so kann der Benutzer den Themenbereich eingrenzen oder erweitern, indem er unter Verwendung des Thesaurus die Deskriptoren verallgemeinert oder spezialisiert, neue Deskriptoren hinzufügt oder überflüssige löscht. Dieser Zyklus kann sich mehrfach wiederholen, bis der Benutzer mit dem Ergebnis der Anfrage zufrieden ist.

In unserem System kombinieren wir den Vorgang des Retrieval mit Hypertexttechniken. Wir verwenden hierzu bekannte Retrievalverfahren und denken, daß durch interaktive Nutzung und Verwendung von Hypertext, Anfragen schneller - da durch den Endbenutzer direkt kontrollierbar - zu befriedigenden Ergebnissen führen werden. Darüberhinaus sollte das System in verteilten Systemen einsetzbar sein. Ähnliche Ansätze werden in [McMath] beschrieben. Wir gehen jedoch noch einen Schritt weiter, indem wir die Formulierung der Anfrage und die Betrachtung der Antworten in das System integrieren. Es soll nicht Ziel unseres Systems sein, neue Retrievalverfahren zu untersuchen. Einen guten Überblick über Konzepte des Information Retrieval und über Retrievalverfahren wird etwa in [Fuhr] gegeben.

2. Hypertext

Basis des Systems bildet Hypertext. Sämtliche Benutzeraktivitäten sollen sich online im Hypertextsystem abspielen. Wir sehen Hypertext als gerichteten, markierten Graphen an, dessen Knoten Verweise zu Informationseinheiten enthalten und definieren Hypertext wie folgt:

Ein Hypertext G ist ein 5-Tupel $\langle K, E, F, I, A \rangle$ mit

K = endliche Menge von Knoten

$E \subseteq K \times K \times A$ endliche Menge von gerichteten, markierten Kanten

I = endliche Menge von Teilinformationen (Karten)

F: K -> I ordnet jedem Knoten eine Teilinformation zu.

A = endliche Menge von Linktypen (Attributen oder Markierungen).

Im folgenden identifizieren wir die Knoten mit den zugehörigen Informationseinheiten und sprechen von "Hypertextkarten".

Genauere Ausführungen des Hypertextmodells würden den Rahmen dieses Artikels sprengen. Sie können jedoch in [Meis90] und [Meis91] nachgelesen werden.

Zum Gebiet der Chemischen Technik existiert ein Thesaurus, der "Dechema-Thesaurus für die Chemische Technik" (vgl. [Dechema]). Dieser Thesaurus enthält die wichtigsten Fachbegriffe des Gebietes. Veröffentlichte Artikel dieses Fachgebietes werden durch Deskriptoren des Thesaurus gekennzeichnet. Die Abstracts der Artikel mitsamt den Schlüsselworten werden von einer Abstractdatenbank verwaltet.

Für den Benutzer, der relevante Artikel suchen will, besteht die Aufgabe zunächst darin seine noch unscharf formulierte Anfrage in Termen des Thesaurus zu übersetzen. D.h. die Suche nach relevanten Artikeln erfordert zunächst eine Suche nach Begriffen im Thesaurus, durch die die Artikel möglicherweise gekennzeichnet sind.

Diese Vorgehensweise diente uns als Vorlage für unser System. D.h. Einstiegspunkt in das System bildet der Thesaurus, der von einem Hypertextsystem verwaltet wird und damit dem Endbenutzer direkt zugänglich wird. Die Suche nach Begriffen im Thesaurus entspricht also einem Browsing im Hypertext.

3. Das Hypertextsystem

Schematisch läßt sich das entwickelte Hypertextsystem wie folgt darstellen:

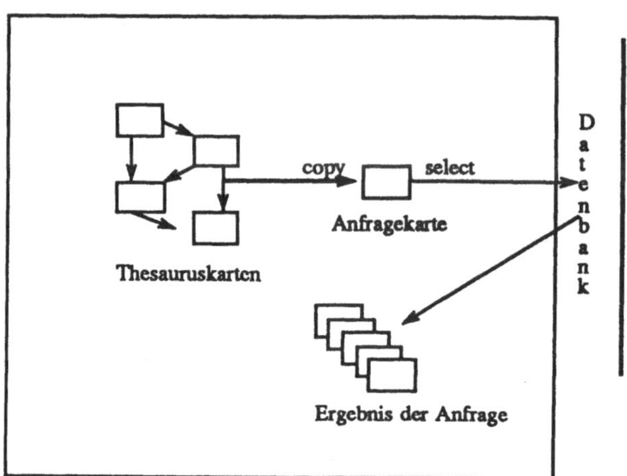

Abbildung 1: Das Hypertextsystem

Der Benutzer blättert im Thesaurus mit den üblichen Hypertexttechniken und kann Begriffe, die im als relevant erscheinen auf einer gesonderten Karte (Anfragekarte) zusammenstellen. Aus diesen Begriffen formuliert er eine Anfrage, die er an die Datenbank übergeben kann. Das Ergebnis der Anfrage wird wiederum Karten des Hypertextes zugeordnet, die der Benutzer dann direkt untersuchen kann.

4. Der Thesaurus

Für unser System haben wir, wie oben schon erwähnt, den "Dechema-Thesaurus für die Chemische Technik" (vgl. [Dechema]) verwendet. Der Wortschatz des Thesaurus umfaßt ca. 30.000 Begriffe. Er ist in 40 Sachgebiete (01-25, 27-31, 33-41, 90) unterteilt. Die einzelnen Sachgebiete sind mit Nummer und Titel ausgewiesen und ihre Nachbargebiete werden angegeben.

Die Sachgebiete sind in einzelne Facetten unterteilt. Ein Sachgebiet kann in den Facetten A bis E unterschiedliche Gesichtspunkte seines Themenbereichs zusammenfassen.

Die Facetten enthalten nun eine Anzahl von Suchbegriffen (Deskriptoren). Wie üblich sind ihnen weitere Begriffe zugeordnet, die als Ober-, Unter- oder Teilbegriff definiert sind. Der Thesaurus ist als Polyhierarchie aufgebaut.

Beispiel: Auszug aus dem Thesaurus (Sachgebiet 01, Facette A)

Fördermittel

  Sy   Förderer

  Sy   Fördergerät

  Sy   Förderzeug

  U   Aufzug

  U   Bagger

  U   Fahrzeug

  U   Flurförderzeug

  U   Handhabemittel

  U   Hebebühne

  U   Hebezeug

  U   Stetigförderer

  U   Lademaschine

Grabenbunker

  O   Bunker

Greifbagger

  O   Eingefässbagger

Greifer

  O   Lastaufnahmemittel

Greiferwinde

  O   Seilwinde

Dabei bedeuten: Sy - Synonym

                 U - Unterbegriff

                 O - Oberbegriff

4.1 Die Thesauruskarten

Wie oben schon angedeutet bildet der Thesaurus die Basis des Hypertextsystems. Er wurde in ein Hypertextformat umgewandelt. Bemerkenswert bei der Umwandlung ist, daß diese automatisch erfolgt und somit auch auf andere Thesauri angewendet werden kann. Diese Transformation kann wie folgt beschrieben werden:

a. Erzeugen von Karten:

    a1. Erzeugen einer Titelkarte. Sie enthält den Titel des Thesaurus sowie die Namen der Sachgebiete.

    a2. Erstellen von Sachgebietskarten. Sie enthalten die Namen der Nachbargebiete, sowie die Namen der zum Sachgebiet gehörenden Facetten.

    a3. Erstellen von Begriffskarten. Sie enthalten die Begriffe einer Facette in alphabetischer Reihenfolge. Sie werden zum Einstieg in den eigentlichen Thesaurus verwendet.

    a4. Erzeugen von Deskriptorenkarten. Diese Karten enthalten die Deskriptoren und ihre zugehörigen Begriffe (Unterbegriff, Oberbegriff,...)

b. Erzeugen von Links:

   b1. Richte Links von der Titelkarte zu den Sachgebietskarten ein (vom Namen des Sachgebiets auf der Titelkarte zur Sachgebietskarte).

   b2. Richte Links von den Sachgebietskarten zu den Nachbargebieten ein. Richte Links von den Sachgebietskarten zu den Begriffskarten ein.

   b3. Richte Links von den Begriffen der Begriffskarte zu den Deskriptorenkarten ein.

   b4. Verbinde die Deskriptorenkarten gemäß ihrer Einordnung im Thesaurus.

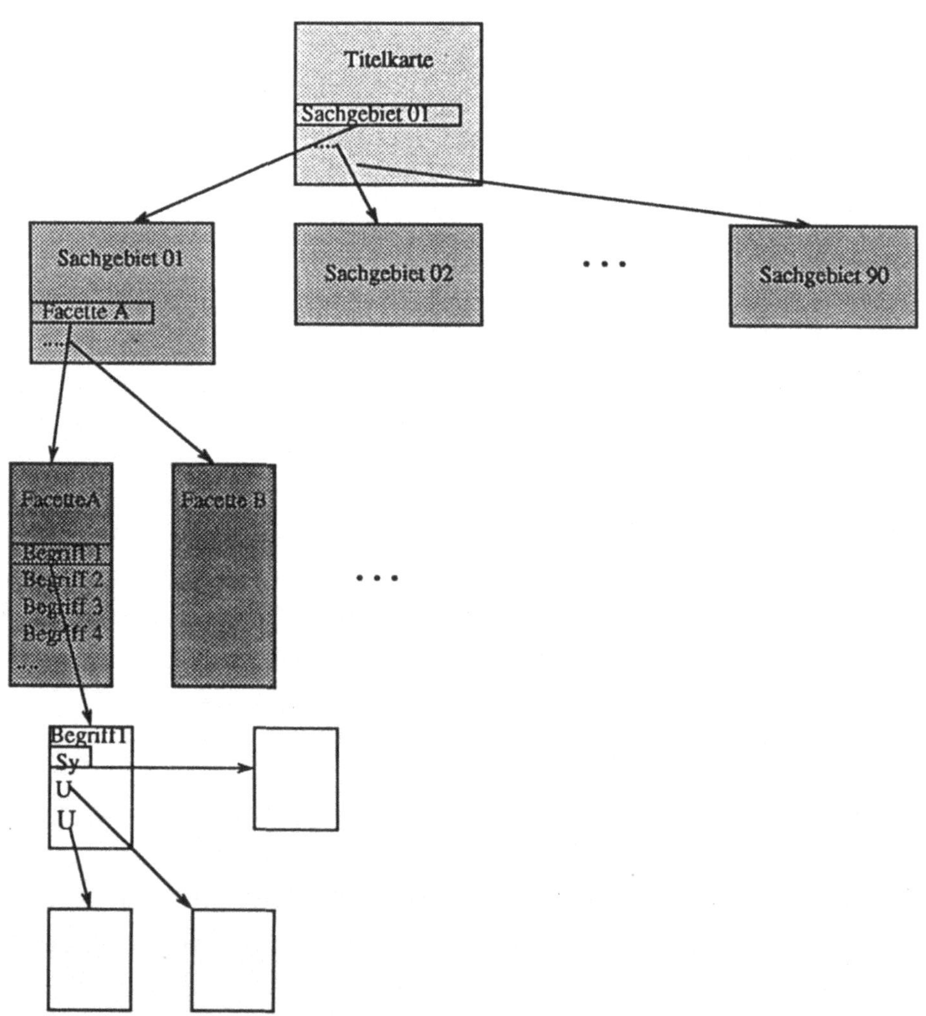

Abbildung 2: Der Thesaurus in Hypertextformat

4.2 Die Anfragekarte

Der Benutzer arbeitet interaktiv mit dem Hypertext, indem er Begriffe sucht und den Referenzen folgt. Ziel dieses Blätterns im Thesaurus ist die Formulierung einer Anfrage mit Hilfe der Deskriptoren des Thesaurus. Zum Erstellen der Anfrage haben wir eine "Anfragekarte" eingeführt. Auf dieser Anfragekarte stellt der Benutzer während des Browsing im Thesaurus seine Anfrage zusammen (Kopieren von Deskriptoren auf die Anfragekarte und Verknüpfung der Deskriptoren). Diese Anfrage wird an das Datenbanksystem übergeben.

Zu beachten ist, daß wir uns nicht auf ein Retrievalverfahren (Bsp.: boolesches Retrieval, Vektorraummodell, probabilistische Verfahren, usw.) festlegen müssen. So können wir beispielsweise Anfragekarten für unterschiedliche Verfahren einsetzen und die Ergebnisse der Anfragen miteinander vergleichen.

4.3 Die Antwortkarte

Die Antwort auf eine Anfrage besteht aus einer Liste von Artikeln, die sequentiell nach einem vorgegebenem Relevanzkriterium angeordnet sind. Zur Einbindung der Antwort in das Hypertextsystem führen wir eine "Antwortkarte" ein. Die gefundenen Artikel werden neuen Hypertextkarten zugeordnet, die durch sequentielle Links miteinander verbunden sind.

Der Benutzer kann nun in den Antwortkarten blättern und so feststellen, welche Artikel relevant sind und welche nicht. Aufgrund seiner Erfahrungen kann er evtl. feststellen, daß noch wichtige Artikel fehlen.

Anschließend kann er wieder im Thesaurus blättern und die ursprüngliche Anfrage kann verändert werden. Dieser gesamte Vorgang wird sich solange wiederholen, bis der Benutzer mit dem Ergebnis der Anfrage zufrieden ist.

5. Erweiterung: Kombination von Browsing und Retrieval

Sind die Artikel der Datenbank ebenfalls als Hypertext organisiert, d.h durch Verweise miteinander verknüpft, so kann das Ergebnis einer Anfrage ein "Browsing" in der Datenbank auslösen. Der Benutzer kann von Artikeln aus Verweisen folgen und kann so ein Browsing in der Datenbank durchführen. Das Ergebnis eines Retrieval löst also ein Browsing aus. Umgekehrt ist es denkbar, daß Terme, die in Artikeln der Datenbank gefunden werden, auf die Anfragekarte kopiert werden. So kann eine Anfrage zusammengestellt werden. Anschließend wird ein Retrieval durchgeführt. D.h. Browsing in der Datenbank löst Retrieval in der Datenbank aus.

6. Literatur

[Dechema]   "Dechema-Thesaurus für die Chemische Technik", Dechema, Frank-
             furt/Main 1974
[Fuhr]   Fuhr, N.: "Hypertext und Information-Retrieval" in Hypertext und Hyper-
             media - IFB249;. S101 ff.; Springer-Verlag 1990
[McMath]   McMath, C.F, Tamaru, R.S and Rada, R: "A graphical thesaurus-based
             information retrieval system" in International Journal of Man-Machine
             Studies, 31, 1989, 121-147
[Meis90]   Meiser, D.: "Die verteilte abstrakte Hypertextmaschine DAHM" in Pro-
             ceeding of IiI, Tuczno 1990, S 248-265
[Meis91a]   Meiser, D: "Konzepte eines verteilten Hypertextsystems" in Proceedings
             Hypertext/Hypermedia '91; Graz; IFB 276, S. 191-204

EINE HYPERTEXT-BENUTZERSCHNITTSTELLE FÜR EIN JURISTISCHES VOLLTEXT INFORMATION RETRIEVAL SYSTEM[*]

Dieter Merkl, A Min Tjoa, SteFan Vieweg
Institut für Statistik und Informatik, Abteilung für Informationssysteme
A-1010 Wien, Liebiggasse 4/3
e-mail: dieter@ifs.univie.ac.at

Zusammenfassung

Die vorliegende Arbeit gibt einen kurzen Überblick über das EUREKA Projekt 359, "Lokale intelligente Benutzerschnittstelle für Volltext-Retrievalsysteme (ITS 90)". Der Projektteil Hypertextschnittstelle für juristisches Volltext Information Retrieval wird präsentiert. Dabei wir der Benutzerin die Möglichkeit angeboten, ausgehend von Rechtsvorschriftenzitaten in Gerichtsentscheidungen mittels Hypertextfunktionen in eine Rechtsvorschriftendatenbank zu verzweigen. Dadurch erhält die Benutzerin die Möglichkeit des Zugriffs auf zwei thematisch unterschiedliche Datenbasen. Mittels Hypertextfunktionen können somit die rechtlichen Grundlagen von Gerichtsentscheidungen durch direkte Betrachtung die zugrundeliegenden Rechtsvorschriften überprüft bzw. nachvollzogen werden.

1. Einleitung

In dieser Arbeit wird ein Teilaspekt des Projektes "Lokale intelligente Benutzerschnittstelle für Volltext-Retrievalsysteme (ITS 90)" (EUREKA Projekt Nr. 359) vorgestellt. Die Laufzeit dieses Projekts wurde mit zwei Jahren fixiert (Jänner 1990 bis Dezember 1991). Als österreichische Projektpartner fungieren hierbei die Österreichische Staatsdruckerei (Wien, Projektleitung Dr. Andreas Manak), Büro für Grundlagenforschung und Systemplanung (Wien, Dr. Werner Robert Svoboda) sowie Institut für Statistik und Informatik der Universität Wien (Prof. Dr. A Min Tjoa). Das Projekt umfaßt im wesentlichen vier Themenschwerpunkte:

---

[*]   Das Projekt wird vom österreichischen Innovations- und Technologie-Fond (ITF) gefördert.

- Automatische Erkennung von Strukturelementen in Dokumenten-
  texten und deren Nutzung für das Information Retrieval
- Automatische Erstellung von Dokumentrelationen
- Verwendung von Hypertextfunktionen in der Benutzerschnittstelle
- Einheitliche Benutzerschnittstelle für Online- und Offline-Daten-
  banken (lokales Gateway)

Schwerpunkt dieses Artikels ist die Darstellung der Hypertextfunktionen. Für die
Hypertextfunktionen wird die besondere Struktur der dem Retrievalsystem
zugrundeliegenden Texte ausgenutzt. Durch die Ausnutzung der Strukturinformation wird
eine höhere semantische Qualität sowohl während der Indexierung als auch während der
Abfrage erreicht.

Der Rest des Artikels ist wie folgt gegliedert: Im Abschnitt 2 wird die Systemumgebung
beschrieben. Anschließend geben wir einen kurzen Überblick über die zur Indexierung
der Dokumente eingesetzten Methoden. Im Abschnitt 4 erläutern wir die Problemstellung
der Hypertext-Applikation. Der Artikel schließt mit einigen Anmerkungen zur
Realisierung der Hypertext-Benutzerschnittstelle.

2. Systemumgebung

Das EUREKA Projekt ITS 90 setzt auf einer CD-ROM Datenbank der Österreichischen
Staatsdruckerei auf. Diese CD-ROM beinhaltet eine Sammlung der Entscheidungen des
Österreichischen Obersten Gerichtshofes in Sachen Zivilrecht (OGH-SZ). Insgesamt
liegen etwa 8000 Gerichtsentscheidungen im Volltext vor. Der Umfang der Rohdaten
(Texte) beträgt zirka 90 MB. Als Restriktion besteht die Festlegung auf IBM-AT oder
kompatible Rechner.

3. Volltextindexierung in ITS 90

Bei der Indexierung der Volltextdokumente wird die besondere Struktur von
Gerichtsentscheidungen berücksichtigt. Diese Art der Texte ist dadurch ausgezeichnet,
daß sie nicht nur aus Wörtern aufgebaut sind, sondern zusätzlich noch Verweise auf
andere Texte in Form von Rechtsvorschriftenzitaten beinhalten. Als Indexterme
fungieren somit im Rahmen des EUREKA Projekts Nr. 359 Wörter und
Rechtsvorschriftenzitate. Die Menge der Wörter wurde zusätzlich durch eine
Beschränkung auf Hauptwörter eingeengt. Zur Erkennung von Hauptwörtern in Texten
wird sehr pragmatisch angenommen, daß Hauptwörter mit einem großen

Anfangsbuchstaben geschrieben werden. Ein Hauptwort ist somit eine Zeichenkette bestehend nur aus Zeichen des Alphabets, die mit einem großen Anfangsbuchstaben beginnt. Eine weitere Reduktion des Indexierungsvokabulars wird durch Verwendung einer Stopwortliste erreicht. Mit Hilfe dieser Stopwortliste werden Wörter eliminiert, die für juristische Texte zu wenig aussagekräftig sind. So werden beispielsweise die folgenden Wörter eliminiert:

Neben diesen in juristischen Texten hochfrequenten Wörtern werden mit Hilfe der Stopwortliste noch eine Reihe anderer Wörter eliminiert, die aufgrund der sehr pragmatischen Hauptwortdefinition fälschlicherweise aus den Dokumenttexten extrahiert wurden (z.B. Artikel, Zahlwörter, Pronomen).

Der Vorgang der Indexierung eines Dokuments läßt sich in folgende vier Teilschritte untergliedern:

- Extraktion von Hauptwörtern aus Dokumenttexten
- Bereinigung von Hauptwörtern um deren Flexionsformen
- Elimination von zu häufig bzw. zu selten in der Dokumentensammlung vorkommenden Hauptwörtern
- Speicherung der Terme als Index zur Dokumentensammlung

Bei der Flexionsformenbereinigung wurde das Hauptaugenmerk auf eine rasche Implementierung eines Prototyps gelegt, der zufriedenstellende Ergebnisse zum Zwecke des Information Retrieval liefert. So wurden keine Strategien implementiert, die eine Flexionsformenbereinigung in streng linguistischem Sinne gewährleisten. Vielmehr wurden linguistische Heuristiken verwendet, die durchaus akzeptable Ergebnisse liefern. Diese Heuristiken liefern in der Mehrzahl der Fälle das in linguistischem Sinne richtige Ergebnis, ohne dabei morphologisches Wissen (wie z.B. Wissen über Wortstämme oder Silbentrennung) zu verwenden.

4. Automatische Generierung von Hypertextlinks

Über die Hypertext-Benutzerschnittstelle wird der Benutzerin der Zugriff auf zwei thematisch unterschiedliche Datenbasen ermöglicht:

- Gerichtsentscheidungen
- Rechtsvorschriften

Ausgehend von Rechtsvorschriftenzitaten in Gerichtsentscheidungen kann die Benutzerin über die von der Benutzerschnittstelle angebotene Hypertextfunktion aus einer Gerichtsentscheidung in das Volltextdokument der zitierten Rechtsvorschrift verzweigen. Als Startpunkt des Links dient ein in der Entscheidung enthaltenes Paragraphenzitat. Die Extraktion von Rechtsvorschriftenzitaten wird durch einen eigens dafür entwickelten Parser vorgenommen [Schn-90]. Mit Hilfe dieses Parsers wird einerseits das Zitat als solches zum Zwecke der Dokumentindexierung extrahiert. Andererseits wird die genaue Position in der Entscheidung zur visuellen Präsentation des Links in der Hypertext-Benutzerschnittstelle festgestellt.

Die Verwendung von Rechtsvorschriftenzitaten zur Dokumentindexierung bietet die Möglichkeit einer semantisch differenzierteren Zuordnung von Gerichtsentscheidungen zu Themengebieten als auf Wortvorkommenshäufigkeiten basierende Clustermethoden, wie sie beispielsweise in [ElHa-89], [Will-88] oder [Salt-89] beschrieben werden. Die dahinterstehende Idee ist eine Verfeinerung der Clusterhypothese [Rijs-75] für juristische Texte:

Dokumente mit denselben Rechtsvorschriftenzitaten behandeln ähnliche Themengebiete und sind daher für dieselben Anfragen relevant.

Dieser Teil des Projekts (Automatische Erstellung von Dokumentrelationen) ist jedoch nicht Gegenstand dieses Artikels, wir verweisen daher auf zu erscheinende Arbeiten zu den Themenbereichen Term- und Dokumentenclustering unter Berücksichtigung von Rechtsvorschriftenverweisen [Merk-91].

Wie oben erwähnt, beginnt die automatische Generierung von Hypertextlinks mit der Extraktion von Rechtsvorschriftenzitaten aus den Gerichtsentscheidungen. Es ist dabei jedoch darauf zu achten, daß sich die Gesetzestexte, auf die sich die Zitate beziehen, im Zeitablauf verändern. Einzelne Gesetzesbestimmungen werden novelliert; Paragraphen können wegfallen (außer Kraft gesetzt werden), ersetzt werden oder neue Paragraphen können in eine bestehende Ordnung eingefügt werden. Wir verwenden in der Folge den Begriff "Zeitschichtung" für die Tatsache der Veränderung von Gesetzen im Zeitablauf.

Das zentrale Problem bei der Verzweigung von Gerichtsentscheidungen zu Rechtsvorschriften ist die Wahl der passenden Zeitschichten. Durch die im Zeitablauf entstehenden Versionen der einzelnen Rechtsvorschriften müssen Strategien entwickelt werden, um die geeignete (d.h. die für die Entscheidung relevante bzw. gültige) Version einer Rechtsvorschrift der Benutzerin anzubieten.

Juristische Texte bilden eine exzellente Basis für die Realisierung einer Hypertext-Benutzerschnittstelle. Einerseits sind Rechtsvorschriftenzitate in juristischen Dokumenten natürliche Referenzen auf andere Texteinheiten und stellen somit Musterbeispiele für die in [Conk-87] beschriebenen Referenzlinks dar. Andererseits bewirkt die Zeitschichtung von Rechtsvorschriften, daß die Generierung von Referenzen zu Paragraphentexten komplexere Anforderungen an die Hypertext-Benutzerschnittstelle stellt als zeitunabhängige Textersetzung.

Bei der Wahl des Gültigkeitszeitraumes einer Rechtsvorschrift sind folgende, die Gerichtsentscheidung betreffende, Zeitpunkte zu unterscheiden.

- Abfragedatum
- Entscheidungsdatum
- Zeitraum, auf den sich die Klage bezieht

In dieser Aufstellung bezeichnet das Abfragedatum das aktuelle Datum der Systembenutzung. Das Entscheidungsdatum ist jenes Datum, an dem der Oberste Gerichtshof die Entscheidung getroffen hat. Dieses Datum ist eindeutig und Bestandteil der Entscheidungsdokumente. Der Zeitraum des Tathergangs (Zeitraum, auf den sich die Klage bezieht) kann nicht eindeutig aus den Entscheidungsdokumenten bestimmt werden. Dieser Zeitraum müßte durch semantische Analyse aus den Textinhalten gewonnen werden. Diesbezügliche Anstrengungen erscheinen jedoch als nicht gerechtfertigt, da der Zeitraum des Eintretens des Klagegrundes nicht aus allen Dokumenten eindeutig entnehmbar ist.

Analysen im Rahmen des Projekts haben gezeigt, daß das Entscheidungsdatum des Obersten Gerichtshofes als Vergleichszeitpunkt zur Zuordnung zu den Gültigkeitszeiträumen der Rechtsvorschriften herangezogen werden soll.

Das sich durch die Zeitschichtung ergebende Zuordnungsproblem von in bestimmten Gerichtsentscheidungen zitierten Rechtsvorschriften zu ihrer im Zeitablauf gültigen Fassung soll durch Abb. 1 skizziert werden.

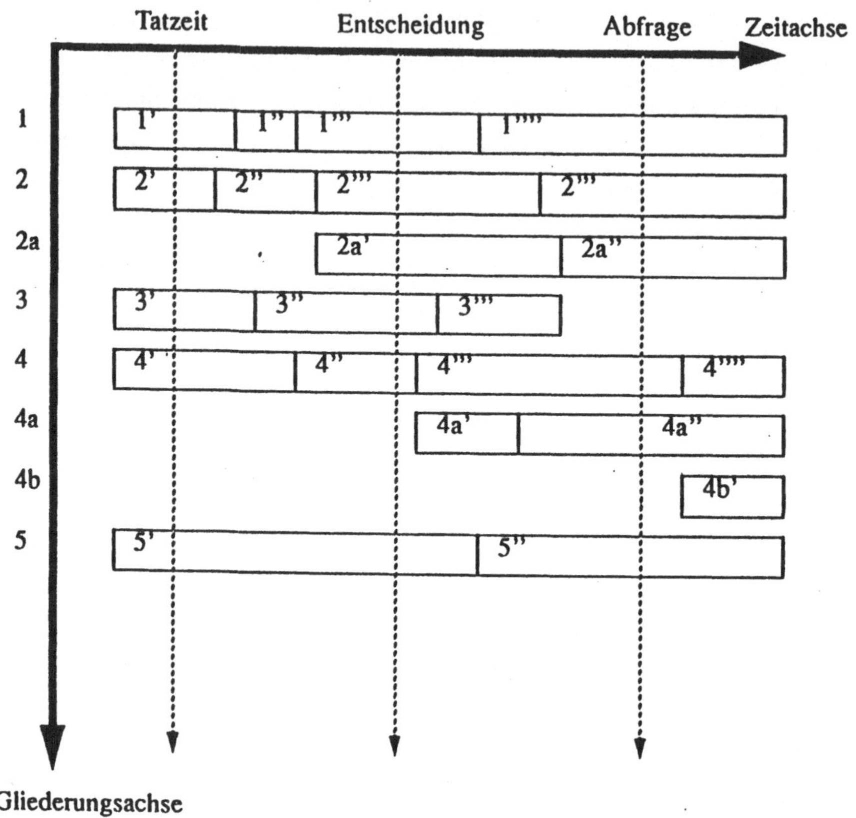

Abb.1:   Zuordnungsproblem von Rechtsvorschriftenverweisen

5. Realisierung

Bei der Implementierung der Hypertextfunktionen wird zwischen zwei Sichtweisen unterschieden werden. Einerseits hat die Benutzerin die Möglichkeit der Verzweigung aus einer Gerichtsentscheidung zu den Volltextdokumenten der Rechtsvorschriften. Andererseits wird ihr die Möglichkeit des Navigierens durch die Rechtsvorschriften geboten. Zur Unterstützung der Navigation wird die Möglichkeit einer Abfrage angeboten. Das Ergebnis der Abfrage stellt in diesem Fall den Einstiegspunkt zur Navigation im Hypertextnetz dar (Query-Unterstütztes Navigieren). Hierbei wird der Einstiegspunkt in die Rechtsvorschriftendokumente nicht von einem in einer Gerichtsentscheidung vorkommenden Rechtsvorschriftenverweis definiert. Die Benutzerin kann durch die Angabe einer Abfrage den Einstiegspunkt in das Hypertextnetz selbst wählen bzw. durch die Angabe von Queries während der Navigation an andere Stellen des Netzes gelangen. Die Benutzerin hat dadurch folgende Möglichkeiten der Navigation:

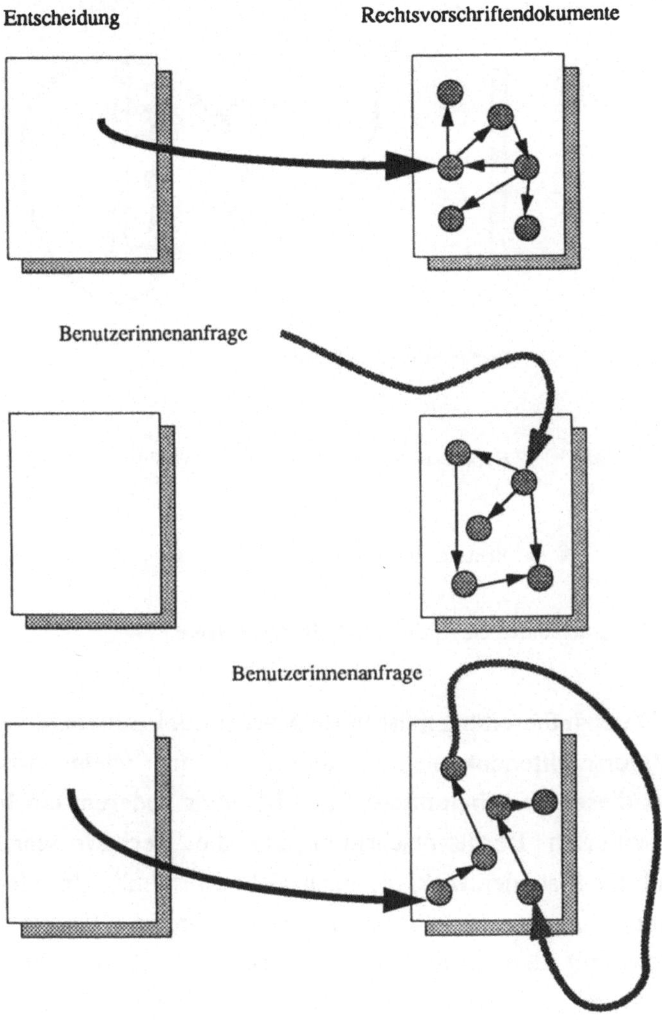
Entscheidung
Rechtsvorschriftendokumente
Benutzerinnenanfrage
Benutzerinnenanfrage

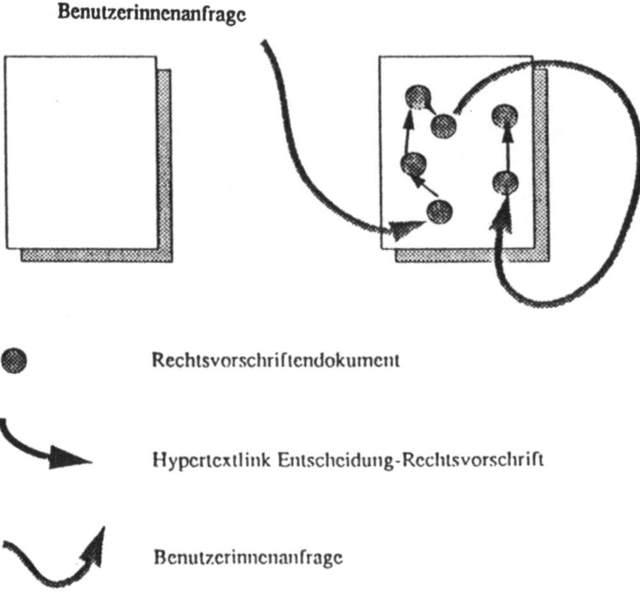

Rechtsvorschriftendokument

Hypertextlink Entscheidung-Rechtsvorschrift

Benutzerinnenanfrage

Abb. 2:   **Navigation durch die Rechtsvorschriftendokumente**

Im Rahmen der Datenaufbereitung müssen zunächst sowohl Entscheidungsdokumente als auch die Rechtsvorschriftendokumente indexiert werden (siehe Abschnitt 3 dieser Arbeit). Ergebnis dieses Verarbeitungsschrittes ist unter anderem ein Index der in den Entscheidungen zitierten Rechtsvorschriften. Da die Rechtsvorschriften nach dem derzeitigen Stand der Systementwicklung noch nicht vollständig (in allen Zeitschichten) datenerfaßt sind, muß der Rechtsvorschriftenindex (Index der zitierten Rechtsvorschriften) mit den tatsächlich vorhandenen Rechtsvorschriften abgeglichen werden. Zitierte, jedoch nicht oder nicht in der entsprechenden Zeitschicht datenerfaßte Rechtsvorschriften dürfen keine Startpunkte für Hypertextlinks darstellen. Die übrigen zitierten Rechtsvorschriften bilden Ausgangspunkte von Links aus den Entscheidungsdokumenten in die Rechtsvorschriftendokumente. Die Rechtsvorschriften werden durch ein Netz von Hypertextlinks nach Gliederung und Zeitschicht verbunden.
Während der Abfrage stehen der Benutzerin somit sowohl Links aus den Entscheidungsdokumenten als auch ein komplexes Netzwerk innerhalb der Rechtsvorschriftendatenbank zur Verfügung. Beim Aufbau des Hypertextnetzes werden, ausgehend von den in den Entscheidungsdokumenten zitierten Rechtsvorschriften und dem Entscheidungsdatum, die passenden Versionen der Rechtsvorschriftentextes ermittelt und Verweise darauf in den Entscheidungstexten abgespeichert. Diese Zuordnung ist zeitinvariant. Daher wurde zugunsten kürzerer Antwortzeiten während der Systembenutzung auf eine getrennte Speicherung der Entscheidungsdokumente und der ausgehenden Hypertextlinks verzichtet.

6. Zusammenfassung

Juristische Texte wurden in dieser Arbeit als Beispiel für die natürliche Verwendung von Hypertextfunktionen in der Benutzerschnittstelle eines Information Retrieval Systems dargestellt. Die dem EUREKA Projekt Nr. 359 zugrundeliegende Volltextdatenbank mit Entscheidungen des Österreichischen Obersten Gerichtshofes eignet sich deshalb ausgezeichnet für die Verwendung von Hypertextfunktionen, da die in den Texten vorkommenden Rechtsvorschriftenzitate gleichsam natürliche Referenzlinks darstellen.

Literatur

[Conk-87] J. Conklin: Hypertext - An Introduction and Survey; IEEE Computer 20(9); 1987

[ElHa-89] A. El-Hamdouchi, P. Willet: Comparison of Hierarchic Agglomerative Clustering Methods for Document Retrieval; Computer Journal 32(3); 1989

[Merk-91] D. Merkl, A M. Tjoa, S. Vieweg: BRANT - An Expert System Approach for Knowledge Based Document Classification in the Information Retrieval Domain; Working Paper; Institute of Statistics and Computer Science; Vienna; 1991

[Rijs-75] C. J. van Rijsbergen: Information Retrieval; Butterworth; London; 1975

[Salt-89] G. Salton: Automatic Text Processing - The Transformation, Analysis, and Retrieval of Information by Computer; Addison-Wesley; Reading, Mass.; 1989

[Schn-90] J. Schnizer: NorA - Spezifikation für ein Programm zur automatischen Suche von Normzitaten in juristischen Texten zum Aufbau einer Normendatei; interner Projektbericht ITS 90; 1990

[Will-88] P. Willet: Recent Trends in Hierarchic Document Clustering: A Critical Review; Information Processing & Management 24(5); 1988

HYPERQUERY — Ein Anfragesystem mit Graphischer Benutzeroberfläche

Jürgen Herczeg

Hubertus Hohl

Matthias Ressel

Forschungsgruppe DRUID

Universität Stuttgart

Institut für Informatik

Zusammenfassung

Das System HYPERQUERY ist ein Informationssystem, das Benutzern den Zugriff auf stark vernetzte multimediale Informationen erleichtern soll. Hierzu wurde ein Hypertext- bzw. Hypermediasystem um eine Anfragekomponente erweitert, die den gezielten Einstieg in eine objektorientierte Datenbasis erleichtert. Das System soll insbesondere Gelegenheitsbenutzern ermöglichen, Reiseinformationen abzurufen. Der Benutzerschnittstelle fällt dabei eine wichtige Rolle zu. Die Implementierungen zweier unterschiedlicher graphischer Benutzeroberflächen der Anfragekomponente werden vorgestellt und diskutiert.

1 Einleitung

Traditionelle Informationssysteme bedienen sich formaler Anfragesprachen, die es ermöglichen, Informationen aus einer Datenbank durch Eingabe textueller Anfragen präzise abzurufen. Der Zugang zur gewünschten Information setzt jedoch gute Kenntnisse und Erfahrung beim Umgang mit der jeweiligen Anfragesprache voraus. Gelegenheitsbenutzern und Computerlaien bleibt der Zugang zu solchen Informationssystemen dadurch oft verwehrt. Neuere Ansätze, wie sie in *Hypertext-* und *Hypermedia-Systemen* verwirklicht sind, ermöglichen dem Benutzer, Informationen durch sehr einfache Interaktionen explorativ abzurufen. Oft ist es dadurch jedoch schwierig, gezielt spezielle Information anzufordern und bei der Navigation in einem komplexen Informationsraum nicht die Orientierung zu verlieren [2]. Einer adäquaten Benutzeroberfläche fällt hierbei eine entscheidende Rolle zu.

Das System HYPERQUERY ist ein Informationssystem mit einer graphischen Benutzeroberfläche, das eine *Browsing-Komponente* mit einer *Query-Komponente* (Anfragekomponente) kombiniert. Der Benutzer kann durch menügesteuertes und direktes Manipulieren textueller und graphischer Objekte Anfragen an eine Datenbasis stellen (*Query*) und die gefundenen Informationen nach dem Prinzip von Hypertext-Systemen inspizieren (*Browsing*). Für die Anfragekomponente wurden zwei verschiedenartige Benutzeroberflächen implementiert: Die eine orientiert sich mehr an generellen Anfragesprachen, die andere mehr an der zugrundeliegenden Anwendung, hier einem Reiseauskunftssystem. Beide Benutzeroberflächen werden vorgestellt und ihre Vor- und Nachteile in Bezug auf die Nutzung eines Informationssystems durch unerfahrene Gelegenheitsbenutzer diskutiert.

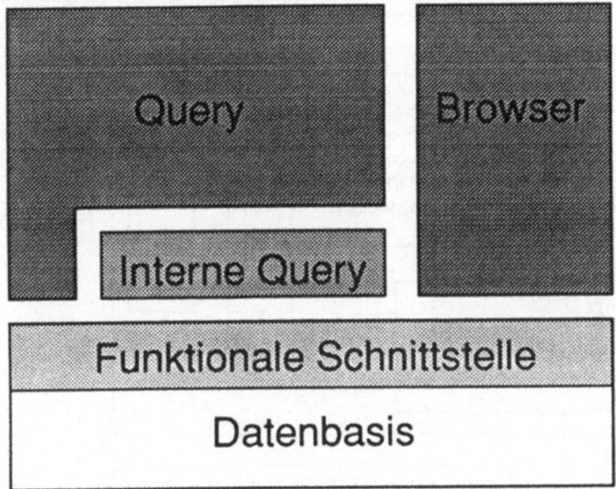

Abbildung 1: Systemarchitektur von HYPERQUERY

2 Das System HYPERQUERY

HYPERQUERY wurde im Rahmen der Forschungsprojekte MCPR (Multimedia Communication, Processing and Representation, RACE 1038) und GUIDANCE (RACE 1067) auf SUN Workstations entwickelt. Innerhalb dieser Projekte wurde das Anfragesystem in eine Hypermedia-Anwendung integriert [6]. HYPERQUERY wurde in der objektorientierten Programmiersprache CLOS [8], die Benutzeroberfläche von HYPERQUERY im X Window System [7] mit Hilfe des Benutzerschnitt-stellen-Baukastens XIT implementiert [5]. Das System gliedert sich in folgende Teilsysteme (vgl. Abbildung 1):

- In der *Datenbasis* sind die Daten in Form von Objekten abgelegt. Das System verfügt im Moment über Daten aus dem Reisebereich.

- Eine *funktionale Schnittstelle* zur Datenbasis, die Zugriffsfunktionen auf Struktur und Inhalt der Datenbasis sowie Funktionen zur Erweiterung der Datenbasis bereithält. Die Anfrage- und die Browsing-Komponente setzen auf dieser Schnittstelle auf.

- Eine *interne Anfragekomponente (interne Query)* zum Erstellen formaler Anfragen an die Datenbasis. Jede Anfrage wird intern durch eine hierarchische Objektstruktur repräsentiert. Diese kann mittels der Zugriffsfunktionen an die Datenbasis ausgewertet werden.

- Die interaktive *Benutzeroberfläche der Anfragekomponente (Query)* zum inkrementellen Erstellen von Anfragen.

- Eine *Browsing-Komponente*, mittels derer die Datenobjekte inspiziert und insbesondere Verweise auf andere Objekte weiterverfolgt werden können. Hiermit wird auch der Zugriff auf multimediale Datenobjekte wie Bilder, Graphiken, Videos, Musik oder gesprochenen Text ermöglicht.

Jedes dieser Teilsysteme kann ersetzt werden, unter Aufrechterhaltung der Schnittstellen zu den darüber- und darunterliegenden Teilsystemen. Beispielsweise kann die Datenbasis vollständig aus-getauscht werden gegen Daten aus einem anderen Anwendungsbereich unter Beibehaltung der Ob-jektstruktur. Beim Übergang zu anders strukturierten Daten ist die funktionale Zugriffsschnittstelle entsprechend anzupassen. Bei der Implementierung der Benutzeroberfläche der Anfragekomponente wurden zwei gegeneinander austauschbare Alternativen entwickelt. Die verschiedenen Teilsysteme von HYPERQUERY werden im folgenden genauer beschrieben.

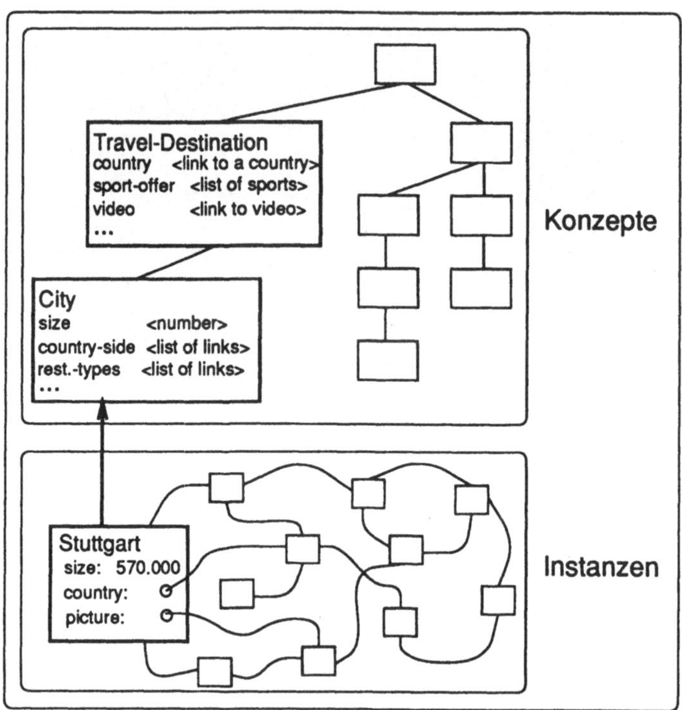

Abbildung 2: Objektorientierte Datenbasis von HYPERQUERY

2.1 Datenbasis

Die Datenbasis von HYPERQUERY wurde objektorientiert realisiert. Sie besteht aus einem Netz miteinander verknüpfter Informationsknoten, die durch CLOS-Objekte repräsentiert werden. Dabei werden zwei verschiedene Arten von Objekten unterschieden: *Konzepte* und *Instanzen*.

- *Konzepte* definieren Attribute von Informationsknoten. Sie sind in einer *Vererbungshierarchie* strukturiert. Ein Konzept kann dabei auf übergeordnete Konzepte verweisen, von denen es Attribute ererbt. Das Konzept *Town* beispielsweise trägt die Attribute *size-of-town*, *country-side* und *restaurant-types* und verweist auf das übergeordnete, allgemeinere Konzept *Travel-Destination*, das Attribute wie *country* oder *sport-offer* beschreibt.

- *Instanzen* sind konkrete Ausprägungen von Konzepten. Sie füllen die dort definierten Attributen mit individuellen Werte, die selbst wieder Verweise auf andere Instanzen sein können. Das Objekt *Stuttgart* beispielsweise ist Instanz des Konzeptes *City* und trägt als Attributwert für *country* einen Verweis auf *Germany*, eine Instanz des Konzeptes *Country*.

Abbildung 2 zeigt eine Auschnitt aus dem Objektnetz der Datenbasis.

Bei Attributen wird unterschieden, ob jede Instanz genau einen Wert oder eine Menge von Werten haben kann und ob die Attributwerte primitive Datentypen, z.B. Zahlen und Strings, oder Verweise auf weitere Instanzen sind. Für jedes Attribut wird dabei in der zugehörigen Konzeptbeschreibung der Attributtyp und der Wertebereich angegeben.

Zur Integration der Datenbasis in eine Hypermedia-Anwendung können die Informationsknoten Verweise auf multimediale Daten enthalten, wie beispielsweise gesprochenen Text oder Videos.

Diese multimedialen Daten werden jedoch von der Anfragekomponente nicht verwendet, der Zugriff erfolgt ausschließlich über die Browsing-Komponente.

Die Größe der implementierten Datenbasis (ca. 300 Datenobjekte) läßt es zu, sie im Arbeitsspeicher zu halten. Es handelt sich also nicht um eine objektorientierte Datenbank im strengen Sinn. Sie ließe sich jedoch für größere Anwendungen bei entsprechender Anpassung der funktionalen Schnittstelle durch eine geeignete objektorientierte Datenbank ersetzen.

2.2 Funktionale Schnittstelle zur Datenbasis

Um die höheren Systemkomponenten von HYPERQUERY unabhängig von der Struktur der Einträge der Datenbasis zu machen, wurde eine funktionale Schnittstelle eingeführt. Diese implementiert Funktionen zum Zugriff auf folgende Informationen:

- Wurzelkonzept der Konzepthierarchie

- Unterkonzepte eines Konzeptes

- Übergeordnete Konzepte eines Konzeptes

- Attribute eines Konzeptes (einschließlich ererbter Attribute)

- Attributtyp eines Attributs

- Wertebereich eines Attributs

- Instanzen eines Konzeptes

- Attributwerte einer Instanz

Diese Informationen werden von den Anfrage- und Browsing-Komponenten ausgenutzt. Außerdem beinhaltet die Schnittstelle zur Datenbasis Funktionen zur Definition neuer Konzepte und Instanzen. Abbildung 3 zeigt beispielsweise die Definition des Konzeptes *Town* und einer seiner Instanzen.

2.3 Interne Anfragekomponente

Die interne Anfragekomponente bietet eine funktionale Schnittstelle, mit der Anfragen vergleichbar mit relationalen Datenbankanfragesprachen formuliert werden können. Eine Anfrage (*Query*) wird intern als eine hierarchische Objektstruktur repräsentiert, deren Komponenten sich an der Konzeptstruktur der Datenbasis orientieren.

- Eine *Query* besteht aus einer Menge von *Konzeptbeschreibungen*.

- Eine *Konzeptbeschreibung* setzt sich aus dem Namen eines Konzeptes, einer Menge von *Attributbeschreibungen* für dieses Konzept und einer Menge von namentlich benannten Instanzen des Konzeptes zusammen. Bei der Angabe von Instanzen wird der Suchraum auf diese eingeschränkt.

- Eine *Attributbeschreibung* beschreibt eine Bedingung für die Werte eines Attributs des zugehörigen Konzeptes. Sie enthält ein Attribut, einen Operator und eine Operandenmenge. Die Operandenmenge besteht je nach Attributtyp aus einer Menge primitiver Attributwerte oder, falls das Attribut auf Instanzen verweist, selbst wiederum aus einer Unteranfrage (*Query*). Für Attribute, die bei jeder Instanz auf genau einen Wert verweisen, sind folgende Operatoren definiert: *is_in* und *is_not_in*. Für Attribute, die bei jeder Instanz auf eine Menge von Werten verweisen, sind folgende Operatoren möglich: *contains_one_of*, *contains_all_of* und *contains_none_of*.

```
(define-concept town (travel-destination)
    "Town" "Towns"
  (size-of-town     (:pretty-name "size of town")
                    (:type (:one-of large medium small)))
  (restaurant-types (:pretty-name "restaurant types")
                    (:type (:list-of (:concept restaurant-type))))
  (country-side     (:pretty-name "surroundings")
                    (:type (:list-of (:concept country-side)))))

(define-instance stuttgart town
  (pretty-name "Stuttgart")
  (size-of-town       large)
  (country            germany)
  (cost               high)
  (beauty             *)
  (cultural-facilities (science-museum art-gallery historical-museum
                        natural-museum zoo disco night-club jazz-club
                        cabaret opera theatre ballet concert music-festival
                        film-festival))
  (sport-offer        (tennis golf hiking fishing canoeing swimming
                        sailing riding cross-country-skiing))
  (special-interest   (spa cure palace castle shopping-mall airport
                        brewery tower university planetarium))
  (restaurant-types   (vegetarian-food chinese-food french-food mexican-food
                        indian-food swabian-food alsace-food))
  (country-side       (hills river vineyard lake forest)))
```

Abbildung 3: Definition eines Konzeptes und einer Instanz

Die Auswertung einer Query ergibt als Ergebnis eine Menge von Instanzen aus der Datenbasis. Sie erfolgt durch rekursives Auswerten der Unterkomponenten der Query nach folgendem Prinzip:

Das Ergebnis $Result(Q)$ einer Query Q ist definiert als Vereinigung (*union*) der Ergebnisse ihrer Konzeptbeschreibungen *conc-descrs(Q)*:

$$Result(Q) = \bigcup_{C_i \in \, conc\text{-}descrs(Q)} Result(C_i)$$

wobei das Ergebnis $Result(C)$ einer Konzeptbeschreibung C sich aus deren Suchraum $Space(C)$ und Attributbeschreibungen *attr-descrs(C)* berechnet:

$$Result(C) = \bigcap_{A_i \in \, attr\text{-}descrs(Q)} \{I \in Space(C) \mid fulfills_{A_i}(I)\}$$

Der Suchraum $Space(C)$ einer Konzeptbeschreibung C zum Konzept *concept(C)* und den benannten Instanzen *instances(C)* ist dabei folgendermaßen definiert:

$$Space(C) = \begin{cases} \{i \mid i \text{ ist Instanz von } concept(C)\} & \text{falls } instances(C) = \{\} \\ instances(C) & \text{sonst} \end{cases}$$

Das Prädikat $fulfills_A(I)$ bestimmt, ob eine Instanz I eine Attributbeschreibung A zum Attribut $attribute(A)$ mit Operator $op(A)$ und Operandenmenge $OpSet(A)$ erfüllt. Es ist wie folgt definiert:

$$fulfills_A(I) = \begin{cases} true & \text{falls} & (Value_I(attribute(A)) \quad op(A) \quad OpSet(A)) \\ false & \text{sonst} \end{cases}$$

wobei $Value_I(attribute)$ der Wert des Attributs $attribute$ in der Instanz I ist und die Operandenmenge $OpSet(A)$ sich folgendermaßen berechnet:

$$OpSet(A) = \begin{cases} operand(A) & \text{falls } query(A) \text{ leer} \\ Result(query(A)) & \text{sonst} \end{cases}$$

$operand(A)$ ist dabei ein (primitiver) Attributwert bzw. eine Menge von Attributwerten und $query(A)$ eine Unteranfrage der Attributbeschreibung A.

Im Vergleich zu einer Anfragesprache für relationale Datenbanken fehlt prinzipiell z.B. der *join*-Operator oder die Möglichkeit, sich in Unteranfragen auf Attribute übergeordneter Anfragen zu beziehen. Im Unterschied zu relationalen Ansätzen ist das Ergebnis einer Anfrage nicht eine Relation sondern eine Objektmenge. Die Attribute dieser Objekte können dann bei Bedarf mit der Browsing-Komponente inspiziert werden. Die Projektion-Operation, d.h. die Auswahl erwünschter Attribute ist deshalb nicht nötig.

Natürlichsprachliche Umschreibungen für mögliche Anfragen sind beispielsweise: „Suche alle Länder, in denen es Ausflugsziele gibt, an denen man Skilaufen kann" oder „Suche alle attraktiven, kleinen bis mittelgrossen Städte in Baden-Württemberg mit Hügeln und Wald, in denem man schwimmen, Tennis spielen, wandern und wenigstens ein vegetarisches Restaurant finden kann" (vgl. Abb. 4).

Durch Austausch oder Erweiterung der Konzepte und Instanzen der Datenbasis lassen sich mit derselben Anfragekomponente Anfragen eines völlig anderen Anwendungsbereiches stellen.

2.4   Benutzeroberfläche der Anfragekomponente

Für die Anfragekomponente von HYPERQUERY wurden zwei sehr unterschiedliche Benutzeroberflächen entworfen. Während die erste, im wesentlichen textorientierte Schnittstelle sich an der internen Repräsentation einer Anfrage orientiert, bietet die zweite, eher anwendungsnahe Schnittstelle eine in der Komplexität eingeschränkte, auf den konkreten Inhalt der Datenbasis zugeschnittene Funktionalität an. Anforderungen beim Entwurf beider Benutzeroberflächen war, daß sie sich für Gelegenheitsbenutzer eignen und leicht erlernbar und handhabbar sind. Da sich hierbei menügesteuerte Systeme als geeignetste Dialogform erwiesen haben [4], wurde bei beiden Schnittstellen vornehmlich darauf zurückgegriffen.

Anfragesprachen-orientierte Benutzeroberfläche

Wesentliches Ziel beim Entwurf der anfragesprachen-orientierten Benutzeroberfläche war, in einer Fenstersystemumgebung eine allgemeine, anwendungsneutrale Schnittstelle zur oben beschriebenen internen Anfragesprache zu schaffen, die einen Benutzer dabei unterstützt, zulässige und sinnvolle Anfragen zu erstellen. Die anfragesprachen-orientierte Benutzeroberfläche wurde in Anlehnung an das System RABBIT [9] implementiert (vgl. Abbildung 4). Eine zu Beginn primitive Anfrage wird

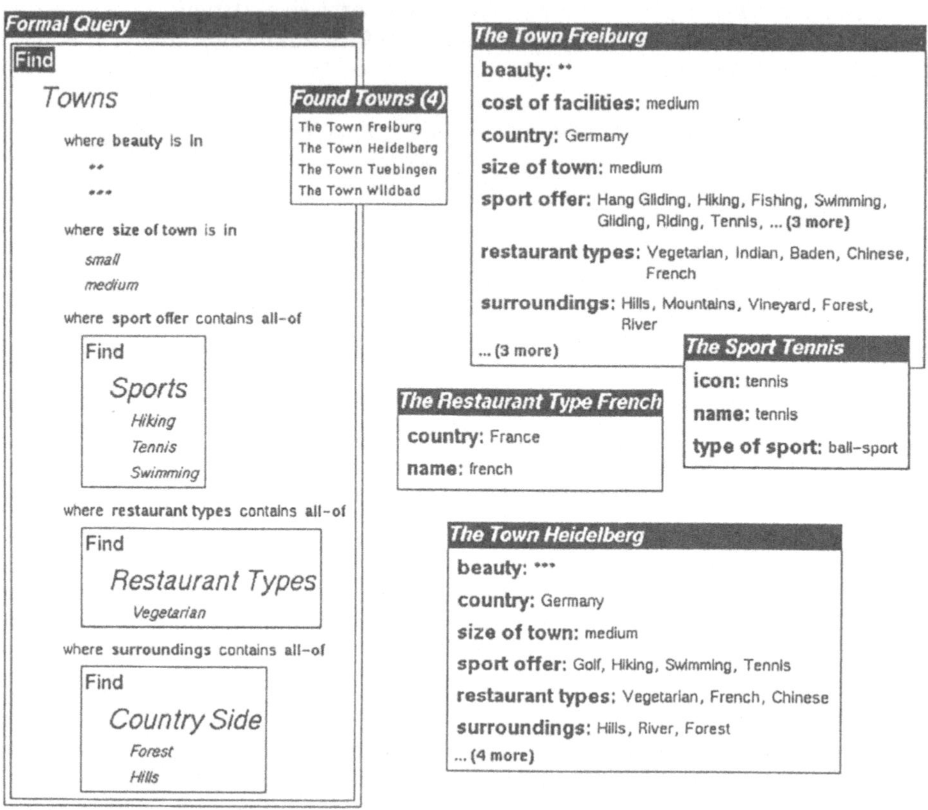

Abbildung 4: Anfragesprachen-orientierte Anfrageschnittstelle

inkrementell modifiziert und verfeinert. Die Anfrage wird dabei vom Benutzer über dynamische Menüs manipuliert. Die Darstellung einer Anfrage orientiert sich graphisch an ihrer im vorangegangenen Abschnitt beschriebenen internen, hierarchischen Repräsentation. Zusätzlich ergibt sich als Text gelesen eine an Anfragesprachen wie SQL [3] angelehnte Anfrage. Wenn der Benutzer mit der Maus einen bestimmten Teil der graphischen Darstellung anwählt, erhält er die möglichen Operationen in Form von Popup-Menüs angeboten. Die in einem bestimmten Kontext zulässigen Attribute oder Konzepte werden ebenfalls über Menüs angeboten, die dynamisch durch den Inhalt der Datenbasis (im wesentlichen der Konzeptbeschreibungen) bestimmt sind. Beispielsweise werden dem Benutzer zum Einfügen einer Attributbeschreibung alle Attribute des betreffenden Konzeptes in einem Menü angeboten. Dadurch wird gewährleistet, daß nur „sinnvolle" Anfragen erzeugt werden können. Dies ist ein wesentlicher Vorteil gegenüber dem Einsatz formaler Anfragesprachen. Hierdurch ist auch gewährleistet, daß die Anfrage immer in einem konsistenten Zustand in dem Sinn ist, daß jederzeit das Ergebnis einer Anfrage (und auch von Unteranfragen) abgerufen werden kann. Die Ergebnismenge wird in einem eigenen Menü angezeigt, die jeweils zugehörige (Unter-)Anfrage wird hervorgehoben. Abbildung 4 zeigt eine Beispielanfrage mit der in einem Menü aufgelisteten Ergebnismenge. Der Benutzer hat dort auch bereits mit Hilfe der Browsing-Komponente Informationen zu den Städten Freiburg und Heidelberg abgerufen.

Die anfragesprachen-orientierte Anfrageschnittstelle bietet dem Benutzer die volle Funktionalität der internen Anfragekomponente und ist unabhängig vom Inhalt der Datenbasis, d.h. universell auch für andere Anwendungsbereiche einsetzbar. Es zeigte sich jedoch, daß ungeübte Benutzer wegen des immer noch relativ formalen Charakters der Anfragebeschreibung Schwierigkeiten mit

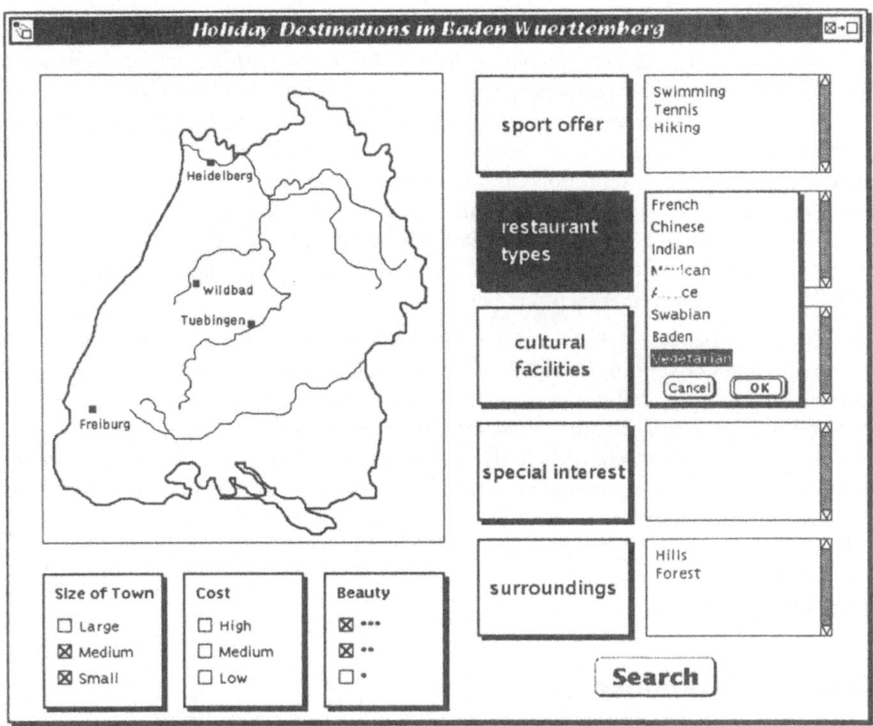

Abbildung 5: Anwendungsnahe Anfrageschnittstelle

der Formulierung einer gewünschten Anfrage hatten. Insbesondere für den Einsatz des Systems in einer Hypermedia-Anwendung, die sich durch anspruchsvolle graphische Visualisierungen, aber einfache Interaktionstechniken auszeichnet, stellte sich diese Art der Benutzeroberfläche als ungeeignet heraus.

Anwendungsnahe Benutzeroberfläche

Zum Einsatz von HYPERQUERY in einem Prototypen eines multimedialen Reiseauskunftssystems, das insbesondere für Computerlaien und Gelegenheitsbenutzer konzipiert ist, wurde eine völlig neue anwendungsnahe Benutzeroberfläche entwickelt (vgl. Abbildung 5). Der Benutzer wählt hier aus einer vorgegebenen Menge von Kriterien und Angeboten die gewünschten Werte aus. Aus diesen Angaben wird eine interne Anfrage erstellt, deren Ergebnis Städte sind, die in einer Landkarte angezeigt werden. Die dargestellten Stadtmarkierungen gestatten dann wieder den Einstieg in die Browsing-Komponente. Diese graphische Benutzeroberfläche ist das Ergebnis des zum Entwurf und zur Spezifikation von Benutzeroberflächen im Projekt GUIDANCE angewandten *Enabling-State-*Ansatzes [1].

Die Funktionalität, d.h. die Menge der möglichen Anfragen, wurde für die prototypische Anwendung eines Reiseauskunftsystems gegenüber der anfragesprachen-orientierten Benutzeroberfläche bewußt eingeschränkt. Zum einen ist der Suchraum beschränkt auf ein bestimmtes Konzept, in diesem Fall Städte. Weiter lassen sich nur „flache" Anfragen stellen, Unteranfragen wie z.B. „Finde alle Städte, die im gleichen Bundesland liegen wie Stuttgart" sind also prinzipiell nicht möglich. Fragen dieser Art werden bei der Entscheidung für ein bestimmtes Urlaubsziel aber auch selten gestellt.

Außerdem ist die Anzahl der Attribute, die spezifiziert werden können, eingeschränkt.[1]

Es hat sich herausgestellt, daß den genannten Einschränkungen eine wesentlich Verbesserung der Benutzbarkeit gegenübersteht. In diesem speziellen Anwendungsgebiet der Reiseinformation reichen schon Beschreibungen weniger, aber wesentlicher Attribute aus, um die Ergebnismenge ausreichend einzuschränken. Diese wesentlichen Attribute werden dem Benutzer ständig präsentiert und zur Modifikation angeboten. Die Interaktion zur Erstellung und Modifikation einer Anfrage vereinfacht sich dadurch entscheidend. Der Benutzer kann somit mehrere Anfragen in kürzerer Zeit stellen, was dem explorativen Ansatz des Hypermedia-Systems entgegenkommt. Die Präsentation eines Anfrageergebnisses in einer Landkarte erleichtert dem Benutzer die räumliche Orientierung und trägt ebenfalls zu einer höheren Akzeptanz bei.

Ein Problem, das sich bei ersten Evaluationen herausstellte, ist, daß die Information, wie mehrere Restriktionen miteinander verknüpft sind, in dieser Oberfläche nicht explizit angegeben ist. So ist es nicht unmittelbar einsichtig, daß die ausgewählten Werte für Größe, Kosten und Schönheit jeweils mit *oder*, dagegen jene Werte für Sportangebot, Restaurants usw. jeweils mit *und* zu verknüpfen sind. Auch ist nicht unbedingt ersichtlich, daß die jeweiligen Restriktionen miteinander wiederum mit *und* verknüpft sind. Die verwendeten Verknüpfungen werden jedoch, soweit dies bisher festgestellt werden konnte, von den meisten Benutzern intuitiv erwartet. In jedem Fall erhält der Benutzer bei inkrementellen Änderungen der Anfrage schnell eine Rückmeldung über die Art der Verknüpfung, je nachdem, ob die Änderung zu einer Einschränkung (*und*) oder einer Erweiterung (*oder*) der Ergebnismenge führt.

2.5 Browsing-Komponente

Die Anfragekomponente von HYPERQUERY liefert als Ergebnis eine Menge von Instanzen aus der Datenbasis. Diese werden auf der Benutzeroberfläche entweder textuell in einem Menü oder graphisch als Einträge in einer Landkarte präsentiert und dienen als Einstiegspunkte in die Browsing-Komponente. Sie dient dazu, ausgehend von einem oder mehreren Informationsknoten detaillierte Informationen aus der Datenbasis abzurufen, z.B. spezielle Attributwerte einer Instanz oder Informationen über damit verknüpfte Instanzen. Die über die Browsing-Komponente zugängliche Information ist nicht auf die Ergebnisse einer Anfrage beschränkt; vielmehr kann sich der Benutzer durch das gesamte Objektnetz der Datenbasis bewegen und hat somit auch Zugang zu Informationen, die ihm zur Zeit der Anfrage unbekannt waren, z.B. Instanzen unbekannter Konzepte.

Als Browsing-Komponente wurde zunächst ein allgemeiner, textorientierter *Instanzen-Browser* implementiert. Dieser wird beispielsweise durch Auswahl eines Eintrags im Ergebnismenü einer Anfrage aufgerufen und·zeigt für die betreffende Instanz die Werte zu einer vom Benutzer gewählten Menge von Attributen (vgl. Abbildung 4). Attributwerte, die selbst wieder auf weitere Instanzen der Datenbasis verweisen, werden durch maussensitive Einträge im Browser-Fenster repräsentiert. Über diese Einträge können nach dem Prinzip von Hypertext-Systemen weitere Instanzen-Browser für die jeweiligen Instanzen aufgerufen werden.

Innerhalb des Forschungsprojektes MCPR wurde eine *Hypermedia-Browser* entwickelt, der es ermöglicht, Multimedia-Informationen in Form von Texten, Bildern, Videos, Musik und gesprochener Sprache abzurufen [6]. Diese werden dem Benutzer in Form von *Dokumentseiten* präsentiert. Dokumentseiten können über Verweise (*Links*) miteinander verknüpft sein und sich so gegenseitig aufrufen. Für Instanzen der Datenbasis, die Verweise auf solche Multimedia-Dokumente besitzen, kann alternativ zum Instanzen-Browser der Hypermedia-Browser aufgerufen werden.

---

[1] Allerdings enthalten die Menüs, aus denen das Angebot an Sport, Restaurants etc. ausgewählt werden kann, weiterhin automatisch alle Einträge, die in der Datenbasis vorhanden sind.

3 Schlußbemerkungen

Erste Versuche haben gezeigt, daß Gelegenheitsbenutzer mit der anwendungsorientierten Benutzeroberfläche besser zurechtkamen und damit problemloser auf die gewünschte Information zugreifen konnten. Dies liegt zum einen an den einfachen Interaktionsformen, zum anderen an der übersichtlichen Informationsdarstellung, die sich auf das Nötige beschränkt und durch ihre Form leicht verständlich und schnell zu interpretieren ist. Die gezeigte Benutzeroberfläche reicht außerdem innerhalb des implementierten Reiseauskunftsystems zur Bestimmung geeigneter Einstiegspunkte in die explorative Browsing-Komponente aus. Lediglich der direkte Einstieg ist schwieriger: Da als Eingabeinstrument nur eine Maus zur Verfügung stand, wäre textuelle Suche nur umständlich zu erreichen gewesen; sie war deshalb auch nicht spezifiert. Eine umfassende Evaluation der Benutzeroberfläche wird zur Zeit im Projekt GUIDANCE vorgenommen. Sie wird sicherlich detailliertere Ergebnisse erbringen.

Bei Übertragung auf andere Anwendungen sind verschiedene Erweiterungen an dieser Benutzeroberfläche denkbar. So ließe sich die Beschränkung auf eine bestimmte, vorgegebene Menge von spezifizierbaren Attributen aufheben, indem die Zahl der angezeigten Attributen in gewissen Grenzen variabel ist und der Benutzer wahlweise Attribute hinzu- oder wegnehmen kann. Die hierfür notwendige automatische Aktualisierung des Layouts ist in der momentanen Implementierung bereits vorgesehen. Weiterhin ist denkbar, daß Unteranfragen gestattet werden, die, in analoger Form, in weiteren Fenstern repräsentiert werden. Die Darstellung der Ergebnismenge müßte hierzu natürlich dem jeweiligen Konzept angepaßt werden. Bei steigender Funktionalität wird es außerdem unumgänglich, geeignete Benutzerhilfen (Hilfesysteme, Undo-Komponente) zu integrieren.

Anmerkung

Die interne Anfragekomponente und anfragesprachen-orientierte Benutzeroberfläche wurde innerhalb des RACE Projektes MCPR (R1038), die anwendungsnahe Benutzeroberfläche innerhalb des RACE Projektes GUIDANCE (R1067) ausgeführt, an dem folgende Projektpartner beteiligt sind: SEL AG; University College London, Ergonomics Unit; Roke Manor Research Ltd.; Britisch Telecom Research Laboratories und Televerket (Swedish Telecom).

Alle geäußerten Ansichten und Meinungen sind die der Autoren und müssen nicht unbedingt mit denen der Konsortien übereinstimmen.

Die Autoren möchten sich außerdem bei Thomas Schwab bedanken, der bei der Entwicklung und Implementierung von HYPERQUERY wesentlich beteiligt war.

Literatur

[1] Paul Byerley, Jon May, Andrew Whitefield, and I. Denley. The Enabling States Approach: Designing Usable Telecommunication Services. *IEEE Journal on Selected Areas in Communication*, 9(4), April 1991.

[2] J. Conklin. Hypertext: An Introduction and Survey. *Computer*, 20(9):17–41, September 1987.

[3] C.J. Date. *An Introduction to Database Systems.* The Systems Programming Series. Addison-Wesley, Reading, MA, 1975.

[4] Dietmar Freiburg. *Ergonomie in Dokumenten-Retrievalsystemen.* Mensch Computer Kommunikation 3. Verlag Walter de Gruyter & Co., Berlin – New York, 1987.

[5] Jürgen Herczeg, Hubertus Hohl, and Thomas Schwab. XIT - A Multi-Layered Tool for User Interface Design. Stuttgart, September 1991. Erscheint in Proceedings of Fourth International Conference on Human-Computer Interaction.

[6] K.-H. Jerke et al. Combining Hypermedia Browsing with Formal Queries. In *Proceedings of INTERACT'90, IFIP Conference on Human-Computer Interaction*, pages 593–598. IFIP, 1990.

[7] R.W. Scheifler and J. Gettys. The X Window System. *ACM Transactions on Graphics*, 5(2):79–109, April 1986.

[8] Guy L. Steele Jr. *Common LISP: The Language.* Digital Press, Digital Equipment Corporation, second edition, 1990.

[9] F.N. Tou, M.D. Williams, et al. RABBIT: An Intelligent Interface. Technical report, Xerox Palo Alto Research Center, Palo Alto, CA, 1982.